Thinking

ONE WEEK LOAN

D0494158

Thinking Differently

Alain Touraine

Translated by David Macey

polity

First published in French as *Penser Autrement* © Librairie Arthème Fayard, 2007

This English edition © Polity Press, 2009

Polity Press
65 Bridge Street
Cambridge CB2 1UR, UK.

Polity Press
350 Main Street
Malden, MA 02148, USA

ISBN-13: 978-0-7456-4573-5
ISBN-13: 978-0-7456-4574-2(pb)

A catalogue record for this book is available from the British Library.

Typeset in 10.5 on 12 pt Times
by SNP Best-set Typesetter Ltd, Hong Kong
Printed and bound in Great Britain by MPG Books Ltd, Bodmin, Cornwall

The publisher has used its best endeavours to ensure that the URLs for external websites referred to in this book are correct and active at the time of going to press. However, the publisher has no responsibility for the websites and can make no guarantee that a site will remain live or that the content is or will remain appropriate.

Every effort has been made to trace all copyright holders, but if any have been inadvertently overlooked the publishers will be pleased to include any necessary credits in any subsequent reprint or edition.

For further information on Polity, visit our website: www.polity.books.com

Liberté • Égalité • Fraternité

RÉPUBLIQUE FRANÇAISE

This book is supported by the French Ministry of Foreign Affairs, as part of the Burgess programme run by the cultural Department of the French Embassy in London. (www.frenchbooknews.com)

I dedicate this book to all the students who attended my seminars at the École Pratique des Hautes Études (VIe Section) between 1958 and 1975, and at the École des Hautes Études en Sciences Sociales between 1975 and 2007.

Contents

Starting Point

New Situations, Old Ideas

Everything in our social life has changed since the 1960s and the 1970s. The student uprisings in Berkeley and Nanterre, which had long-lasting repercussions in many countries, loudly announced a change of era. At almost the same time, economies were leaving behind the post-war years of interventionism and embarking upon an era of neo-liberalism that was exacerbated by the accelerated globalization of production, finance and mass culture. The very system of production was transformed. We were leaving industrial society behind and entering what certain pundits call the communications society or the knowledge society. The world map changed considerably: while Europe's economies stagnated, the United States outstripped other countries in developing new technologies. China, quickly followed by India, embarked upon a period of uncontrolled growth, and overtook Japan as Asia's strongest economy.

The world that is being transformed so rapidly also feels fragile and threatened by all kinds of ecological, biological and demographic disasters. The idea of progress, which the Communist movement had taken over from the democracies, has been abandoned everywhere, and has been replaced by a combination of uncertainty and fear, especially in an Africa whose population is being decimated by AIDS. The twenty-first century began, finally, with a military and religious clash between the United States and the new religious and political expressions of Islam that have replaced the nationalisms of Nasser, Mossadegh or the Iraqi and Syrian Baathists.

But do we have new words to describe so many new situations? The decline of Marxism, which was largely a result of the collapse of the Soviet Empire that made it its official ideology, did not just lead to the disappearance of the Communist Parties; although there was no denying their economic and social success, the social-democratic regimes did not prove very inventive when it came to social thought, and were content to provide an effective framework for supplying humanitarian aid to the poorest countries, which was in itself a positive step. The eminently French category of intellectuals disintegrated because so many of them had, at some point in their lives and without much courage, accepted the leadership role of the Communist Party and refused for a long time to recognize and denounce the crimes of the Soviet and Chinese leaders. The retreat of ideologies also had its good effects, especially in France and Italy, where sectarianism led, in one case, to a terroristic dogmatism, especially between 1970 and 1975, and to the turbulent and bloody 'years of lead' in the other.

The long nineteenth century, which was not yet over in some parts of the world, was a period of liberation as well as of the transition from British imperialism to American hegemony. The labour movement in all its forms – national liberation movements and feminism – forced us to see history in terms that were at once tragic, heroic and violent. The most significant social movements were based on the idea that political and social history, the history of ideas and biographies of actors of all kinds were inseparable, and as a result social thought centred on economic themes such as labour, capitalist profits and the class struggle. For a long time, the central schema created mainly by Marx seemed to be applicable – and was applied – to all situations and all parts of the world. In one rather curious variation on that schema, a positivist, secular and nationalist middle class succeeded in taking power from the oligarchies and the church. That type of government has not yet completely disappeared, especially where, as in France, it formed an alliance with political forces from the world of labour. But in most countries that had become part of the industrial society, the economic worldview prevailed.

That era is now over. In Russia, in Mexico, in a Europe that had been devastated by the First World War and then by the Soviet Revolution, Italian fascism, and above all the ideology of death known as Nazism, revolutionary and counter-revolutionary upheavals, put an end to the idea of progress that embodied a faith in the economy. Marxism, liberalism and even the early social democracies were consumed and annihilated by wars and revolutions. In the Soviet Empire, a heavy silence was imposed on everyone. In a divided Europe, it was increasingly impossible to come to terms with the new situation.

Some did try to do so, but the most significant works of this period were closer to a philosophical approach and were therefore far removed from any analysis of the contemporary world. It was at that point that it began to be claimed, in certain countries and especially France, that there was nothing to understand: there were no more actors because the world was trapped in the dictatorship of capitalism and, of course, the dictatorship of Leninism-Maoism and the disorders of post-colonialism. The social sciences were swept away by the destructive idea that consciousness was always a false consciousness, that we had had to abandon the attempt to analyse human behaviours in terms of the value-judgements that motivated them, and that they could be explained only in terms of an understanding of their economic, political or even demographic determinants. Sociology, defined as the study of other-oriented normative behaviours, was abandoned and denounced in Europe, in Latin America and in many of those parts of the planet that were still known as the Third World. This double vision of the impotence of social actors and the omnipotence of global economic forces became widespread and put down deep roots in intellectual life. References to the labour movement, to liberation movements in colonized countries, and even to feminism became rare. The social sciences faculties emptied. Some of their work was taken over by philosophy, and some by the departments of economics.

Such was the situation we have lived through. We realized that the old ideas had been destroyed, and many of us tried to elaborate new ones. But in France, more so than anywhere else, anything to do with the state and with revolution, defined as the violent seizure of state power, aroused much more interest than anything to do with social life and democracy. The resistance of these 'Jacobin' ideas, combined with the attractions of a purely technological and economic worldview, trapped living thought into very small spaces. It became difficult for countries to communicate, to say nothing of continents. For long decades, social thought was suffocated by what I have termed the *dominant interpretive discourse*, which was created not by political leaders, but by intellectuals and opinion-makers who looked to their memories of the past to find the weapons that could help them to fight new ideas. Not all members of a society shape or disseminate representations of social life; it is not the richest or most powerful categories that create the explanatory language that best suits their purposes. The powerful do invoke ideologies as they pursue their self-interest, but the ideologies concerned serve mainly to justify their power. The colonizer depicts the colonized as 'savages', as inferior beings. Similarly, many of the ideologues of industrial societies described workers as lazy creatures of routine and, like F. W. Taylor, explained that we had to use both the carrot and the stick to get them to do anything. Male chauvinism thought, finally, produced more and more images that made women look inferior by insisting that they were not rational beings.

But societies also produce self-representations that are much broader and more complex than ideologies. What I call the *dominant interpretive discourse* spread the idea that historical realities became meaningless when the labour and socialist movements came under the control of Soviet totalitarianism or drifted into a new conservatism. At the same time, the most radical forms of *dependency theory* explained that action and reforms were impossible in Latin America, and that guerrilla warfare was the only meaningful solution.

But at the end of the century, the end of the great totalitarian systems of Central and Eastern Europe, the failure of most of the new nationalisms, and the rapid spread of new communications technologies brought down the barriers that had trapped social thought into self-negation. The illusions foisted upon us by those who no longer believed in collective action became increasingly intolerable as they became more and more out of step with lived experience. We are now well aware that the social stage is not empty, and that it is the ideologues who are trapped in the past. They are plunging the stage into darkness at a time when incomprehensible or deafening noises are becoming louder. We are already aware that everyday life is making new demands, and that words and ideas we thought had gone for ever are back. We are looking for new categories that will allow us to understand the initiatives that we see, as well as the destruction and the upheavals.

This requires a twofold effort. We must first try to formulate, as coherently and clearly as possible, forms of thought that explain our situation and our behaviours to us. And we must then go back and make a critique of those representations of social life whose dominant influence has prevented us for so long from shedding light on social realities.

It seems to me preferable to begin with a critique of what I have termed the *dominant interpretive discourse*, as that will do more to illustrate the need for new ideas that can, I believe, provide the insights we lack.

A Reversal of Perspective

The object of these remarks is not to bring about a break or mutation in the economic and social situation. A revolution in ideas has taken place in the absence of any major economic or social crisis. What has been called into question is the way we look at things and the words we use to formulate and interpret the transformations that are taking place before our very eyes. It is the method of analysis that has to change, not the object of the analysis. What were, in the recent past, the most widespread of ideas no longer explain anything; they ring hollow and simply widen the gulf between the political and social world and the intellectual world. The divorce between realities and the meanings we lend to them seems to me so extreme, and ideas have so often been replaced by quotations, that we have to transform what appear to be our firmest principles, our most 'classical' representations of society and social actors, or even abandon them. The most profound thing about the social thought we inherited was the positivistic conviction that modernity meant the elimination of not only religious expressions, but also of any kind of reference to the consciousness of actors. We were taught to content ourselves with two principles when it came to analysing behaviours: the rational pursuit of self-interest or pleasure, and the fulfilment of the functions required by the perpetuation and evolution of social life. Neither of those finalities left individuals any room to construct themselves as free and responsible beings. Compared with this type of social thought, the Declaration of the Rights of Man of 1789 seems to mark the end rather than the beginning of an era. It referred to natural rights at a time when, or so we were taught, everything was becoming material, instrumental and quantitative. French *laïcisme* or secularism reinforced that tendency, as did British utilitarianism. In many countries, much of political life is still dominated by this secularized vision, which appeals to all the figures of reason. What might be called the 'critical functionalism' of thinkers on 'the Left', which defines the workings of the social system in terms of mechanisms of domination, is not far removed from that general line.

What I am suggesting here is that we require a change of attitude and a different interpretive approach. We have to abandon what is now an exhausted evolutionism. We were convinced that we were making a transition from community to society, or in other words from a definition of what everyone was to a definition of what everyone does. We have in fact moved in the opposite direction, and the communitarian spirit is reappearing everywhere in all its forms, from those that are fairly positive to the most execrable. Social and cultural apparatuses are no longer able to provide the framework for all aspects of lived experience; controls over sexuality, in particular, have almost completely disappeared. We are learning to recognize differences and protect minorities. All these transformations exemplify the same general change: legitimacy and the definition of good and evil are no longer supplied by institutions, be they secular or religious. What we most desire is the recognition that individuals and groups have an implicit right to be recognized and respected, irrespective of all the laws and norms that are secreted by institutions. This demand, which is being voiced all over the world and in many different forms, often takes a communitarian form but, more often than not, it is also a demand for the individual right to live in conformity with our self-image, and to do so freely and responsibly.

That goal dominates representations, which in their turn orient our behaviours. There is a danger that the word 'individualism', which is mentioned so often, will lead to a misunderstanding: it is not a question of saying that everyone should act in accordance with their interests and desires, but of recognizing that all individuals tend to appeal to their 'right to have rights', to use what has become the classic expression. This become perfectly obvious to me when I heard the women we were listening to, either individuals or in discussion groups; for them, the most important thing was to construct themselves as women, mainly through their sexuality. This spontaneous discourse is the complete opposite of the discourse that speaks of women only as victims, and which demands, at best, equality with men, or even the elimination of all references to gender in most situations, and especially in job-selection procedures.

In similar vein, the sociology of religions has long taught us to see that the retreat of the churches and other religious institutions does not signal the triumph of rationalism and instrumentalism, but the emergence of a set of very different behaviours: the assertion that individuals are responsible for their own salvation on the one hand, and, on the other, the reconstruction of social controls, even though we know that they can never recover the power they had in a different society. We are moving beyond the once-powerful image of a secularized society, and while we are not necessarily reverting to a defensive communitarianism or a nostalgia for 'holistic' systems, the individual is increasingly portrayed as being, by definition, someone endowed with rights that cannot be suspended or denied by either force or the law. This is happening all over the world.

This transformation of a self-consciousness that is becoming stronger than any awareness of the rules and norms, and stronger than the demands of the system within which we live and act, makes it necessary to recall something that is so often forgotten and even violently rejected by many: the idea of the *subject*, or in other words of an individual who is recognized as being his own creator, and therefore as an individual who can demand the right to exist as an individual endowed with rights that extend beyond his or her material existence.

This reversal of perspective is so complete as to be dizzying. In order to get over it, we have to go back to the past and rediscover the presence of the subject in places and times where the subject was not spoken of directly, as now happens, but was implicit in religious, 'progressive' or revolutionary visions.

These figures of the subject represent cultural models that were the focus of major social conflicts. In industrial society, the main social conflicts were defined in terms of class and class-consciousness. In earlier types of society, it was the theme of the freedom of the citizen, as opposed to the power of the monarch, that carried the greatest symbolic weight, while religions, and especially the monotheistic religions, portrayed the subject as a god, or as a representative of a god who was responsible for the applications of God's law. At all stages, and all over the world, the organization of society was governed by a more or less anthropomorphic image of transcendence. Which forces us to accept that a society cannot be reduced to a production line or a system of exchanges. Similarly, laws are not just ways of organizing economic and social life and protecting interests. In both its practical and theoretical expressions, the domain of ethics and law appeals to value-judgements, or in other words to conceptions of human beings, their rights, and their duties with respect to others.

It was at the moment – which was in fact quite brief – when society saw itself in purely economic terms that it became possible to imagine that value-judgements and de facto judgements would increasingly merge into one, and that a rationalist conception would explain everything. The expressions 'civil society' and 'bourgeois society' (*Bürgerlische Gesellschaft*) referred to that very specific situation, but they could not provide a full description of it. Even in that society, we saw conflicts which, at least in the most serious cases, implied value-judgements. Those conflicts force us to see that even bourgeois society could contain figures of the subject, and they demonstrate that we cannot be content with a positivist conception of society.

Those who reject this approach will find it more and more difficult to denounce this individualism as a mere breakdown of social bonds or a surrender to the blandishments of the market. This individualism, which I would prefer to describe as the creation of the subject or *subjectivation*, is, rather, a way of defending the rights of all – which are universal – against all forms of social integration. I am very suspicious of the eminently classical vocabulary of integration, socialization and the collective consciousness. I become even more suspicious when, as is so often the case, individualism degenerates into the communitarianism that I regard as the greatest threat facing the new century.

We therefore have to get away from anything that defines sociology as the study of social systems and their functions. It is now possible to break the silence that surrounds all conceptions of the subject, and of the subject's representations and struggles. We have to find a way to shed light on the dark period that has plunged us into the obscurity of the *dominant interpretive discourse.*

The Other Danger

As soon as new ways of thinking about life and social actions emerge, one question always arises: what happens when the ideology of progress and its quantitative criteria disappear, and when qualitative differences becomes more important than quantifiable inequalities?

This question, which I am formulating in cautious terms, is the dominant question of our era, just as class conflicts or the struggle for political freedoms were once the dominant issue in different societies. There are two main answers to it.

The *first* is that differences no longer know any bounds, that we are all trapped into one or more communities, and that we are obsessed with our identity and the purity of our 'people'. Once we begin to go down that road, we inevitably find ourselves caught up in Samuel Huntington's 'clash of civilizations', and even if we are critical of that notion – and I am – we cannot deny that it does describe a powerful trend that can lead to the outbreak of new wars of religion or ethnic wars.

The *other* answer is not so simple, and most of this book will be devoted to its exposition. It says that the most important thing is that the behavioural conformity is no longer imposed by particularity of a culture of society, but by the way everyone is constructed as a subject who has universal rights as well as an individual being.

The difference between the two answers can be seen everywhere. Europe's Muslims, for example, are divided among themselves and have reached the parting of the ways. The future of all Europeans depends on the extent to which they can help the Muslims of Europe to reconcile the universalist individualism we have inherited from the Enlightenment, with an awareness of the particularities of all culture and all societies.

The debate about education is just as passionate. Many people are more concerned with public security than with giving every child the chance to construct his or her own identity. If we cannot resolve that problem, schools will become factors that produce greater inequality because they refuse to take into account the psychological, social and cultural particularity of every individual, and that refusal will harm the weakest and the most oppressed.

The dependency of women, the rejection of ethnic, religious, cultural or sexual minorities, and the difficulties young people face at school and in their personal lives are three vast domains of social life in which the inversion of social – finds its field of application, and calls for ideas, feelings and policies that can transform our personal and collective lives. I hope to demonstrate the need for that inversion. Now that we no longer see history as a staircase that everyone can climb, either quickly or slowly, it is up to us to choose between new wars of religion and the recognition that individuals are subjects who are equal but different.

Finally, we must rule out one objection that is as surprising as it is common, namely the claim that an 'idealism' based upon the idea of the subject masks social conflicts, the most important of which in reality stem, they tell us, from the nature of an economic system based primarily on the exploitation of workers by capitalists. Surely conflicts, strikes and even revolutions are responses to a crisis in capitalist domination? In my own defence, I would point out that I have spent the greater part of my life studying social movements, and especially working-class consciousness, and that I have shown that the latter is not an effect of the contradictions of capitalism, but a defence of the autonomy of labour against methods of rationalization designed to boost capitalists' profits. The new industrial disputes are themselves defensive attempts to resist the introduction of a 'flexibility' that reduces the lives of wage-earners to a series of temporary jobs and periods of unemployment and destroys their awareness of being in charge of their own lives. The same point can be made with respect to many other domains. Freedom of choice in terms of sexual behaviours, freedom of conscience, and especially religious freedom, are so many instances of the struggle to defend everyone's right to be a subject. A subject is not a victim but an actor who wants to establish a free self-to-self relationship, rather than being integrated into a community. This inversion of the meaning of such conflicts, which then become liberation movements, is bound up with a rejection of totalitarian regimes, because we are not simply defending one particular dimension of existence against a totalitarian regime. The only way we can fight totalitarian regimes is by appealing to a principle that is itself total: the right to be freely oneself, to choose one's own life. Any attempt to contrast a sociology of the subject with a sociology of conflict would obviously completely contradict the spirit of my analysis.

Part I

A Blind Society

1

Doing Away With the Dominant Interpretive Discourse

When we realize that we are no longer in control of events or that we can no longer understand them, we look back and ask ourselves if the events that had the greatest influence in the recent past might not have led us astray, and left us blind and unable to act. Such a situation would not be too serious if it were simply a matter of making up for lost time, as we have done when it came to using certain technologies. But this is quite different: it concerns our self-representations and our interpretation of our lived situations. Our unease becomes all the greater when we discover that we have become trapped into a vision of social life and of ourselves that deprives us of all freedom and all creativity, into a vision of a society in which there are no actors and which is completely subordinate to external determinants. Such a vision quickly becomes an obstacle to both action and thought. Many of us – all of us, to some extent – refused to see the blind alley into which it had trapped us and blamed everything on the globalization of the economy, American hegemony or the far Left or the far Right in France, rather as though we had never been able to influence the course of events, take decisions or transform culture and politics.

It is not too late to get out of this blind alley; indeed, if we wish to regain the ability to understand and act, making a critique of our past mistakes is a matter of urgency. And this is the ideal moment for such a rereading of the past few decades and the ideas that dominated them.

France experienced serious rioting in the *banlieues* of Paris and other cities in 2005; in 2006, France voted against the proposed European Constitution when many countries voted in favour of it, while the breadth of the youth movement that protested against the bill to introduce a 'First Job Contract' [*Contrat Premier Emploi*] revealed that young people felt they had been marginalized and denied a future. French society – and I will be talking mainly about France – is disoriented and no longer has a set of analyses that allows it to understand its present, past and future. We feel that the reality of our individual and collective lives is becoming further and further removed from both institutional norms and great principles, and is beginning to break free of categories that no longer have any meaning and because so many people in today's society feel that they are in a weak position, in precarious jobs and threatened with exclusion.

This crisis is making us so fearful that we immediately tend to lay the blame elsewhere. While that option is often successful in terms of public opinion, it sheds no light on the situation because what we might call the dominant ideology or the spirit of the times always tries to understand it in terms of external determinants. We have to abandon the conception of social life and personal experience that had a dominant influence on our recent past. We have to force ourselves to make an original analysis of new ways of thinking, acting and speaking in order to free ourselves from our current feelings of impotence and emptiness.

The Cold War Era

The half-century I am referring to began with the fall of Nazism and Japanese militarism, and then with the Soviet seizure of half of Europe. It was then transformed by a vast decolonization movement and by a big rise in both production and consumption in one part of the world. It ended with the fall of the Berlin Wall and the Soviet Empire. Some think, however, that it lasted until 11 September 2001, when the Al-Qaeda group's kamikaze terrorists flew their planes into the towers of the World Trade Center in New York and the Pentagon. These historical markers – 1945–1989–2001 – have been so widely adopted that it would be pointless to challenge them. It is true that they refer to political history rather than the history of ideas, but these dates marked such tragic moments that they are certainly good observation posts for looking at and understanding the historical fields that came before and after them.

Although this book is not about war, peace, the international crisis, the threat of military invasion or the nuclear threat, it does refer to the major international conflicts that constantly preoccupied those who lived through this period. That provides a first explanation of why we find it so difficult to understand ourselves. Everything we did and said in most countries was dominated by the very recent memory of Nazi totalitarianism and by the even closer presence of Soviet totalitarianism on the other side of the Iron Curtain. The clash between empires and ideologies weighed so heavily on our lives that we always doubted our ability to make our own history and to choose our own destiny.

It is impossible to discuss the French or Italian Left during this period without admitting that those countries' Communist Parties were totally bound up with the Soviet Union and Kominform, and that a major fraction of European intellectuals did not denounce that situation, and did not even have the courage to pass judgement on the regime created by Lenin and Stalin at a time when they were denouncing the United States as the source of all our woes.

Everything got off to a false start. When we said 'Left' or 'Right', we were in fact thinking of the two sides that clashed in the Cold War. People on the Right defined themselves primarily by condemning the Communist world; the only thing that people on the Left had in common was their hostility to the United States. It was difficult to analyse societies, social actors, collective movements or cultural transformations at a time when we were developing and thinking in the shadow of Empires that were struggling to dominate Europe, or even the rest of the world.

The Singularity of France

All European countries suffered from the effects of this confrontation. Countries on the other side of the Iron Curtain certainly experienced much more suffering and repression than those in the West, but all Europeans lost much of their ability to make real choices and to act on the basis of their own problems and internal debates.

Within Western Europe, France found itself in a different situation from that of other countries. This was not because French society was very different from the society of its neighbours but because the French had for a long time subordinated their vision of their society to their own conception of the state: no matter whether it was defined as a nation state, a people's state or a revolutionary state, it was always the guardian of what had come to be called 'civil society'. So long as social and political movements were directed against the state and gave birth to and transformed citizens, France played an avantgarde role in thought and social action but, as Marx said, while the French were ahead of other peoples when it came to politics, they were behind when it came to analysing the transition from politically dominated societies to societies dominated by economic realities and their social expressions. In France, Marx's argument still holds. The trade unions have almost always been dominated by the political parties, and for the last third of the twentieth century, the French Left was dominated by François Mitterrand, whose brilliant strategy consisted in undermining the Communist Party by allowing the new Socialist Party to adopt the spirit of its demands. The outcome was that, in 1981, the Left was full of enthusiasm for new nationalizations and for the assertion of the higher rights of the state, including the architect-state that embarked upon *grands projets* that a parliamentary government could not successfully complete. It is true that this state supremacy did have some positive effects and was by no means limited to what some call the bureaucracy or techno-bureaucracy.

In the second half of the twentieth century, France was saved from shame and collapse by General de Gaulle, who loved France much more than he loved the French. As in many other countries, it was the state that reconstructed France. It was the Gaullist state that embarked upon great scientific and technological projects that have not been updated or have been replaced by others. More recently, it is the state we have to thank for holding out at the UN Security Council against the campaign of lies that President Bush used to justify war against Iraq. This state has been undermined, and often perverted, only when it was no longer capable of understanding social demands and creating the pre-conditions for the emergence of a new cultural space.

The 'Dominant Interpretive Discourse' (DID)

This image is, however, inadequate. There is always, at least in a free society, a set of principles, ideas, memories and judgements that is not simply determined by the national and international political environment. The composition of what we still call the 'spirit of the times' is more diverse and changeable: that is the difference between it and the official policies and lines that authoritarian governments dictate to writers and businessmen. This apparently confused mass is, however, consistent enough to make it an essential intermediary between the creators and those who wield power. In the case of France, the spirit of the times was not dominated by subordination to the state but, rather, by the creation of a décor that painted a very dark picture of many aspects of social and cultural life. There is nothing exceptional about this. On the contrary, we must remember that these mediations and influences are always autonomous, and that they determine the actions of both producers and consumers and outwit the strategies of public relations firms and especially the media.

We underestimate the importance of these levels of experience to such an extent that we often deny their existence and look to the state and the international economy to find a direct explanation for our behaviours. Events, decisions and forms of social organization are in reality perceived only through our representation of them. As a result, the explanations given by the social sciences always consist in finding some correspondence between external determinants and the demands of individual and collective actors, which are sometimes expressed directly, and sometimes through the medium of movements, innovations or prophecies. But between the two, we always find the fluid but opaque mass known as the 'spirit of the times'. While it is often the case that individual histories are determined by major historical determinants trends, there is therefore always a divorce between the two, so powerful is the mass that shapes interpretations and so great is its ability to create categories, judgements and forms of organization. It always feels fragile, but it can stubbornly resist anything that opposes it.

It is at the intermediary level of the dominant ideological discourse that intellectual choices are made, and that conditions of communication are shaped. The latter impose rules, pay attention to some and not to others, and sometimes even succeed in making us accept as natural and objective what is no more than a product of some free-floating construct of social reality that is important only because of the role it plays. This ideological discourse is as far removed from state power as the authority of science or the influence of creative intellectuals. We can use the expression *dominant ideological discourse* to describe this set of representations. They are mediations, but what is more important is that they construct an overall image of social life and individual experience.

In some cases, this dominant interpretive discourse (DID) is associated with a dominant economic or political power, or even a monopolistic or authoritarian power. That situation corresponds to what that power's opponents call the 'dominant ideology'. But in many countries, and especially France, the dominant ideology is not the ideology of the ruling class or state power. Nor can it be said to be the creation of intellectuals in the general sense. Most scientists have nothing to do with this discourse, and nor do many of the 'professionals' who live in a world defined either by a discipline or a profession, or by the law and its institutions and rules.

We therefore cannot locate this DID with any precision, but nor can we deny its reality or its strength. Its strength is the strength of influence, but it can also be that of constraint. The dissociation between the DID and power demonstrates that the construction of reality is an important element of reality itself. Objectivist visions of social reality are unacceptable. The history of ideas is proof of that, as it is very difficult to find a concrete social and political reality behind the expression of even abstract ideas in sociology, history or political science. It is therefore impossible to understand any thought unless we situate it in historical and social terms. The intentionality of action and the historical nature of its presence and use are the two principles on which the social sciences are based, and that is the difference between them and the natural sciences and what we might call human natural sciences such as linguistics or some parts of anthropology.

The characteristic feature of the DID is that it designates a content that is both ill-defined and changeable. Its weakness does not detract from its importance. It is certainly easier to say that social life is no more than a discourse or a construct or, conversely, that it is determined by economic, ethnic or religious realities. But in most cases, and especially in societies that enjoy freedom of expression, these extreme positions are untenable. Biologists have long insisted that the innate and the acquired cannot be divorced. The same is true in the social sciences: those who believe that they have discovered an important truth by saying that food, size and sex are not natural realities are stating the obvious. But to conclude from that that sex is nothing more than gender, which is a social construct, is an immense step, and one that must not be taken. Similarly, what Marxists call the social division of labour is, as a general rule, inseparable from the technical division of labour, but the two things are by no means the same.

The same general caution should be applied to relations between the dominant interpretive discourse and social classes. Of course neo-liberals are closer to business leaders, and socialists to wage-earners, but the correlation is now much weaker in countries where wage-earners make up 80 per cent of the active population. In France, liberal and social-democratic ideologues have always been timid, and few have ever had the talent of a Raymond Aron, who was able to produce a liberal-inspired body of work that used a terminology that was acceptable to the Left, and which many intellectuals of that persuasion privately admired.

The DID I am describing is a historical reality that is constantly changing, but it always has a dominant effect. In the United States, post-war social thought was dominated by functionalism, with Talcott

Parsons as its most sophisticated advocate. At that time, French thought was dominated by a Marxism tinged with both nationalistic sentiments and an anti-Stalinism derived from Trotsky. In both cases, works that deviated from the DID had difficulty in finding an audience, as Wright Mills in the United States and Raymond Aron in France learned to their cost.

This domination-effect is sometimes grounded in some great work, but in most cases it is also produced by transmitters such as teachers, journalists and editors, and even those politicians who cling to an overall vision of society.

The effects of the dominant interpretive discourse are essentially negative: it erects barriers that have no official discourse but that are difficult to get around, and they restrict our understanding of the facts by giving an *a priori* interpretation of them. In the France of the second half of the twentieth century, a Marxist-inspired DID, defined mainly by its refusal to accept a logic of actors, to say nothing of the idea of the subject, which it tried to reduce to a class ideology, had a dominant, but not total, influence on the way we thought about society. I will demonstrate why and how that dominant interpretive discourse paralysed or perverted many of French society's self-representations, because it did not correspond to social reality and could neither perceive nor express what was going on in France and the world at that time.

In the case of France, which will be analysed here but which is not an isolated case, it tried to justify itself by invoking the predominant role played in industrial society by the thinking of the labour movement and especially by anti-capitalist thinking. That discourse, which was mainly intended to replace an action that was on its way to becoming a thing of the past, was elaborated at a time when the labour movement was becoming exhausted because it had been destroyed by the way it had been interpreted by the Soviet Union and then Mao's China, and when the trade unions were beginning to lose their influence in the Western world, and especially in France. That is the main reason why, while action is always full of motives, projects, emotions and risks, the dominant interpretive discourse constructs a world without actors that is dominated by implacable logics that infiltrate all categories of knowledge and social organization. It is not a vision of the whole of social history or even of social relations, and it is not an analysis of class consciousness or political consciousness; it is a purely critical vision of social life, and believes that social life is governed by some absolute power.

The success of Michel Foucault's *Discipline and Punish*, which is remarkable in terms of both its talent and its documentation, can be explained in terms of the fit between the book and this dominant interpretive discourse, so much so that many readers overlook, as we shall see, other aspects and other phases of Foucault's work.

This dominant interpretive discourse finds expression in books, articles and discourses that are real only to the extent that they are part of it. But it is still widely diffused and becomes an almost official discourse for certain categories of teachers, students, journalists and other media professionals. It was at its strongest in France during the aftermath of May 1968, and that confirms my initial hypothesis: a discourse that sometimes took the form of a catechism and sometimes that of a Little Red Book (which is more serious), and that did a lot of damage in the academic world, emerged from the ruins of the spirit of 1968 and the May movement, especially between 1970 and 1974. It continued to wreak damage until the first mass-market editions of Solzhenitsyn on the one hand and the 'carnation revolution' in Portugal on the other revealed the threat of a possible victory by the Communist Party, which terrified both the Leftist supporters of Otelo de Carvalho and Europe's social-democrats.

The Survival of the DID

The transformation of the Socialist Party at the Épinay Congress, and the *Programme Commun* drawn up with the Communist Party, which intermittently supported it until 1981, did nothing to undermine the influence of the dominant interpretive discourse. On the contrary, François Mitterrand ensured its survival by taking it away from the Communists and Leftists and making it part of the socialist heritage. The years 1981–4, which so rapidly demonstrated the failure of an economic policy that tried to swim against the current, also saw a revival of this discourse, which sometimes took as extreme a form as at the beginning of the 1970s.

General political developments certainly made it less powerful and less visible, but it emerged once more in the late 1990s and especially with the great strike of 1995, which not only expressed French fears about rising unemployment but also saw the revival of discourses that were very similar to the earlier ideological model and what were in truth pathetic political attempts to reconstruct a political action 'to the left of the Left' that was fully in keeping with that discourse. Once the threat of terrorism, which was as real in France as it was in Germany, though less so than in Italy, had been eliminated, Leftist policies, including tactics and strategy, were little more than an illustration of a DID that was totally divorced from practice.

The hypothesis that seems to suggest itself is indeed that the content and influence of this interpretive discourse, which were considerable and sometimes even dominant, compensated for the growing weakness and disorientation of the entire political culture that the French describe as republican, socialist or communist. The capacity for action was undermined in every sector, primarily because the socialist or communist idea was identified with the Soviet regime, many of whose fellow travellers, who knew the truth, could not go on hiding either its totalitarian nature or the extent of its repressive programme for ever.

French political life was characterized by the weakness of the liberals on the one hand, and that of the social democrats on the other. Even the term 'social democracy' was often excluded from the vocabulary of the Left. Alone in Europe, the French Left consistently rejected the idea that the social objectives of equality and justice, which should have been its objectives, could be combined with an openness to a world market which, with the active approval of the parties of the Right, wanted to be free from all constraints. It was obviously easier to think along those lines so long as the Cold War forced many moderates to ally themselves with the American model and its army, which seemed to them to be the only real powers that could stand up to Soviet pressure. That discourse did not, however, fade away when the Berlin Wall came down. It was heard once more fifteen years later, still unchanged and suddenly exposed when the French voted to reject the proposed European Constitution. A clear majority on the Left opposed the treaty and, more generally, both the market economy and any social-democratic attempt to combine political and social objectives, even though many examples, in Europe itself and especially in the Scandinavian countries, had demonstrated that such a combination was both possible and fertile.

One cautious remark to end: the influence of this dominant interpretive discourse can be seen everywhere, but the most important works to a large extent escaped it. We find in the broad theoretical movement that is variously described as post-structuralist, post-Marxist or post-modern, themes and many works that do rise above the clouds on the dominant interpretive discourse. On the other hand, that discourse did not, except in some fairly borderline cases, have any real power. Even in those universities it had penetrated most deeply, it was associated with a certain intellectual permissiveness that proved to be very innovative, whereas the discourse itself was, even in professional milieus, no more than a widely prescribed doctrine.

On the other hand, the critical analysis of French political and intellectual history outlined here should certainly not lead us to conclude that this is the exception to the general rule. A dominant interpretive discourse does not disappear in any country or at any point in time, so long as it is bound up with state power or a ruling class or, at the opposite extreme, so long as it is bound up with religious traditions or debates within the intellectual world and university institutions. 'Objective' explanations of social behaviours in terms of economic or other determinants are not acceptable in any country. What is largely specific to France, a country whose collective memory is based upon the Revolution, the violence of repression, a lively working-class consciousness and plans for political transformations, is the very broad agreement that we live in a society in which there are no potential actors, no independent movements and no creative inspiration. One example among many clearly demonstrates this: in France, feminism was devoted almost entirely to struggles against women's dependency and the violence they suffered; its positive perspectives have, from Simone de Beauvoir onwards, been restricted either to the demand for equality or to the quest for a society in which gender-differences would no longer be pertinent. Sociologists have written almost nothing on the innovations and struggles initiated by women themselves. Women historians are more insightful, but even today most feminist studies concentrate on revealing the extent to which women are victims. That is certainly necessary, but it could never be said that it is enough.

This specificity is, to a large extent, explained by the fact that the labour movement or, to be more specific, trade unionism, was not seen in France as a force for social transformation but merely as a disruptive force from which political parties – and especially the Communist Party – could extract a political meaning. This had disastrous effects on democracy, because democracy presupposes that social actors, their collective movements and their aspirations, take precedence over the action of parties, especially when the latter are defined in terms of a struggle to the death with a political and economic power.

To conclude this analysis, we have to defend the idea that other discourses can also interpret this era, and above all that representations, interventions, ideas and policies that are very different to those that play the central role can take shape and can even have the good fortune to make themselves heard in political and union policies, as in social thought in general; that the feeling of crisis and impotence, or even of the loss of meaning we are now experiencing, could be overcome if we looked to the recent past for forms of action and thought based upon the belief that action is possible, on the importance of social movements and on the need for cultural elaborations relating to all aspects of life in all countries, and especially those countries that are suffering mainly because they have theorized their impotence, dependency and woes.

This book therefore does not just explore a past that is already slipping away from us; it is an attempt to see the destructive effects of the dominant interpretive discourse as one of the main causes of a situation that has long urgently appealed for other interpretations that did not have a central role in recent decades but which have every reason to combine social thought and social action in the decades to come.

Such a critical reflection on the past and especially the present is urgently required because, no matter what the dominant interpretive discourse has been saying for so long, we do not live in an empty world in which we have no capacity for actions or in which there are no liberation struggles. At the same time, we are in a better position than we were to understand that the worldwide triumph of a capitalist economy that has been freed from all social and political controls leads to ruptures, means that more and more people have no security, and increases inequalities. No one is tempted to go back to trusting blindly in the progress of production, consumption and communications; we have lost for ever the illusions that led the 'great powers' to regard themselves as the sole guardians of the rule of reason and the future of the world. We see new demands, new representations and new ideas wherever we look. Wherever we look, we can see that the historical stage is not empty, and that it has not been completely taken over by military-style conflicts, invasions and mass destruction. Although they have a huge impact on the world, such catastrophes do not mean that those who have always said 'We cannot do anything' are right and that those who have always said 'We can do something' are wrong. It is worth making the effort, and we can make a contribution that is as great as the efforts that have been made to transform institutions and to create new organizations which promote collective action.

I am therefore trying to kill two birds with one stone; first, to make a critique of what were the dominant modes of thought and to show the need to eradicate them, even though they are still there in many heads, discourses and institutions; and, second, to suggest that we invert our representations of social life to bring them into line with the observable facts, and especially observable practices. There is an enormous gulf between the false and arbitrary thinking that dominated what is still a recent past, and the need to analyse and understand a world that is undergoing a profound and permanent transformation. The gulf is so great that we are dazzled when we move out of the shadows and into the light.

A radical critique of a mode of thought that has already lost its capacity to invent would be of no more than retrospective interest, were that not the road we have to take if we are to construct a new representation of both individuals and society. Such a representation presupposes, first of all, that we can *see* what exists, listen to those who are speaking, protesting and making proposals, and that we can agree to learn from our experience and observations, rather than the arbitrary assertions of the dominant interpretive discourse.

The fact that we do not live in a world that is dead or that has been reduced to silence is enough to dissuade us from indulging in the feeling of relief which followed the collapse of the ideologies that once cluttered up the intellectual scene. You ask if there are new actors, or if the stage of history really is empty? Then stop looking in the opposite direction and covering up your ears! There are actors, ideas, beliefs, conflicts and innovations everywhere. Women are not just victims, as so many women authors would have us believe; they are asserting themselves, have a new self-confidence and are leading all of us – men and women – into a new cultural world. The societies and cultures that were hidden and destroyed by colonization are showing their faces and demanding that we rewrite a history that overlooked them. The religious phenomenon, which was thought to be in decline or a survival of pre-modern illusions, is increasingly visible and is making itself heard more loudly day-by-day. We constantly ask ourselves how we can be both equal and different, how we can both respect particular cultures and remain true to the universalism without which there can be no communication. We also wonder day-by-day about what the real roles of schools should be, about whether prisons serve any purpose, especially since François Mitterrand and Robert Badinter abolished the death penalty in France for reasons of principle. They acted in the name of the highest principles.

We constantly have to remind ourselves that the air is full of words and screams, protests and proposals. That is the only way to get away from the false idea that nothing happens any more, and that we are living through a series of catastrophes that make all thought impossible and pointless, and which encourage us to blame television or the internet for the death of all civil consciousness. None of these problems and none of these innovations is new. Many of them were already there when ideology completely concealed the emergence of new behaviours. But it is not too late to construct a representation of social life, both collective and individual, that is stronger than the one that deafened us for so long. It will give us the means to understand what is happening to us and around us, even though we are in such a hurry not to notice what it is.

This book evokes neither a return to an era that has gone nor the revelation of tendencies that have only now become visible. Its *raison d'être* is that most social thought has been buried beneath an ideology born in the ruins of what were industrial societies. Their social actors were then imprisoned or lied to by totalitarian regimes. This book's sole ambition is to teach them to look and listen once more.

2

The Imaginary Revolution

Nostalgia for Revolution

The dominant interpretive discourse is based upon one more central
assertion: the reason why society is empty is that it is dependent upon
the state, and the need for revolution is such that social actors count
for nothing.

Western Europe has lived through a long period of glaciation.
Faced with the Soviet world and its deportation camps, it remained
true to its attachment to the defence of basic human rights. Its intellectuals enjoyed an almost total freedom of expression. And yet it
was widely believed that Europe, like the rest of the world, was in a
pre-revolutionary situation. For many long years, no political figure
was more popular than Fidel Castro, with the possible exception of
Che Guevara, who, after having taken part in the successful guerrilla
campaign in Cuba and holding high office in the Cuban state,
embarked on his Bolivian adventure with his group of revolutionar-
ies. It was doomed from the start and ended with his death, but he
also achieved exceptional glory as the figure of Christ the Guerrilla.
For a long time, weaker voices in Paris kept repeating: 'One solution,
revolution' and 'Elections are a mug's game.'

Why speak of *revolution* in a part of the world where it was the
last thing on anyone's mind? First and foremost because Europe was
divided in two and because the great post-Liberation projects for
social transformation had been forgotten in Western countries. As a
result, socialists and social-democrats were content to manage economies and societies that had been remodelled at the end of the war.
Few structural reforms were implemented during these long years.

All over the world, the a Left was torn between a social-democracy that had been undermined and had no plans for change, and Trotsky-ist, Maoist and other groups for whom the idea of revolution was the only way of expressing their frustration and lack of any political perspective. This was especially true in France, where the categories of the state remained more important than those of society.

This half-century can be seen as the transition from societies that were dominated by their states to societies that are incorporated into the international economy and in which economic choices outweighed political decisions. This idea is reinforced if we look at the construc-tion of Europe, which gradually deviated from its original ambitions after they reached their high point under the presidency of Jacques Delors. After that, Europe became increasingly obsessed with the almost insoluble problem of how to integrate the former countries of the Soviet sphere into an organization created by Western Europe. The same idea can be expressed in different words. The transition we lived through was a transition from an analysis in terms of systems to an analysis in terms of actors, and especially those actors who can be regarded as subjects. We can also say that we were emerging from an industrial society in which actors and system were two sides of the same coin, and entering a society in which the categories that define situations have become completely divorced from the categories that define actors. It was this divorce that eradicated the idea of revolu-tion, which is based upon the idea that economic mutations will bring about a complete upheaval in both organization of society and social attitudes. It is, then, the interdependency of all aspects of social life that can, in certain situations, trigger a revolution. In the kind of social situation in which we find ourselves, by contrast, the complete divorce between actors and the system means that we suffer from an inability to act collectively rather than from the fear that we will be swept away by some revolutionary current.

The French find it very difficult to accept this idea; they see it as a roundabout way of abandoning all political voluntarism and allowing themselves to be guided by world markets. They are still living in the shadow of the Great Revolution, and are therefore convinced that no far-reaching social reforms can be implemented, or even envis-aged, unless we adopt a revolutionary perspective. Hence the ubiq-uitous use of the adjective 'revolutionary', even though only a few small groups were in fact prepared to embark upon a total struggle with a view to bringing about the equally total collapse of the old society. The main effect of this survival of the revolutionary idea was to make political France incapable of implementing reforms, trans-forming its worldview or making greater allowance for popular demands, especially in the workplace. It was as though the Communist Party, which remained a powerful force for a long time, and then the Socialist Party, which had been bequeathed its heritage by François Mitterrand, had blocked the possibility of reform. The enthusiasm sparked by the major legislations of 1981, and especially the new nationalizations, exhausted the energies of the French Left, and it quickly realized that its policy of swimming against the tide had failed. The subsequent failure to act lasted long after the end of François Mitterrand's second presidency. The French Left was still largely unable to do anything as Jacques Chirac's presidencies came to an end.

This representation of social life became extremely widespread; it was not adopted by everyone, but it did become the dominant interpretive discourse and had an influence on everyone, all the more so in that few social analysts were prepared to break completely with the earlier model for thought and action for fear of being taken in the opposite political direction. No one died, but everyone was influenced by a vision of social life whose formulations were becoming further and further removed from any observable reality. On the other hand, the paralysis this created should not be overstated: some major thinkers with a philosophical bent were able to write important books that were out of step with both this outdated vision of social and personal life and its political antithesis.

So far as I am concerned, I concentrated, perhaps for too long, on trying to understand Western industrial society's real actors and social movements, popular and democratic uprisings against the Soviet regime, and Latin American debates about the theme of dependency: the path I took protected me to some extent from the intellectually destructive effects of the dominant interpretive discourse. On the other hand, it also explains why I remained within the intellectual framework of industrial society for so long. Despite my interpretation of May 1968, and despite my studies of what I myself called new social movements, I found myself, in the 1980s, having to admit that those movements had ended in failure, and to radically revise my own theories.

Critique of Revolution

The idea of revolution and the assertion of the subject are contradictory. That statement may seem surprising because we view revolutions as the crucial moment in a liberation that is made impossible by institutions and cultural processes. The idea of revolution is based upon the conviction that no positive and reformist action is possible, and that our main task is to seize state power, and either destroy it or transform it. This has the effect of creating a new order that has no more reason to respect the rights of the individual than its predecessor. The dominant interpretive discourse described in the first chapter is full of revolutionary intentions and memories that lead to the rejection of democracy because the two themes are antinomic. Revolution is not a road that leads to democracy and, because of the freedom it confers, democracy cannot be regarded as the instrument of revolution. The idea of revolution subordinates the actor to a 'natural' logic, which may be either biological or historical. It destroys all subjectivity as well as all rights. It is true that history often uses these words in a confused way. We all speak of the Great Revolution, meaning either the French Revolution or the first Russian Revolution of the Spring of 1917. What happened in 1789 was in fact not so much a revolution as an assertion of human rights and the overthrow of a system that denied or destroyed those rights. It was only from 1792 onwards that a logic of war at home and abroad set in, and it led to the mobilization of all resources and the annihilation of all freedoms. As everyone knows, the oath of the tennis court, the Declaration of the Rights of Man and the Citizen and the abolition of privileges during the night of 4 August were great moments in human liberation, and were therefore very different to the *journée* of 10 August, the September massacres or the Great Terror in both the provinces and Paris.

We have to contrast *democracy* with *revolution*. Of course there is more than one type of democracy, and more than one revolutionary process. But this contrast has such intellectual influence, and the growing contrast between revolution and democracy has become so obvious that we can use it to define the 'spirit of the times', or what I have called the dominant interpretive discourse of the second half of the twentieth century. For it is true to say that the best way to identify that discourse is to go on seeing it as revolutionary. The idea of revolution implies a break with an entire institutional system – and not just an economic system in which the actor – the class nation or minority whose cause is being defended – can no longer find in those institutions the means to achieve its objectives, obtain the reforms it is defending, or do away with an injustice or an intolerable inequality. Once the break becomes more important than the reform, the objective is to overthrow a government or to seize power rather than to resolve the initial social or cultural problem. We then adopt a definition of the historical situation in which there is no room for actors.

Of course no theoretician or historian of revolutions describes the historical theatre as empty. On the contrary, they describe a stage that has been invaded by the masses or by popular groups, such as the image of the Château of Vincennes being invaded by the Parisian mob in October 1789. But in this case, the actors are no more than the agents of a break that is as inevitable as it is necessary. The people of Paris or the soldiers and sailors of St Petersburg in the Spring of 1917 are the passive agents of history; they do not create it and give it a meaning. Hence the tragic nature of all revolutions, which always take place under the sign of death. The execution of sovereigns is more than a symbol of a radical break; it signals the rejection of any analysis and makes it impossible to describe any action in terms of interests, orientations or antinomic values. That is why the word 'people' describes the actors of a revolution so well. The 'people' is not a social category; it is what the state calls itself when it tries to define itself in social terms, and it is therefore what those who are making the transition from society to state, from the social to the political, call themselves.

Most Western societies have experienced revolutions and the elimination of what they called 'anciens régimes'. Many parts of the world that were isolated within Empires that maintained order rather than organizing change, or that were subjected to colonial domination, were forced to go down the revolutionary road and therefore created regimes that subordinated society's actors to a state apparatus, old or new, more completely than ever. But why does that revolutionary model seem to have survived in a France that had, to a large extent, already been modernized, that had undergone major institutional transformations and that had a positive self-image immediately after the First World War? Why did the French Socialist Party join the Third International en masse when those who, like Léon Blum, chose to remain in *la vieille maison* were using a language that was almost as revolutionary as that of their adversaries? Why did French miners embark upon revolutionary strikes after the Second World War, and especially in 1947 and 1948? Why did France remain true to the revolutionary model to such an extent that the Communist Party went on playing the leading role on the Left while the socialists failed to redefine themselves as social-democrats through a Cold War in which most Western countries identified with the democratic ideal and not the revolutionary idea? Why was most French peoples' rejection of the proposed European Constitution couched in terms of a truly revolutionary discourse which insisted that a market economy was incompatible with a policy of social justice and equality? Why did the 'left of the Left' in all its forms enjoy some success in France when it called for an open break with capitalism, even though the vast majority of French people were completely unaware of what its consequences would be? Why did a current of opinion that was convinced of the need to break with the market economy and its corollaries still look like a possible option for the Socialist Party in 2006?

The question I am asking about the success and survival of the revolutionary idea in France also applies to the dominant interpretive discourse. I find it constantly present and I am now trying to understand why it has done so much to encourage a sociology in which there are no actors and no subject.

The only possible answer lies in the way France has always privileged the problems of the state. The French have never been able to think about social phenomena other than in political terms. They have never shown any great interest in economic problems. They tend to regard every social problem as a particular 'front' in the class struggle. They are happy to express anti-parliamentarian views, but are convinced that society can be transformed by starting with the state, and not vice versa. It seems to be impossible to get beyond this classic explanation, which has been given by so many good analysts. It is the state that created France in territorial terms, that defended it in arms, that modernized it from the time of Colbert onwards, and that industrialized it, thanks in part to the armaments industry. And above all, it was the state that created a state society within society. Some call it the public sector, while others, like Pierre Bourdieu, see it as subordinating society to the state nobility.

France has always witnessed attempts to strengthen society and to free it from the tutelage of the state. But all the talk about 'civil society' has usually served to cover up clientelism or even corruption. In recent years, Pierre Mendès-France and then Michel Rocard, Jacques Delors and others made significant attempts to strengthen society and did briefly take away some of the state's power, but their views never convinced François Mitterrand, a cunning and all-powerful representative of the statist view of society who insisted that political analysis and action took priority over any understanding of society, its actors and its problems.

It is, however, easy to go too far in that direction and to forget that France is a parliamentary democracy, and that basic freedoms, and especially freedom of expression, are on the whole respected, which cannot be said of all countries in Europe. It therefore seems difficult to provide any satisfactory explanation as to why the French prioritize political action, and even revolutionary action, over all forms of social action and especially collective bargaining. We have to content ourselves with the explanation that is usually put forward, and it does in fact explain this long-standing tradition. France is the homeland of *laïcité*, or in other words a centuries-long confrontation between church and state. As André Siegfried demonstrates in a classic study, the French Revolution's creation of a schismatic church had long-lasting effects. Debates over education did much more to dominate the nineteenth century than industrial conflicts, and the most lasting image of the Vichy regime is its anti-Jewish policy and its constant calls for a return to Christian values and a state that defended religious values. For a long time, the conflict between Right and Left meant a conflict between Catholics and secularists rather than one between antagonistic social groups, and especially social classes.

Intellectuals did a lot to elevate the state above society, but the state, with its concealed arbitrariness and violence, was also the main target of their criticisms. The education debate died down, but a radical and revolutionary Left survived and could easily be brought back to life. The Left appealed to the state rather than society, and especially the globalized economy. This Left remains convinced that the only way to defend French society effectively against economic globalization is to strengthen the state, and especially public services. There is no real equivalent in other countries to the way the words 'state', 'republic', 'public sector' and public service' are used in France. For many French people, there is an inevitable and necessary clash between a capitalist system that is seeking to dominate the whole world under American hegemony and what we might call French 'civilization', in the sense in which Samuel Huntington uses that word to describe an indissociable set of elements, including the economy, political management, the organization of the administration, education, and so on. The idea of *laïcité* itself does not refer only to the necessary separation of church and state; it further implies that the whole of public life is dependent upon the will of the state, and that, while they are not confined to the private sphere, 'religions' are marginal to public life, as is so clearly indicated by their de facto absence from the school curriculum and the state's monopoly on conferring university degrees.

Every French generation passes on a national heritage: the French Revolution, the rights of man, great struggles such as the Dreyfus Affair and the Popular Front, the need not to give ground to religions and particularisms of all kinds, and so on. This has to be accepted or rejected *en bloc*. And yet it is this that produced the dominant interpretive discourse I have referred to so often. Even the critique of the state usually adopts the viewpoint of a state that is above society and its workings. There has always been a family likeness between the

French state and the Catholic Church, but the members of this family have fallen out badly, not that that prevents them from looking like one another and having common interests.

Parallels with Latin America

It is not in France's neighbours that we really find the problems that social thought encounters there: it is in Latin America. *Dependency theory*, which is based upon solid studies by the UN's Economic Commission for Latin America and the Caribbean, places the emphasis on the structural duality of Latin America and on the concentration of income in social categories that are small in numerical terms but capable of becoming markets for European or North American products. This is an almost perfect replica of France's dominant interpretive discourse, at least for the majority of dependency theorists, who see dependency as the hegemonic determinant of the economic and social situations that prevail in the sub-continent. These theoreticians have adopted the political line taken by Fidel Castro, which is based upon a rejection of the national-popular regimes to be found in most Latin American countries. It is this that led to the creation of guerrilla groups, which were certainly not localized social movements or even revolutionary vanguards in the Leninist sense, but mobile action units that tried to strike the dependency system at its weakest point, namely nation states that were often very corrupt or under the control of local oligarchies. They were formed by students or young people, many of them from the urban middle classes and highly skilled in the use of revolutionary ideology. None of these guerrilla campaigns was successful, and the most disastrous failure occurred in Guatemala, where an attempt to establish links between the guerrilla fighters and the Quiche peasants through the intermediary of American priests triggered a campaign of military repression that ended with the Quiche being massacred. The general public learned about it from Rigoberta Menchu's books. This was not then a peasant movement, but the type of *foco* action defined by Régis Debray, and its primary goal was to undermine a dependent state. The importance given to guerrilla groups and the huge popularity of Che Guevara's theory of guerrilla warfare in Bolivia is a clear indication that this type of action was seen as a response to a foreign-inspired domination that extended to every aspect of social life. This made mass social movements and political mobilizations impossible. Colombia's guerrilla groups, and especially FARC, belong to a very different type of political actions in that they are not mobile and have remained for many years in vast but sparsely populated areas. Popular Unity in Chile was still further removed from the classic guerrilla groups, and therefore from the extreme forms of dependency theory, as there was a democratic component to Salvador Allende's government. Indeed, one might take the view that that was its most important feature. We therefore should not exaggerate the importance of the guerrilla campaigns but, in terms of the intellectual life of Latin America, the most radical forms of dependency theory did have a profound influence and, as in France, were associated with an increasingly violent rejection of the political system, so much so that Che Guevara embarked upon his Bolivian adventure without even trying to win the support of either the miners' union, whose influence was decisive at the time, or the Bolivian Communist Party.

A minority of sociologists defended a more moderate form of dependency theory. Inspired mainly by Fernando Henrique Cardoso and Enzo Faletto, they supported the idea that class struggle and problems of national integration coexisted alongside the problems of dependency, though they by no means denied the importance of the latter. The intersection between these three dimensions of political life created an autonomous arena for truly political actions, even though the most radical theorists denied that any such arena could possibly exist. But, specialist debates aside, these complementary and contrasting trends within dependency theory had major political and intellectual effects. Not only did the moderate version's most important defender become a politician who was twice elected President of the Republic of Brazil; at the level of social ideas, the continent is still greatly influenced by radical forms of dependency theory, which still enjoys the support of influential sociologists such as Pablo Gonzalez Casanova in Mexico. A similar balance sheet can be drawn up for France, taking into account the important difference between the two regions in terms of infrastructure and intellectual production. In both cases, the dominant interpretive discourse was a major obstacle to the intellectual renewal and the open discussions that shape new ideas. The most important development is not the renaissance of a very radical discourse, with President Chávez in Venezuela, and sometimes others, but the fact that there do not appear to have been any changes in the intellectual climate, and that the younger generations maintain a cautious silence or have gone in very different directions, partly because many of them studied at foreign universities.

The important point is, however, that the most radical forms of dependency theory, which argue that no reforms can be implemented even by opposition political parties, blocked the emergence of new ways of thinking in both Latin America, France and other countries in Europe. Some have overcome the obstacle, perhaps more obviously at the political level in Latin America and in the truly intellectual domain in France. But there are some remarkable similarities between the two continents, and the dominant interpretive discourse has had the same negative effects in both. It would not be difficult to extend the comparison to other parts of the world, or even to the United States, where this dominant interpretive discourse has been developed in some places. There is therefore nothing specifically French about this; these are indeed international manifestations of a conception of society that denies the possibility of autonomous reformist social and political actions. To put it in political terms, we might say it had led to a rejection of social-democracy in Europe, and to a rejection of all variants on national popular regimes in Latin America. The rejection of both those alternatives means that there is a lot of pressure to keep research perfectly in line with that interpretation.

In both cases, the real world has little in common with the image of it given by theories that see only subordination to a system of domination, the action of very strict determinisms, an absence of actors, and a vigorous rejection of any concept of the subject that appears to be independent of relations of domination. This 'no exit' vision of social realities, which are held to be subject to general domination, is an insurmountable obstacle that blocks the development of the social sciences. What is worse, it is increasingly inclined to oppose any initiative, either political or intellectual, that attempts to get societies out of the blind alleys in which intellectuals tell them they are trapped, even though the parties concerned do not necessarily take the view that there is no way out.

The Two Lefts

Having reached this point, the reader will, perhaps, argue that my criticisms are directed mainly at the far Left, and lay none of the blame at the door of the moderate or social-democratic Left, the Right or, more paradoxically still, the far Right. The case that can be made against the moderate Left is, however, so obvious that we have to recall the meaning of this analysis, which is no means hostile to the Left as such. No one would imagine for a moment that we can define the situation in a country, or in the world as a whole, without evoking the action of the big financial centres, problems with energy or the rise, in a lot of European countries, of xenophobic movements and pro-fascist parties. But the semblance of completeness means that such a vision is of no interest. Indeed, my analysis is designed to go against such panoramic views because it is designed to introduce, as well as economic and social determinants whose importance no one would dream of denying, elements that relate not to the situation, but to the actors themselves. Resisting all psychological or even psycho-cultural temptations, it looks at those who, to a certain extent, influence our actions. We could call them 'diagnosticians', but the word 'interpretation' comes closer to what I am calling the dominant interpretive discourse. The way in which the actors construct reality is not to be confused with its economic determinants, and the content of a DID is not determined by the state of the economy, or even of political relations. As everything I have said so far indicates, I regard this DID as an instrument that is designed to eliminate the actor as subject, to deny the presence of the actor. It would not be wise to use the same notion to speak of the ideology or, more generally, the culture of a social movement, because such movements pertain to the demands of the actor and the subject; a social movement always speaks of freedom, equality, justice and, more generally, rights. Although they vary greatly, DIDs, in contrast, try to demonstrate the impossibility of any action that is not determined from the outside, and of actions that are free because they are freedom-oriented.

It is still true to say that the same operation can be observed 'on the Right', or that DIDs are elaborated on the Right to demonstrate the existence of determinisms that work to the advantage of the masters of the economy. A comparison of Right and Left is, however, somewhat unfortunate in that it is in the very nature of right-wing or neo-liberal thought to argue that, the fewer voluntaristic interventions there are, especially on the part of the state, the more likely it is that the economy will function rationally. It is therefore no accident that right-wing neo-liberal thought should be poor and usually unsophisticated, while the authoritarian or conservative Right, and *a priori* the fascist Right, should be voluble, albeit simplistic and brutal in most cases. Xenophobia and racism express themselves in crude terms, and their formulations can be so exaggerated as to look caricatural. They are, alas, not caricatural, the Nazi language that determined the Führer's every action being only one example.

When, on the other hand, it is actors who resist the power of money, the state or a theocracy that are under attack, the discourse that is designed to deny the existence of actors, intervenes in much more subtle ways. It might be said that this is a strange way of going about things, but it could not be more common for all that. The Left and the far Left create modes of thought that are so determinist that they sometimes use the same analysis as their enemies, as was the case with Marxism, whose expectations were in fact the same as those of the neo-liberal economy. The Left does not trust actors, as we can see from the French education system, which refuses to take into consideration the characteristics of its pupils and identifies completely with the universalism of the knowledge it has to transmit. The Left is naturally suspicious of all appeals to consciousness because such appeals are systematically used to undermine any resistance to the ruling order by inducing a paralysing feeling of guilt.

The dominant interpretive discourse is therefore not a set of vaguely associated ideas: it is a weapon to be used against anything that defines social actors as beings whose actions are primarily intended to allow them to assert themselves and to defend their rights. This is not a deviation in the sense that we might speak of a Stalinist, Maoist or even Leninist deviation within the labour movement, and such deviations were in fact pathetic, given the historic importance of the phenomena concerned. It is a counter-current, or something that resists what should naturally be the strongest current: the assertion of the freedom of subjects. The closest equivalent on the Right is the nationalist discourse that tries, as authoritarian German thought in particular tried, to found the nation on the notion of a people that is at once natural and cultural (blood and soil).

The reason why all sides try to eliminate the actor and the actor's appeal to his freedom and rights, is that the actor is the worst enemy of all power systems. No power can believe that it is based entirely upon consent: power feels self-confident only when it can speak in the name of some necessity, be it that of economic laws or that of the destiny of a people. That necessity appears to it to be much more profound than the difference between Left and Right, though that difference is always there. The contrast between the logic of power and the logic of the citizen, worker or cultural agent is obviously still present, but while the Right is defined primarily by the trust it puts in natural mechanisms, the Left is torn between two antagonistic positions. One Left puts its trust in social movement and liberation campaigns that affect private life, but a second Left always mobilizes against that marked tendency, struggles to take power and finds support in organizations of all kinds and in education systems. It is because the contrast is much more pronounced on the Left than in the ranks of the Right that political life depends much more heavily on the Right than on the Left, while economic policy is really determined by the Right rather than by the Left. France, as we said from the outset, finds it easier to thinks in terms of the state rather than society, and to think in terms of the dominant interpretive discourse than in terms of the language of social movements, be they rank and file organizations or highly organized top-down movements.

The opposition between the two Lefts sometimes find expression in the internal debates of the big parties of the Left, but it extends beyond them to an increasing extent. It is, in particular, observable at every level where pubic opinion is shaped. The statist Left's sharp hostility to the media is, however, understandable because, while the media do support a right-wing politics that reduces everything to consumption, they also defend the many private demands that find expression in public life, as is the case with religious beliefs and practices. I can think of no country where what might be called the 'social' Left has won a complete victory over what one might call the 'statist' Left. The revolutionary Left is one of its highest expressions. Over the last half-century we have just lived through, the statist Left has been much stronger than the social Left – the Left of the social movements – and had much more influence because it had the support of the Soviet bloc. Most of the CGT (Conféderation Générale du Travail) was part of the statist Left, and it was always much more powerful than the CFDT (Confédération Française du Travail). Edmond Maire did transform the latter into a social Left, but then backed down in the face of the major crisis of 1995, which saw the statist Left re-emerge as a real force.

How can anyone fail to be struck by the constant weakness of the social and cultural Left in France? Independent direct-action unionism controlled the life of the unions for only a few years, and by 1910 it was unions with links to the state, or that were in other words based in the public sector, that took over the leadership of the CGT. The civil servants led the way, followed by unions in the private sector. When Taylorist and Fordist methods penetrated industrial life at the very beginning of the twentieth century, a sudden wave of strikes gave the social Left more influence, as in both the United States and Germany. After the Second World War, however, the CGT split into two confederations. One looked to the West, while the other became part of the Soviet system, which had the paradoxical effect of giving the Communist Party more power than ever before. The two Lefts clashed openly in May 1968, and the most general meaning of that moment, when social struggles were at their height, lies in the clash between the two. May triggered a long general strike, with mass demonstrations and factory occupations, and that movement quite logically resulted in an agreement that the unions did not really negotiate; it was forced upon them by the state. On the other hand, many revolutionary political groups attempted to lend their support to the classic union movement, but the major factor was the emergence of new social and cultural demands emanating from women. This supremacy of the social movements did not last. Acting in the name of the democratic spirit, the union movement began to turn to the state, and increasingly identified the defence of the public sector with the defence of the general interest.

A coalition between a social Left and a Right that espouses almost the same contents is all the more difficult to imagine in that neither has proposed many solutions to the day-to-day problems of French people. It is not enough to restrict the Jacobin spirit in France, because the now classic opposition between republicans and democrats is another way of describing the difference between the two Lefts we have just mentioned. The hold of the state is so strong and it can count on so much support within society itself that there have been few actions prioritizing the defence of rights and therefore social movements. State schools are by far the best example. State schools have made it a rule that teachers must ignore problems, old or new, relating to the personalities, social origins or cultural background of their pupils. Teachers have defended citizenship against the influence of communitarianisms, which was both essential and what public opinion demanded, but they have also demonstrated that they are extremely suspicious of all aspects of cultural diversity. This contradiction weighs more and more heavily on the Ministry for Education, and political institutions in themselves cannot resolve it.

The Intellectuals Divided

We now have a broader and clearer definition of the notion of a dominant interpretive discourse. It was initially introduced as a descriptive term, but it does not in fact refer solely to the ability to mobilize resources or to negotiate with state power. It is a way of revealing two very different conceptions in every domain. Pedagogy is one example. One of these conceptions, which might be termed the *republican* school, is increasingly taking over from what should be called that of the *democratic* school. Indeed, the education system has become an obstacle to the integration and upward social mobility of the children of foreign minorities or children who do not have an adequate command of the national language. The most important point is, however, understanding the lack of symmetry between Left and Right, and the negative role played by the dominant interpretive discourse on a Left that is still tempted to think that resorting to impersonal processes is essential if we are to explain human behaviours and if we are to respond to the different forces that are emerging within all minority groups.

It was once possible to hope that the fall of the Communist Party and the internal struggles of the Trotskyist groups would decisively weaken the state Left and allow what might be called 'the human rights Left' to take on a central importance. But the employment situation does not encourage stronger grassroots initiatives. On the contrary, the employment situation explains why the unions are turning more and more to the state. The current situation is weakening both the state Left and the social Left, and this helps to give access to power to a Right that does not leave much room for what might be called the 'democratic Right', even though such a current could play a useful role by allying itself with the social Left to bring about profound changes in pedagogical practices or to find new ways of thinking about the role of immigrants in French society, and to stop supporting the status quo that makes France waver between a statist Right and a statist Left and ignore expressions of any demand for social innovations, irrespective of whether they emanate from the Right or the Left.

Among intellectuals, the situation has become confused, especially in the United States where liberal – or in other words left-wing – intellectuals are divided over what to think of President Bush's action in Iraq. Some condemn it, while others ultimately approve of it and speak of the need to overthrow an authoritarian regime. These doubts have now, with some delay, penetrated the world of French intellectuals, where we have seen the beginnings of a drift to the Right, though it is in fact a drift upwards rather than downwards. Rather than listening to the demands of groups and individuals, our intellectuals look to the state and its interventions.

The representation that sees society as being structured by class relations that were shaped in industrial society is in crisis, and probably in decline. That vision is becoming more and more out of step with the post-industrial societies in which we live. The DID is therefore very much in favour of the state and state control over society, and even goes so far as to deny the existence of actors and social movements. The combination of these two deviations explains both why that vision of society persists, and is even becoming more widespread, and why it finds it too difficult to perceive and understand new realities.

This dominant interpretive discourse does not drown out everything else, but it is sufficiently powerful to influence other currents of social thought, and even to cast them out into the outer darkness, should their opposition to the DID prove significant. We might also emphasize the serious effects of the deformations of social thought, which has been slow to address the growing need to find new interpretations of new situations. As I said earlier when I spoke of the transition from one paradigm to another, from one state of social consciousness to another, we need a change of attitude.

It is, of course, true to say that not everything about the way the intellectual arena is constructed is negative. For my own part, I was very influenced by a mode of thought based upon the realities of industrial society, but it is not difficult to see the artificiality of my theories because, in my early work, I stressed the importance of class consciousness as a response to the way working-class autonomy in the workplace was eroded by so-called 'scientific management' methods. That theme had been ignored by Marxist-inspired thought, which had, as the Althusserians wanted, become increasingly trapped into a very economistic conception of Marxist thought.

It is tempting to describe the conditions of intellectual life in eminently material terms, and to speak of its poor organization or lack of funding. Those constraints are real, but they do not constitute insurmountable obstacles. All the social sciences have benefited from the interest taken in them by the major figures in the public sector who have developed a certain idea of France. The main obstacles that prevent our type of society from functioning efficiently lie in representations and not resources.

The dominant interpretive discourse's hold throughout this period cannot be divorced from the major role *intellectuals* played in the political field. This has been a constitutive feature of French political life for two hundred years, and it has no equivalent in other countries. It is based upon the idea that those who are in possession of a certain knowledge and who have reflected upon human life can, and indeed must, intervene in the life of society and, ignoring party rivalries, defend certain basic principles that are not just moral principles, such as the defence of human rights, and oppose all forms of political action that stand in the way of progress, and therefore both reason and rights. The combination of a rationalist, and often scientistic, belief in progress and the defence of human rights inspired the protests of French intellectuals, whose action was both significant and courageous in many dramatic moments in history. It was the intellectuals who called for the formation of a Popular Front to resist the threat of a fascist coup d'état in 1934. A generation later, a few intellectuals were brave enough to oppose the Algerian war and the French army's use of torture; once again, they spoke in the name of human rights based upon the idea of progress, which was, in the last analysis, defined as the triumph of reason at every stage in the modernization of society.

And yet the same belief in 'progress' led so many intellectuals to support, or at least not denounce, the Soviet regime and to claim that the Soviet and Nazi regimes were completely different. These intellectuals, many of whom were scientists, were attracted to what looked like the triumph of reason and the rational organization of social life over privileges and arbitrariness. Many intellectuals remained loyal to the Communist Party, not only after the end of the war, but even after 1956 and the revelations of Khrushchev's secret report. Before then, many of them violently rejected victims' eye-witness accounts of the arbitrary nature of the Soviet regime and its deportation camps. It was this fascination with Moscow that destroyed the intellectuals' unity and brought them to a crossroads. The prioritization of a rationalist and scientistic vision could easily come to terms with despotism, and even unenlightened despotism, as it did in the eighteenth century. On the other hand, the defence of human rights could take on a moral meaning freed from all ties with historical evolutionism.

The reason why intellectual life remained so lively in France was that many intellectuals adopted a critical stance from the 1950s onwards and especially after 1956, which was also the year of the Hungarian revolution and the Potsdam uprising. In 1968, those intellectuals who had broken with the Communist Party and the entire Soviet camp strongly supported the Prague Spring, even though the effects of the May movement concealed the changes that were taking place in Czech society and especially the workers' councils movement, which survived the Soviet invasion. The decisive moment was, however, the short life of Solidarity in Poland. Many intellectuals passionately committed themselves to the defence of that great social movement and, in more material terms, the Polish people, especially after the declaration of a state of war on 13 December 1981. Force Ouvrière had supported the Polish trade unionists from the start, but it was the CFDT that called for unity between intellectuals and trade unionists. The intellectuals who took part in these joint actions shared the conviction that top priority had to be given to a movement that brought together trade unionists and democrats at a national level. This exceptional moment brought together Michel Foucault and Claude Lefort, Pierre Bourdieu and Jacques Le Goff, Michel Wieviorka, François Dubet and many others, myself included, who were inspired by the same need to defend the Polish workers and, indeed, a whole people that was fighting for its freedom.

At the same time, the distance between the alliance of trade unionists and intellectuals and François Mitterrand's government made itself felt. Increasingly, voices began to speak in the name of human rights, and not in the name of a philosophy of history. They were therefore not transmitting an image of the ideal society, but clearly establishing the preconditions for an acceptable regime. Even though a certain number of the intellectuals who lent Solidarity their support were far from opposed to the dominant interpretive discourse, the image of intellectuals who were committed to the defence of human rights was clearly becoming divorced from the image of the type of society that republicanism had created. Those intellectuals who had so often demonstrated their independence were therefore, at least at certain significant moments, more visible than the 'fellow travellers' who did not dare to denounce totalitarian regimes or to defend civil, social and cultural rights so as not to undermine the dominant interpretive discourse. It is not only that the journal *Esprit* and other less prominent journals never abandoned this new alliance between the defence of the workers and the assertion that human rights had to take priority in all collective actions; the theme of human rights, which had lost almost all its influence during the long period of Marxism's dominance, acquired a new and growing importance. So much so that it completely transformed the image of the intellectuals, who now came to be seen as the defenders of those rights. But the divorce between the two categories of intellectuals as actors of history led to the disappearance of that category, and to the disappearance of the very notion that gave birth to it. The physicists who dominated the intellectual scene at Liberation were replaced by biologists, and then by the 'French doctors' of Médecins sans frontières and Médecins du monde.

The theme of the disappearance of the intellectuals, or of the 'great intellectuals', as we sometimes prefer to call them, has become a banality. It has to be added that, in the contemporary period of our emergence from industrial society and entry into a different type of society, which was prefigured by the rise of social movements and economic mutations, the role of social thought is unimportant. The main reason for this is probably that so many intellectuals are still strongly committed to the intellectual cadres of the past. Most feminist researchers in Europe, for instance, devote themselves to the ultra-classic study of inequalities at work and wage inequalities or to the study of violence, while the important work that is being done elsewhere, and especially in the United States, has already indicated new lines of research. The dominant interpretive discourse's capacity for resistance is greater than we think. That is not enough to confer upon that ideology a great capacity for intervention, but it is enough to prevent the formation of a new intellectual movement that can supply the new social or political actors with analytic tools.

These remarks are certainly not intended to distract our attention away from what was, if we look at it in terms of the history of ideas, a remarkable period. It is, however, difficult to deny that the role of the dominant interpretive discourse has frustrated all attempts to bring about an intellectual revolution in the social sciences.

One would like to be able to describe the transformations that are now coming about in social thought in the terms that were used in the nineteenth century, when we saw the intellectual field being invaded by economic and social problems that were bound up with the advent of the industrial society and capitalism. But the fact of the matter is that we do not have to choose between two strong discourses, but between two very different forms of nothingness. The form with which we are familiar, and which I call the dominant interpretive discourse, was an attempt to demonstrate that action is impossible to the extent that domination is impersonal and beyond reach, and to the extent that any reference to subjectivities and actors seems to stand up against the 'petty bourgeois' ideologies, many of which are in the service of dominant forces that could not be further removed from the discourses they encourage. One of the main reasons for the silence of the intellectuals, on the other hand, is globalization itself. Now that economic decisions are taken at a global level and that it is difficult to make political and social interventions into economic life, intellectual milieus, which are often bound up with national institutions, have lost their capacity for analysis and the ability to make themselves heard. Mass culture does not in itself dispossess intellectuals of their critical and prophetic role; but if what intellectuals are saying is to reach the vectors of mass culture, it must first be translated into an economic or cultural language that has been globalized, and that happens only very rarely. Self-confidence is a precondition for the formation of intellectual discourses, but the world of confidence has been replaced by a world of defiance, uncertainty and fears for the future. In Europe, that fear is heightened by an awareness of the massive eruption of other continents, other cultures and other political systems into the management of world affairs.

In these countries, it is all too common for intellectuals to be reduced to the role of ideologists, or even stooges for political movements, who have no real influence on those movements' ideas and strategies. This situation will not necessarily last, as it is a transitional period during which roles are being transformed, and that does not encourage the formation of new ideas and new worldviews. This makes the task of constructing and promoting new modes of analysis all the more urgent, especially in societies that are at once sufficiently adult to be self-reflective and young enough not to fret and wear themselves out by rehashing memories of a past that has gone.

3

Killing the Subject

The dominant interpretive discourse wishes to pursue to the end the long war it is already waging against the subject. It associates the image of an empty society in which there are no actors and which is incapable of any action with that of an all-powerful state, and therefore with the revolution that is the only thing capable of transforming it.

Decline of the 'Bourgeois Subject'

The image of the human subject bequeathed to us by the philosophy of the Enlightenment is such a long way off! That subject, which was the heir to all theories of natural law, and therefore human rights, seemed to transcend the harsh realities of social life. It is only a short step from that to talk of a bourgeois subject, or in other words a subject identified with men who did not have to work with their hands, who had some wealth, if not a fortune, and who were responsible for the defence of the social order. This image of a free subject was offensive to a working-class world that was crushed by relentless production rates, low wages, and poor working and living conditions. How could those who were subjected to such enormous constraints that all they could dream of was survival be described as 'subjects'? And the same argument applied to all the categories that were inferiorized by the ruling elite: women, children, the colonized . . . The universalism in whose name that subject spoke sounded like egoism and an unfair domination.

All the great schools of thought that revolutionized our intellectual life at the end of the nineteenth century wanted to destroy this image of the subject. Marx taught us that economic actors were subordinated to the logic of the capitalist system, which was a logic of class domination. Nietzsche contrasted social and religious morality with the strength of the drives and self-assertion and Freud, who was influenced by him, contrasted the libido with the law, the id with the superego, and left the domain of consciousness in the pathetic position of being the point where psychic life came into contact with the outside world.

The image that made the subject a principle of order seems very remote. We now live in a mobile society that is either competitive or at war, that is brutal and repressive, and that constantly forces workers to increase their productivity. To the extent that opposing forces have limited this capitalist domination, they ensured that the workers were given some protection, guarantees and finally a welfare state, and they have done a lot to liberate individual consumerism. If we also add that mass consumerism and mass communications were born and then developed rapidly in the second half of the twentieth century, we can see that all principles of organization and social order have broken down, and that we have witnessed the triumph of an individualism that suits the purpose of those who define social life solely in terms of consumption. How can we go on talking about the subject, when the human beings we observe are increasingly motivated by individualism, specific desires and an economic strategy for managing their income and expenditure, as well as by their cultural, social and family heritage? While personal histories can be explained in general terms, they are increasingly individual.

This individualism is not in itself reprehensible. It has the positive effect of giving every individual greater freedom of movement and initiative, and the freedom to succeed or fail. Its obvious weaknesses are more disturbing than the false universalism of the bourgeois subject that dates from the philosophy of the Enlightenment or enlightened despotism. One suspects, however, that this description is incomplete, and that a social organization that has its weaknesses, but which is ultimately governed by the logic of the interests and reactions stimulated by economic power, can reproduce itself. In what became a successful formula, Michel Maffesoli stated that this supposedly individualist society is in fact a society that is made up of 'tribes', gangs and local or wider communities. In our century, and especially in its last decades, both historians and sociologists observed the break up of groups and social life in the United States. Robert Putman's *Bowling Alone* provides the best description of this process. This destructured and individualized world tends to be organized not on the basis of the citizenship of the philosophy of the Enlightenment but, on the contrary, on the basis of a new communitarianism that subordinates individuals to the beliefs and practices forced upon them by their involvement in one or another community.

The last half-century has been dominated by the creation of absolute states that impose upon individuals the disciplines that are inherent in their desire to reconstruct a social order based, not upon the natural rights of *individuals*, but the *collective* rights of communities. It is this new social philosophy that has led to the triumph of the idea of *difference*, and it does not concern itself with the issue of how completely different societies can communicate with each other. Even though it is not the one that is usually given, the strongest response to this major problem admits that relations of war or peace take priority and that the friend–enemy opposition is more important than any other, and this leads to what Samuel Huntington has called a *clash of civilizations*. Even those who enjoy the protection of the public freedoms and social rights created by rich Western societies have to admit that the second half of the twentieth century and the beginning of the twenty-first were increasingly dominated by totalitarian systems ranging from the scientistic pseudo-rationalism of Leninism and Stalinism to the religious fanaticism of so many cults, and by the re-emergence of theocracies as minorities retreated into their difference rather than attempting to become part of something larger. One by one, the institutions created by what has been called the liberal bourgeois society of the nineteenth century have disappeared or have been transformed into one or another variant of the totalitarianism I have just evoked. The assertion of identities and difference has gone hand in hand with the undermining or break up of nation states, as we saw in the Balkans in Europe, and as we are now seeing in the Andean countries of Latin America. Such 'communitarian' movements are positive and necessary reactions to all forms of internal and external colonialism, and they lead to the rediscovery of identities that were destroyed in the name of the introduction of a universalism that usually came down to the imposition of the law of the victors.

Yet while this critique of the pride of colonizers and dominant powers is justified, it also becomes seriously inadequate and even dangerous if it does not take into account its inherent dangers. The appeal to identity always implies exclusion; the celebration of differences makes it impossible to communicate with the other. At every level of social life, from individual and inter-individual behaviours to the way great political or cultural ensembles behave, we are seeing the reappearance of the laws of community which, Tönnies predicted at the end of the nineteenth century, would be transcended by the more complex organization of societies. Is it possible to discover a principle that allows us to resist this obsession with identity, this entrapment in difference, and even the spirit of holy war, which reduces contacts with the other to violence? Whereas everything was once overburdened with meaning, nothing has a meaning, and we are discovering that non-meaning is everywhere. The result is the necessary elimination of the strongest element of social life, as conceived by the eighteenth century: consciousness. History, the nation, liberation and the *de jure* subject now look like so many hypocritical forms of a freedom that applied only to the few and that led to the growing subordination of everyone else.

Public opinion appears to be quite naturally heading in that direction. Trapped inside the fortresses of identity, everyone refuses to have any awareness of the other and no longer wants to revive the hopes of progress. We now feel that we are being crushed by the pressures of a consumerism that is at once stimulated and threatened with destruction at the hands of the monsters of identity. Is it possible to imagine the emergence of a new figure of the subject in such a climate?

After the Labour Movement

The crisis in an ideology that holds that progress will be guaranteed by reason and technological efficiency has being going on for so long and is so profound that we do not need another description of a theme that has been commented on so often. It is more helpful to recall that this philosophy of history was strongly criticized by the socialist ideologies which held that a combination of the will of the people and modernization would bring about the progress that the egoism of the bourgeoisie had corrupted, provided that we add that this new belief in progress, which was more combative and passionate, has itself been in decline for a long time, and that the void it left behind is the most direct explanation for the success of the dominant interpretive discourse.

The labour movement as such gave birth to a philosophy of progress that was also a certain conception of justice, freedom and solidarity. For a decade, it embodied, albeit not always consciously or deliberately, a more direct and realistic figure of the subject than that of bourgeois liberalism. That figure represented the significant transition from the evolutionism that came before it to more direct analyses founded only on the concept of the subject examined in Part II below.

Now that Marxist thought is in retreat and that the forces of unionism and the socialist 'grand narrative' have been crushed by Communist totalitarianism and its fellow travellers we must, rather than baying with the hounds, recall the greatness of the labour movement and its activists, even when they were under the sway of national and international Communist powers.

Above all, we must put some order into our perception of reality. We are assailed by two contrasting discourses, and we know very well that both are partial and unacceptable. On the one hand, we are told that the industrial world is dying, that we have moved en masse from the secondary sector to the tertiary, and that class consciousness has dissolved. Some add that there are no more workers, and think that they are imitating Henri Mendras, who was speaking of 'the end of the peasantry' some fifty years. The difference is that he was right. On the other hand, we hear the words 'socialism' and 'workers', with whom the Left has always been identified, even though few wage-earners and few of the unemployed vote for the Socialist Party, while many of them vote for the National Front. Serious statisticians, for their part, do not find it very difficult to describe a 'condition of the working class' and its evolution. Who should we be listening to? Finding the answer to that question is less difficult than it might seem.

From the wage-earners' point of view, industrial society is a society in which the most decisive social relations are those that bring employers and wage-earners into conflict in the workplace, the workshop, the factory or the branch. Relations between employers, wage-earners, and the government or other political actors are shaped at a more organized and integrated level. The highest level, finally, is that of the local, regional, national or international community; at that level, the dominant point of view is primarily concerned with the organization of economic life, the national interest and an awareness of threats, such as competition or aggression, that call whole societies into question. As we move from one level to the next, the basic value of solidarity extends to the collective defence of social rights, and then a 'progressive' consciousness that proclaims that the interests of the workers are bound up with an increase in production, rising standards of education, and an awareness of the need to defend just causes, both at home and abroad. That pyramid no longer exists. Where we once had a working class, we now have more and more people who are unemployed, who have no job security and who have been excluded from society. Where we once had the creators of a new society, we have only victims. At a higher level of perception, the factory seemed for a brief period to be the principal social actor, but it is now the market, or capitalism in the most direct sense, that controls everything, all the more so in that it is now organized at a global level. Categories of labour are beginning to disappear and are being replaced by job categories. Sociological analysis gives way to economic calculations.

Such is the main transformation or reversal of perception that takes away the central role that social relations of production and the subjectivity of the workers played in a social life that they dominated for so long. We can no longer talk about wage-earners in class terms, but only in terms of the threat of unemployment, political alliances or social plans. The dominant interpretive discourse owed its strength to the decline of the labour movement, and actually speeded its decline by subordinating social actors to the logic of an implacable system of domination.

The rejection of the idea of progress leads to the disappearance of any reference to ourselves as agents of progress. The idea of progress identified the subjectivity of the actor with developments that had a certain purpose evolution and with transformations in the situation and the environment. Yet in reality, the idea of progress has taken us in quite the opposite direction to that indicated in this book. The idea of the subject, which will becomes increasingly important here, is incompatible with any philosophy of history, no matter whether it comes down to being an apologia for progress or describes progress as a process that that will lead to a human happiness that has little to do with individual self-reflexivity or the assertion of individual rights. It is only when the individual or the social group stands out from the background into which they were incorporated that the self-reflexive process can lead the subject to a new definition that has little to do with any definition that philosophies of history could supply.

In order to give a clear account of the links between this representation of society and the dominant interpretive discourse, we must first take certain precautions and admit that this French ideology does have some positive content. We have so often heard the appeals to human rights and the Enlightenment spirit, but also to the implacable struggle between labour and profit; they have given rise to battles, sacrifices, ideas and eye-witness accounts that count for a great deal in the image we have of this French spirit, irrespective of whether we support or denounce it. I would add that, in the course of the last half-century, intellectuals have more than once rebelled against the policies of a state that wanted to take control of society, but which also became bogged down in Indochina and then used torture in Algeria. For my own part, I feel that I belong to industrial society and its industrial conflicts in more than one sense. But an awareness of its greatness makes the need to make a critique of it still more urgent, and that critique must be made primarily in the name of the labour movement. The French state so often claims to be its interpreter, but leaves the workers so little power to determine their own future.

In the industrial domain, France is a country that has done practically nothing to build a system of collective bargaining. When so-called collective bargaining does take place, the employers and the unions are in fact summoned together to be told about the decisions the state has taken. In France, it is the law and not collective agreements that plays the main role in organizing and transforming industrial relations.

The real confrontations take place in the realm of ideas. My criticisms concentrate on the dominant interpretive discourse, because it seems to me that it is that discourse that is paralysing French society, and preventing it from understanding and transforming itself. We do not have to look at the organization of economic power or at the unequal situation of the various provinces to find the reasons why France finds it so difficult to transform itself. In a country in which trade unionism scarcely exists, they find expression in repeated strikes in the big state sector companies, even though they give their wage-earners major privileges, and in the chronic nature of the crisis in education, on which the reforms that are always being planned seem to have no effect. There is nothing wrong with France's arms and legs, but there is something wrong with its head. I refer to France's self-representation, its conception of the world and, to be more specific, the dominant interpretive discourse. That is why my analyses and criticisms concentrate on it. These criticisms have two goals: to demonstrate that a false consciousness had had an undue influence on all French thought, and to convince the reader that it is by making a critique of that dominant interpretive discourse and then getting rid of it that we can find a solution to France's problems. And that means going back to the subject.

A Neo-Liberal DID

Surely the triumph of neo-liberal policies and ideologies has taken away much of the power of the dominant interpretive discourse. Surely the statism and the concentration of decision-making that I am criticizing are things of the past. Do not the most neo-liberal forms of management now have the greatest influence, and should we not be criticizing them in their turn? Have we not seen the emergence of a dominant interpretive discourse with a neo-liberal content, and has it not replaced the discourse I am criticizing, which was very closely associated with the leading role the state once played in French society?

If that were the case, the long analysis of the voluntaristic and statist dominant interpretive discourse made here would be of purely historical interest. That is in reality far from being the case. The thing about a dominant interpretive discourse is that it is not just an ideology that protects and stimulates the interests of a ruling group; it is a truly intellectual creation, a representation of society, of the actions of institutions and of the individual and collective behaviours that come between the state and economic and political powers on the one hand, and the framework for social and collective action on the other. It is actually an arena that shapes interpretations, and it is a characteristic of what we call the Left or, to be more accurate, of those who shape public opinion in a so-called left-wing climate or a so-called left-wing tradition of opposition and resistance to a neo-liberal ideology which certainly exists, but which has not eliminated the dominant interpretive discourse. The distinction I am making here divorces the ideological level, which supposedly corresponds directly to interest groups, the ability to take decisions or political powers, from the level of the dominant interpretive discourse that creates, in autonomous fashion, a representation of society that has effects on politics and economics, no matter how they are managed. The divorce between the two is all the clearer in that we live in a democratic country, and the case of France is all the more extreme in that the intellectual, administrative and institutional capacity to create a dominant interpretive discourse is all the greater there. France has almost never, at least during periods of democratic freedoms, been governed solely by the dominant interests of the economy or the state; the creation of a mode of interpretation that can resist both the interests of the state, the interests of the economy and trends within public opinion, has been just as influential. Hence the importance of an analysis of this dominant interpretive discourse, and hence the need to see it as the source – both directly and indirectly – of many of the weaknesses of our social policy, and of many of the difficulties we encounter when we try to apprehend and analyse new problems, both theoretical, political and practical. We therefore have to draw a map of the borders between institutional practices, forms of economic and administrative organization, economic power, the dominant interpretive discourse and a dominant ideology that is bound up with the economic and political interests that are at work in society.

The divorce between the dominant interpretive discourse and the dominant ideology is clearly perceptible, as one is solidly implanted in the public sector, while the latter enjoys more influence in the private sector. There are many institutions, both large and small, where the interventions of neo-liberal ideologues are relentlessly honed and analysed. Those interventions have less influence on companies in the public sector, and are often absent from academic debates and the journals that discuss general problems. This is more striking in France than in other countries, but it can be seen as a European characteristic if we compare the great countries of Europe with the United States or the very different case of Japan.

Intellectuals still play an important role in a country where freedom of expression is respected, despite the triumph of a neo-liberal ideology. Politicians and senior civil servants avoid – not always, but usually – stirring up conflicts with a milieu that is not supposed to wield any power but which has considerable influence on the whole country and the whole of society. All the more so in that it deals with problems that are far removed from the management of the economy. Indeed, one of the riches of the intellectual field in European countries is their ability to make a neo-liberal ideology coexist alongside a more statist and interventionist dominant interpretive discourse. Both have their good sides and their bad sides. This is another way of saying that we have not seen statist DID being replaced by a neo-liberal DID over the last fifteen years. If we made that error of judgement, we would make it impossible to understand much of the workings of cultural and even social life in France. This observation brings us back to a truism. It is unusual for anyone to speak of 'right-wing intellectuals', unless they are referring to a few independent minds, while the expression 'left-wing intellectuals', which is virtually synonymous with 'intellectuals', had an almost institutional collective meaning. This corresponds to the analysis I am making here: the space of the intellectuals is on the Left, no matter how we define that term. The Left is the birthplace of a set of interpretive categories that have much more influence than is usually thought on other intellectuals, but also on politicians, administrators and union leaders. The same could not be said of Germany, Russia or the United States.

Are we to conclude that we have reached a stage at which left-wing intellectuals, or intellectuals as a group, are absent or have disappeared? No: just as the DID described here is, after having dominated French intellectual life for so long, in a state of decay and has lost its power and even some of its influence, so modes of thought that seemed to be very isolated in earlier decades are becoming more visible. This strengthens the hypothesis that the DID concealed a whole side of French intellectual life that is now reappearing and which may play a much more creative role in the near future.

I maintain that, in France, living social thought cannot come into being on the right of the political spectrum. In recent decades, it was possible to think with categories other than those of the DID, but those differences were 'on the Left', or in other words on the DID's home territory.

The orientations that I have always defended turned their back on the DID, but that difference mattered only to the extent that has brought what often appeared to be similar ideas into conflict; and that is why I was so passionate about going down the road that leads to a strict determinism. The image of a society in which there were no actors, and which was subject to strict determinism and crushed by systems of domination that infiltrated everything, had a lot in common with a revolutionary spirit that was all the more fiery, especially among young people, in that it no longer had any opportunity to express itself in any concrete way. The same revolutionary spirit made it almost obligatory to accept certain analyses of guerrilla activity and other movements that were at work in Latin America, even though a slightly more attentive analysis showed that they were out of step with reality. The intellectuals who created the DID offered the public a representation of social and political life that corresponded to a demand for revolutionary action that could not, at least as a general rule, be satisfied in the contemporary world. That frustrated revolutionary spirit and the construction of a discourse of society that eliminated actors reinforced one another. This suited the purposes of both the government and political parties that were only too eager to take the place of a public opinion and social movements that seemed to be in a state of decay, torn apart by internal struggles and reduced to silence. Such a combination of feelings and discourses can be hugely influential and can lead to those who refuse to adopt that dominant ideological viewpoint being classed as marginal or deviant.

The constitution of a dominant interpretive discourse therefore occurs in what might be called 'Left' political situations, but the converse is not true: the dominance of the Right does not encourage the creation of such a discourse. In such situations, direct pressure is brought to bear by economic forces and political decisions that work in their favour, and often by a neo-liberal ideology that usually comes down to a demand for as little intervention as possible in market mechanisms because it is believed that any voluntaristic policy will have less rational and less positive effects than market forces, which, it is assumed, automatically make the best choices.

Decline of the DID

The latter situation is, however, far removed from our current situation, which is a product of the decline of the voluntarism of the post-war period. The rejection of both the ideology of dominant interpretive discourses and 'social projects' creates a silence that can sometimes be interpreted as meaning that there are no more projects for the future. That is only partly true. The contemporary triumph of neo-liberalism has certainly undermined political, and especially intellectual, debates to a remarkable degree. Neo-liberalism, understood in the economic sense of the term, leads to an almost complete absence of intellectual and political debate. In the United States, it was the transformation of the Right when the neo-conservatives unexpectedly took centre stage that revived the ideological scene, but that occurred at the precise moment when a neo-liberal vision dominated by the economy gave way to a quasi-prophetic vision of the United States' world role as the defender of democracy who would overthrow dictatorships and allow the axis of good to triumph over the axis of evil. The intellectual out-put of the 'neo-cons', many of whom came from the far Left, and their influence over a significant part of the academic world, might be regarded as the appearance of a new dominant interpretive discourse. It seems more accurate to say that, once President Bush had came to power, thanks in part to the support of the 'neo-cons', not to mention the war in Iraq, a void was created in European countries. That did not lead to a purely pragmatic policy with exclusively economic goals, but to the absence of any response to an ideology of power in countries that were increasingly obsessed with their own loss of power. This was true even in the case of Great Britain, which was willing to follow the United States down the road to war in the Middle East in order to share in America's hegemonic power. This is no time for critiques of old ideologies, or even for a forced conversion to the dominant interpretive discourse to which I accorded such importance in the case of France. It therefore comes as no surprise to see new and virulent expressions of that discourse emerging in France, when the proposed European Constitution was rejected, and even when political attempts, which may well have seemed pathetic but which had considerable influence, were made to prevent the Socialist Party from putting forward new proposals or even from taking a stance on events as serious as the riots in the *banlieues* in the Autumn of 2005.

The current political void must be seen as a sign of the final exhaustion not only of ideologies of Left and Right, whose content is so weak that they can easily be redefined whenever the situation changes, but also of a dominant interpretive discourse that has much more density, stability and internal coherence. This is particularly relevant to France: the distance between this dominant interpretive discourse, and social and economic reality is now so great that it is difficult to see how the country can go on living in an ideological and intellectual world that is completely different from that of its neighbours. The continued survival of a revolutionary Left and radical anti-capitalism seems impossible, given that it has no role to play in a world that is dominated by the globalization of the economy and by America's political and ideological hegemony. One can understand the appearance, for short periods, as after the rejection of the proposed European Constitution, of unrealistic discourses that serve the far from negligible purpose of expressing a stubborn refusal to admit that we have seen the demise of an intellectual and political world that inspired major actions, and created an interpretive discourse that could for a long time exercise, if not a real hegemony, at least a dominant influence. The decline of that discourse, which may, if institutions are reformed and if a new political class emerges, become a factor that will transform French political life in the period that has just begun. Its decline must lead to the creation of a new type of representation of society that is completely different from the one that has paralysed us for so long.

Like it or not, the theatre of history will not remain empty. The political and ideological languages that have enjoyed success for so long will eventually be replaced by others, and they will be based upon what has been so constantly rejected, even though it is quite in keeping with observable practices: individualism, defined in the highest sense of the term, which is bound up with the idea of the subject, will rise from the grave where its adversaries thought they had buried it beneath tons of books and discourses. The themes of human rights and the subject, and debates about truly ethical issues, will increasingly take over the political stage, where their presence will become increasingly visible, thanks especially to the feminist movements. Only then will we see the end of the long history of the dominant interpretive discourse which, in many countries and especially France, began to believe that it was immortal from the 1970s onwards and which imposed its ideas and slogans with as much, if not more, vigour as the 'neo-con' discourse has since done in the United States.

Such political and ideological changes are, however, difficult, as they are part of what I call a general change of paradigm or a transition from socio-economic categories to cultural categories to explain the whole of our collective and individual experience. We must develop critical ways of thinking that can provide us with new analytic categories and bring about profound changes in our representations of society and ourselves. It often seems that philosophers have a monopoly on thinking. That must not be the case. Even when it works at the level of the most general hypotheses, sociological thought always refers to concrete data and concrete analyses, and we cannot do without its fecundity. We must be active at every level and look in all directions: the only imperative is to think in new ways, without prejudices and without taboos. More important still, we must remain as close as possible to lived experience, to debates old and new, and to comparative studies.

It is never too late to remind those who have already forgotten it: no era is completely dominated by one current of thought, unless it is imposed by the state. We are still victims of the dominant interpretive discourse's tendency to over-estimate its own influence, even though intellectual life has always been richer and more diverse than it thought. This renaissance may, however, be delayed by an active central power that is intelligent enough to profit from its adversaries' weaknesses and to impose its own discourse. That is what is happening in Nicolas Sarkozy's France.

Free of all Commitments

Intellectual life is not in fact the only thing that is at stake. The French are being crushed by their pride in living in the 'fatherland of human rights' on the one hand, and their negative attitude towards all social movements on the other. They could be a people defined solely by their relationship with the state, its history and its struggles. But the dominant interpretive discourse cannot conceal something that escapes it and that gives French society a warmth and a luminosity that its interpreters fail to perceive. What the great discourses and the organized movements do not show is that, because they reject interpretations of their feelings, the French can be swayed by emotions, generosity and even an anger that can lead to violence but that usually promotes solidarity. They rose up to help the Chileans who were forced into exile by Pinochet, sent foodstuffs, printing equipment and messages to the Poles who were imprisoned by Jaruzelski, just as many of them took in Jews, and especially Jewish children, who were being hunted down by the Gestapo. It is not that they do better – or more – than other people but, because they are reluctant to mobilize, their emotions are free of all political or religious interpretations, because the dominant interpretive discourse has cast into the darkness, or even forbidden, anything that could promote feelings, ideas, movements and politics.

4

Defensive Policies

It is dangerous to claim that any particular policy has hugely negative effects on the life of society, as we run the risk of defining the mechanism that is at work too vaguely. The images I have just given of French society, its dominant interpretive discourse and its neo-liberal tendencies do not allow us to conclude in any real sense that these cultural and political orientations have either a harmful or a positive effect on social policies. We can, however, identify a certain number of truly cultural problems that French society seems to find particularly difficult to handle. It fails to respond to them in such as a way as to reconcile the need for change with the preservation of a certain continuity. Let us look at some of the obstacles that have to be overcome:

(a) in the name of equality, the educational system fails to take into consideration the individual's psychological, social or cultural characteristics. As a result, it favours those who are helped by their background and penalizes those who have to rely solely on their schools;

(b) a second difficulty, which is related to the first, is the stubborn resistance to all forms of cultural plurality and the defence of a so-called 'French exception'. This is exacerbated still further by the weight of prejudice against the *banlieues* and those who live there and results in a real rejection of a whole population, even though it is becoming integrated despite its repeated failures;

(c) the problem of industrial relations appears to be insurmountable;

(d) there is a deep hostility in France to anything that puts decision-making outside its national boundaries, be it the construction of

Europe or the globalization of the economy, which is identified with the American Empire. What is at stake here is more difficult to define: what can or must a national consciousness be in an economy that has been globalized, and in a world that has been divided by major politico-religious confrontations and by the difficult construction of a Europe that increasingly devotes all its efforts to its internal management?

These four problems are not the only things that are holding French society back: at least as much emphasis has to be placed on the difficulty of getting the political system to work, and especially on its resistance to equal opportunities for men and women. It is, on the other hand, futile to repeat the criticisms that have so often been made of the statist or administrative ways in which many sectors of the nation's activities are managed. We should, rather, concentrate our attention on French society's ability to know and understand itself, and on the changes that must be introduced into the process of political decision-making.

In short, the way in which France sees itself appears both to prevent it from planning for the future and blind it to both its needs and problems. Before we begin our analysis, we have to reject the simplistic view that any intervention, even for social and political reasons, is negative, and that giving the market complete freedom would produce the best possible results. Such statements have no real content in a society where half the national income is not managed by the market, and especially in one in which the dominant discourse combines a basically critical vision of society with a haughty conception of the nation.

The French Exception: The 'Great Nation'

The social conception that has been most influential in France is the notion of the individual who is recognized as having universal rights, irrespective of his or her social or cultural background. The individual's citizenship does not coincide with his or her membership of the nation, but reflects the creation of a free community defined by its respect for the rights of all. This is a liberating and revolutionary notion, and it is difficult for any individual brought up in French political culture to reject it. The universalism of citizenship must always take precedence over all communitarian loyalties. Such is the so-called French conception of the nation, even though we know that its main representative – Renan – did not overtly contrast it with the German conception of the nation as a shared destiny.

There is, however, a danger that something that is to be admired as a general principle can lead many people to lose their cultural rights. There is even a danger that it might lead to the destruction of all cultures, as it can be deduced from this that French culture is not a particular culture because it promotes universal rights. In more concrete terms, this rejection of cultural specificities leads to the devaluation of all other cultures, which can be represented on a scale, with only a few Western nations, and especially republican France, reaching the top. This argument has long been accused of being ethnocentric, or of ignoring or despising other cultures. It was in the name of republican universalism that so many colonizers took up arms, including those who used guns and torture to fight national liberation movements. And how can anyone fail to see that this republicanism is the greatest obstacle to the upward mobility of people who come from elsewhere or who are descended from slaves?

How do we get out of this apparent contradiction? Thanks, firstly, to a policy that is easy to describe but difficult to implement. Human rights initially applied to citizens, but what is the point of being a free citizen if you are a slave to your work? Many went so far as to claim that the only real rights were social rights, and that political rights were no more than an illusion in capitalist society. It is only a short step from that to saying that only workers have rights. The outcome is a dictatorship that is imposed in the name of the workers and that quickly transforms workers into the slaves of a party-state. For one hundred years, our history was dominated by the clash between two equally dangerous ideas: the refusal to grant social and cultural rights to all who are subject to any form of domination, and the imposition of a dictatorship on all in the name of a class, party, religion or nationality. Clashes over such massive and fundamental problems will never end, but the progress of democracy can be measured in terms of the attempts that have been made to reconcile what appear to be diametrically opposed positions. What we call social-democracy, which was first invented by the English and the Germans at the end of the nineteenth century, was a great step towards the extension of citizenship to the whole of social life. We are far from having made the same progress in the cultural domain, but we have to advance in that direction.

A false republican universalism exacerbates the dependency of the majority, just as the triumph of 'rationalism' in France once gave all men the right to vote and denied all women the vote. The point is not to denounce an unjust and repressive conception, but to get to the heart of the problem: how can universalism be reconciled with the rights and diversity of cultures? Which leads us to ask a difficult question: why are young people, and especially young people of Arab origin, so violently rejected by the majority of the population? These young people are descended from immigrants and live in the *banlieues*, but they have French nationality, speak French and went to school in France; in many cases, they no longer have any personal ties outside France. It is therefore not their normal behaviour that results in their rejection; it is the image the French have of themselves. They see themselves as living in the land of reason, and quite readily allow immigrants to acquire French nationality. But those who do not recognize their superiority effectively become their inferiors.

I have no wish to caricature the French, who are not all racist – far from it – but it is true that many of them genuinely believe that France, the country of the 'Great Revolution', is the homeland of human rights, and that newcomers should integrate. And they did integrate into post-war France when upward mobility was a reality. Many of the children of that generation believed that they could improve their position in that society; that is no longer the case. At the same time, the growing number of contacts and exchanges between different cultures means that we must do more to recognize differences. We should not, however, conclude that France is different from other countries that have experienced similar forms of immigration. The events that France has experienced in recent years have been less violent and less bloody than the ethnic clashes that took place in Britain, and especially inner London, a generation ago, or the great urban crises the United States experienced, especially in the Los Angeles suburb of Watts, which is still a tragic symbol. There has, on the other hand, been a great deal of resistance at the level of French citizens' representation of their country, which they see as the embodiment of a higher level of civilization and freedom. Even if we reject gross simplifications and support the idea that citizenship is superior to communities, we come up against resistance and a lack of understanding on the part of some French people. Fortunately, the arrival of new generations of immigrants appears to have gone some way towards removing these obstacles.

Each of the problems evoked here is of great importance, because the way we deal with them determines our relations with others. They are central to the work that is now being done in sociology, and Charles Taylor's work on the 'recognition' of the other is of particular importance here.

The Republican School

We cannot keep going on about the 'Republic's hussars' struggle against confessional schools. We have long accepted that the church, the army and economic powers formed a reactionary bloc in France in the nineteenth and early twentieth centuries. The Dreyfus Affair will convince anyone who still has any doubts about that. But historians remind us of the need for caution: republican and confessional schools were less different than it is sometimes said, and France did not need Jules Ferry to teach it to read and write.

But let us leave these historical reminders on one side. Let us ask more pressing questions, and above all get away from a dominant interpretive discourse which, for ideological reasons, ignores or even refuses to recognize the most urgent problems facing the French education system. And yet pointing out its weaknesses, which are so serious as to require radical changes of direction, could not be easier.

The first, which has already been mentioned, is the false egalitarianism that forces teachers to regard their pupils as all the same, to overlook the fact that some are rich and some are poor, that some have been here for a long time while others are newcomers, and that there are psychological differences between them. The underlying reasons for the impersonality of teacher–pupil relations may well deserve respect. They are meant to be a safeguard against the pressures brought to bear by the wealthiest and most influential categories. But the fact remains that this egalitarianism has disastrous effects, as schools should be helping their weakest pupils by giving them the same equal opportunities as pupils living in better educated milieus.

The second weakness is a deformation that is so systematic that we no longer even see it. Our primary schools and *lycées* are obsessed with the issue of what is and what is not permitted and, to put it in more concrete terms, are afraid to punish their pupils. Teachers often identify with a world of rules and norms, while the need to explain facts, be they scientific, historical or whatever, is marginalized. While many teachers' primary aspiration is to transmit knowledge, our schools seem to the pupils – and, increasingly, their parents – to be places where they learn the disciplines they need to live in society.

We must not be afraid to say that both these weaknesses are both holding France back and failing its schoolchildren. It is the quality of the teachers, who are on the whole good, that makes up for the negative effects of these archaisms

These themes have not been studied or discussed for decades. And the dominant interpretive discourse is content with facile tirades about social inequalities in our schools. It now seems almost incredible that it was denied for so long and so completely that there are reasons for the social inequalities in our schools. The schools that wanted to ensure equal opportunities for children who started out from a low level have become not only transmitters of inequality; they have been a major factor in promoting it.

Having identified these basic themes, it also has to be said that pupils are badly advised and that their teachers are poorly trained. The public sees only the conflicts between teachers and didacticians, especially over mathematics, history and reading. Professor Meyrieu is one of the very few people to have argued the case for a pedagogic approach. And what do the teacher training institutes teach their students about the psychological problems of adolescents, or about relations between different cultures? There appears to be a particular taboo on observing teacher–pupil relations, even though it should not result in any accusations or condemnation. The problem of education cannot be reduced to being merely an appendix to the more general problem of inequality or capitalist domination. But the theoretical and practical void in the domain of education is such that going against the dominant interpretive discourse is now a matter of urgency: we have to look in very concrete terms at the internal workings of our system of education in all types of schools.

The old position is now indefensible, as study after study has shown that teacher–pupils relations, and especially the way teachers define their role as transmitters of knowledge, have a major effect on the results achieved by schools. When teachers define themselves as a group that is communicating with a group of pupils, and take an individual interest in every pupil, pupils perform much better. The fact that such huge and important problems cannot be solved in a few sentences, and that arguments with very different implications must be compared, explains why debates about education are so heated. But the important thing is that we must not lose sight of reality. And yet, considerations such as those evoked above, and especially the assertion that the schools' central preoccupation has to be the personal development of pupils, are indignantly rejected by many teachers, and by much of public opinion. This growing blindness is alarming because, while the number of children attending private schools has not risen in percentage terms, there has been a steady rise in the number of parents who send their children to such schools for limited periods of time.

At the same time, it has to be stressed that the young teachers who are sent to work in difficult sectors, on completing their training have not been given any special further training. They find it very difficult to relate to their pupils, and this causes them real difficulties. A high proportion of teachers working in difficult areas quickly request transfers and experience serious personal problems, mainly because they feel that they are being treated unfairly and deserve more professional respect. The fact that so little research has been done and that the work of groups of teachers, such as those at the school in the rue Vitruve in Paris's twentieth *arrondissement*, who have taken more initiative, has aroused so little interest, shows that the republican spirit can no longer keep teachers' hopes alive and can even lead to greater inequalities among pupils rather than to any equality of opportunity. No other domain of social life demonstrates more clearly the need to transform the French model, and to take a much more innovatory look at the relationship between a universal that must be clearly defined, and pupils' psychological, social and cultural characteristics, which teachers must take into account.

Laïcité

We encounter the same set of reactions and problems when we look at republican universalism in schools and at general attitudes towards religion and especially Islam, which, given the high number of immigrants from Islamic countries, is now the most active religious force in France, and the one that is expanding most rapidly. And yet anything to do with religion awakens so many echoes and has such an effect on the French collective memory that a particular analysis has to be elaborated if we are to assess the role of the social thought whose orientations and attitudes towards religion I have been criticizing.

The word *laïcité* in itself condenses all these elements, as it is used in only a few countries such as France and Turkey, and is in fact untranslatable in many countries, including the United States. The terms of the separation of church and state in 1905 were moderate, but they were also part of a long war between the Catholic Church and a state that was (as in Brazil, Argentina and Chile at the same time) strongly influenced by an anti-clerical or anti-religious feeling. It implied more than recognition of the churches by a state which, in return, did not finance any one denomination; it asserted that citizenship, and therefore the sphere of political life and public freedoms, was completely divorced from the religious world. A hundred years later, France objected to the suggestion that the Christian origins of European civilization should be enshrined in the proposed European Constitution, not because it was trying to deny an irrefutable historical reality, but because it rejected the view that democracy and political life had a religious basis. There is a striking difference between the situation in France and that in countries that do have a state religion, and where priests are paid out of public funds – but where the churches often have little influence – not to mention those democracies that associate the rules of democracy with the principle of Christian morality. Nowhere is this more obvious than in the United States, where government meetings begin with prayers and where President Bush frequently said that he was fighting the axis of evil in the name of Christian values.

Given that I have always been critical of the French dominant ideological model, especially in schools, I unhesitatingly support the French position on *laïcité*, in the sense that it bases a model for social organization on non-religious principles. The outbursts of anti-clericalism and anti-religious feeling we have seen in France are much less dangerous than any attempts to justify politics or the school curriculum in moral and religious terms. Even used by committed democrats, anything that evokes the formula *Gott mit uns* ('with God on our side') seems to me to be a recipe for holy war, and therefore increases the likelihood of a 'clash of civilizations' based upon religious principles. There is a danger that societies that derive the principles on which their institutional unity and objectives are based from a belief will see all conflicts as part of a global confrontation.

It is now impossible to discuss relations between religions and political life as though there were no crusade and no counter-crusade: the confrontation between the two poses too many serious threats to the whole world. The term 'Islam' should, however, no more be applied to all countries where the Muslim religion is dominant than the term 'Christendom' should be applied to all those countries – including France – where the Christian churches were once attended by the vast majority of the population. On these basic points, I feel that I have much more in common with the supporters of *laïcité* than with their enemies.

Anyone who adopts this general position has to recall the debate about the bill banning the wearing of the veil in schools. When I sat on the Stasi Commission, which was asked by the President of the Republic to give its opinion on this question, I, like others, defended a position that might seem to contradict my usual position as a supporter of cultural diversity. While the number of women wearing the veil has risen, this is not for strictly religious reasons. It is obviously necessary to give the Muslim religion, and the way of life that prevails in Turkey or the Arab countries, a normal visibility and, therefore, better safeguards than it had in the past. At a deeper level, the religious phenomenon in general – Christianity, Jewish thought and the Islamic world – is, in my view, marginalized by the official curriculum, and that is stupid. This mention of my usual position by no means contradicts the stance I took as a member of the Stasi Commission.

Wearing the veil at school is not just a matter of cultural diversity: girls are perfectly free to wear the veil outside school. What is at stake is the defence of a space that can be shared by all. It is by no means contradictory to wish for greater cultural diversity, as opposed to the 'one' culture with which we are so often asked to identify, and to give *citizenship* priority over *communities*. And nor is it contradictory to defend a *laïcité* that is more respectful of religious modes of thought and expressions of religious feeling, even when they are not under the control of any particular church. I would add that Parliament and French public opinion were hugely in favour of a law banning the veil, and that no big Muslim organizations called for protests over the issue.

The heated discussion over this issue, which preoccupied the whole of France for over six months, provides me with an opportunity to state my position clearly. I unconditionally defend *laïcité* and I am suspicious of states that seek to impose their will on the whole of society; rejecting all hegemonic tendencies, I try to make room for the human subject in both social reality and social analysis. We have to reject the hegemonic pretensions of both the state and the churches if we are to develop a way of thinking that subordinates the analysis and evaluation of social facts to a principle that is both alien and superior to established powers, no matter whether we call it self-consciousness, human rights or solidarity. But this defence of *laïcité* must always go hand in hand with a better understanding of and greater respect for cultural diversity.

The *Banlieues* of the Republic

The educational system's problems are part of a general crisis in contemporary societies, and especially their political systems. In France, they reveal society's reluctance to accept any change in the social and cultural paradigm. This difficulty was seen with particular clarity during the riots of November 2005, which led to uprisings in some *banlieues*, especially in the area around Paris. They were on an unprecedented scale but had no religious content, and cannot be explained in purely economic terms. Most observers agree that they were triggered because young people of Arab, Turkish or African origin, who have been badly hit by unemployment, feel that they are the victims of discrimination. Whereas immigrants and the descendants of immigrants did achieve some degree of integration over the space of two generations, the present generation – the children and grandchildren of the first immigrants – appears to have been caught up in a process of 'de-integration', as many 'native' French people actively discriminate against them. Boys are especially affected. It is often impossible for a young *Beur* or African to get a job. If they change their names, they get interviews, but are rejected when they show up. The rejection is compounded by a retreat into their family and community, and this gives elder brothers an increasingly repressive control over girls. The gap becomes wider, and eventually leads to a real segregation.

These points have to be made. Collective phenomena have to be located in time and space, and it is essential to define the nature of the emerging crisis or conflict. How can we fail to be astonished to find that no analysis of the issue has been outlined before now? And yet the problems have been piling up in recent decades and some good observers, such as François Dubet, with his pioneering book *La Galère, jeunes en survie* (1987), Mathieu Kassovitz with his film *La Haine*, and Didier Lapeyronnie, have supplied a lot of information and have offered interpretations of the lives and actions of the young people of the *banlieues* or *quartiers*. Despite that, and with a few remarkable exceptions, French society and its dominant ideological discourse have nothing to say about these mass phenomena, which are, in their imagination, marginal. Efforts have been made to find an explanation, but its content is purely economic or demographic. No one has talked to the populations concerned. We criticized the council estates, the rundown state of the tower blocks and the poor transport links with the city centres. It was unusual for anyone to voice criticisms of the local authorities, which were often praised despite their inability to do anything. The police, on the other hand, have come in for virulent criticism. Few people talked about school, and almost no one talked about the family life of the young people concerned, or about their position with respect to employment. The most common image was that of a population that had been desocialized or that was regressing. It was likened to a group whose leader has used violence to acquire a power similar to that of the males that dominate the pack. Traditional language did have one category at its disposal – the underclass (*lumpenproletariat*), but that category took no account of the situation's ethnic dimension. Nor did it take into account the illegal economy known as '*le business*'. When riots broke out, or when the occupants fled the estates, they were seen as 'marginal' phenomena. The same word was used to describe people who displayed little capacity for upward mobility because they were poor and belonged to cultural minorities.

What were the reasons for this refusal to understand? We take the complacent view that any change, even when associated with rapid modernization, has its dark side, and that we have to accept that the marginal or the excluded will be with us on a more or less permanent basis. For a long time, economic problems, cultural loyalties, forms of family life, the position of women, relations with the welfare system and the local authorities, and inter-ethnic conflict were simply lumped together and left almost unexamined, as though every individual were made up of a number of isolated compartments. The silence of the ideologues could not have been more in keeping with the silence of a society that complacently accepts a combination of a little police repression and a few humanitarian interventions. SOS Racisme certainly set in motion a broad solidarity movement on the part of those passionate believers in freedom who had made France a welcoming place. Those reactions aside, France's professionals and intellectuals paid little attention to the problems and behaviours of the descendants of its Islamic immigrants. That is why, when SOS Racisme realized that its action was supporting national or nationalist groups rather than individuals who were in difficulties, it organized a working party to decide which direction it should take. The Elysée, which had always had a direct influence on the movement, urged it to adopt the most prudent position, as it did not want to give the impression that the French government was supporting the Kurdish PKK in particular. Once again, the discussions got nowhere and came up with the same tired formulae.

My goal here is not to offer a hasty interpretation; it is to show that the dominant interpretive discourse prevented the analysis from going any further, made it impossible to compare interpretations, and prevented new ideas from emerging. It was as though there was nothing to be said about these people, as though they were an undifferentiated grey mass. The 'March of the Beurs' mobilized lots of young people and won over so many sections of public opinion that, when it reached Paris, the President of the Republic, François Mitterrand, invited its organizers to a reception in the Elysée. The silence and the confusion were so complete that the uprisings in the *banlieues* took everyone by surprise. The failure to make any distinction between fire-raisers, dealers and the unemployed youth meant that no analysis was possible. Even the young people concerned often gave up trying to understand who they were, what they wanted and what they could do.

It is quite natural for a society in which there are supposedly no actors to see its own problems in terms of a crisis of de-integration, without ever mentioning the existence of protagonists who have a past and a future, who make choices and who have their lived experiences. If we share that view, we have to admit that it was a complete success: for the dominant interpretive discourse, these young people, who were not necessarily all that young but who were men and women, *beur* and African, simply did not exist.

Conscious and Organized?

Self-consciousness cannot emerge from a void, and the spirit of freedom cannot be born of a loss of freedom. All too often, such observations mean that a central role is given to an elite that comes from outside because that is the only thing that can transform the dominated into liberators. This is a central theme in Zola, seen especially in *Germinal*. This idea was widespread in the nineteenth century, when it seemed that a proletariat that had been to some extent marginalized could not bring about its own liberation. The socialist movement, and especially Marxists, endorsed the idea. Even Stalin, who was the least educated of all Lenin's comrades, had studied at a seminary, and most of the others were real intellectuals. The twentieth century was dominated by the belief in this approach, and the triumph of the idea that the class struggle had to be led by a vanguard meant that power was seized and became a dictatorship *over* the proletariat and, more generally, the whole population.

The idea of the subject allows us to understand both exploitation and the domination of liberation. The fate of all liberation movements is decided by the interplay between the appeal to a freedom that comes from above and convinces the new rulers that it was they who freed the dominated, and brought in liberation movements in the true sense. Such movements destroy the enemy and their fortresses, but they also represent a desire to be a subject. A people in revolt that destroys spiritual works, desecrates graves and burns books quickly becomes the slave of those who teach it to see itself solely in terms of its domination rather than to look for evidence that the subject is at work within it. If, on the other hand, the dominated liberate themselves, if they are aware that they are freeing their inner creative forces, and if – which is more difficult – they feel that their liberation will give everyone, including their rulers, access to freedom, there is a surge of subjectivism, freedom and creativity.

Modernity cannot come into being, and rationalism and individualism cannot be linked, unless individuals break out of their social definitions and see themselves as subjects. But there is something missing from that formulation: how does one individual-subject recognize the other? The usual answer is that recognition of the other as subject complements the recognition of the self as subject, but if we look at post-feminism, it becomes obvious that this facile answer is not enough. Women do not simply want to be on equal terms with men; they fought the discrimination and the inequalities suffered, but their real aspiration is to construct themselves as women. They accord, in other words, as much importance to their relationship with themselves as to relations with the other, and that cannot be an end in itself. The other is no more than a means – and usually a very important means – to the end of constructing a self-to-self relationship.

All this flies in the face of the long intellectual and political tradition behind an interpretive discourse that still plays a dominant role in intellectual and political life in France. It was given a new lease of life by François Mitterrand. It drove Michel Rocard out of power and gave the victory to the supporters of a 'no' vote in the referendum on the proposed European Constitution. Many French people still suspect that talk of actors leads to a subjectivism that will be manipulated by very conservative forces, and especially religious forces. For a long time, many people believed that, because they were supposedly less rational, women were more likely to be influenced by the church and were, it was said, more inclined to subjectivism and, therefore, conservative ideas. While it is true that these objections have gradually become more muted and that actors are emerging throughout the social sciences, and while it is also true that the theme of the subject, which was violently rejected for so long, has re-emerged everywhere, the strength and influence of the dominant interpretive discourse are still so great that we must adopt a more polemical term if we are to fight it more effectively. For my own part, I will continue to prioritize the need to reconstruct a reflexive social thought.

5

Light and Shade

After Jean-Paul Sartre

The dominant interpretive discourse, which was the main character in earlier chapters, cannot be understood outside the historical context in which it exerted its influence. The Cold War destroyed initiatives and revolts on both sides of the Iron Curtain, but it used different methods to do so. If we wish to arrive at a better understand of this dominant discourse's *raison d'être* and logic, we have only to read the best of the authors who popularized it.

The most influential was Jean-Paul Sartre, who was attacked more than anyone else by those who loathed his humanism. Their failure to understand him is strange, as the theme of the end of bourgeois society and the labour movement is present throughout Sartre's work, while his support for Communist policies from 1956 onwards leaves us a taste of solidarity until death rather than any hope for a radiant future. Jean-Paul Sartre does not belong to the dominant cultural and political model, which is why he appears here and not in my analysis of the DID. He simply paved the way for it by sweeping away everything that came before him and leaving a vast empty space where the dominant interpretive discourse could spread like a weed. Sartre's ambiguity makes him the best and most influential witness of the post-war period up to 1956 and even 1968. He is an ambiguous figure because he portrayed individuals who were victims of the illusion that they could find truth, justice and meaning, when they were in fact blind to the realities that surrounded them on all sides. Some of his characters identified with serious-mindedness and virtue, and were not even capable of any self-understanding; others were so completely dominated that one could approach and meet them only at the lowest level, or by accepting the brutal dialectic that teaches that wallowing in evil is the only way to do good. That point is often made by Goetz in *Lucifer and the Lord*. Goetz is the most extreme character in any of Sartre's plays: he finally takes command of the German peasants, which he had previously refused to do, and leads an extremely brutal rebellion. But the social masses are not historical actors for Sartre. There is no social movement, but only the social pseudo-life that finally overcomes Roquentin in *Nausea*. There are no capitalists or businessmen, just self-satisfied bourgeois who are more concerned with the established order than with creating an industrial society. And nor is there any social movement to be found in the 'dominated' class; its domination is so complete that no actor can emerge, and no actor can speak. The leaders who speak in its name are very distant from the people and its lived experiences. This history, which has no historical content, tells us the truth about a period in which the labour movement no longer existed, either because it had been annihilated by the Communist Parties, or because it had been absorbed by the brutal capitalist development of countries in which it could not restore a new balance.

Sartre's main concern is with the highly ambiguous intermediary categories that are home to those Francis Jeanson so accurately called 'bastards'. According to Jeanson, the word plays a central role in Sartre's work: the 'bastards' are also referred to as 'impostors', and Sartre himself is one of them He appears in disguise in the plays, before becoming the only character in *Words*. But it is impossible for him to become completely absorbed in this self-hatred, which was never as violent in France as it was in the Germanic world. There is therefore the gentle Sartre – or a 'soft' Sartre, as those who want to drive him out of our memory would say – who wrote *Existentialism and Humanism*, and who embarked upon the *Rassemblement Démocratique et Révolutionnaire* adventure of the RDR with David Rousset and Gérard Rosenthal. There is in fact something very unreal about this Sartre, whose image dissolved into the increasingly radical positions he took from 1956 onwards. This was the year in which Khrushchev's secret report revealed Stalin's crimes to the world. Sartre went so far as to adopt very disturbing positions, supporting class justice and terrorism, even though he had discovered its vacuity, and lent his support to the Baader-Meinhof gang in Germany. The Sartre who sold *La Cause du peuple* outside the gates of the Renault plant in Billancourt was not only pathetic but trapped into a misunderstanding. The history to which he committed himself was a history without actors, without conflicts, without reforms and without any positive consciousness. It is this consistently negative account of a vision of a society in which there is no meaning but a lot of bad faith, and which is full of individuals who have lost all their illusions about sense and meaning, that explains both Sartre's importance and his great success. The period in which he wrote was indeed a dreary period.

The novel *The Age of Reason* did not enjoy the same success as Sartre's plays, or even *Nausea*, but it supplies the most powerful vision of the empty world in which Mathieu, who is the main character, succeeds in resisting the lies and temptations of an artificial action and opts for a life in which there is no meaning but only defeats; its only unity and strength is the lucidity that prevents him from losing his self-control but leaves him with no energy to face up to his most immediate problems, such as Marcelle's abortion. Mathieu is of course a subject who constructs his life without submitting to any authority or external ideology, and even a subject who protects us from both mobilizations and good manners. But he is a subject who exists only because he does not act and does not confront evil, injustice or ignorance. None of the characters in the novel – not even the Communist militant Brunet – has any individual reality, for the theme of the novel is the denial that the preconditions for action exist. The void, the impotence and the refusal to commit may well be figure of the subject, but they are the subject's degree zero. While his characters defend a space of freedom against an impotent or cowardly bourgeoisie, Sartre's lucid judgements reduce them to a non-existence.

If we put Sartre where history put him, or at the starting point for the intellectual movements of the 1950s, the 1960s and even the 1970s, it is clear that he is not on the side of what we might call the 'post-Marxists'. That is why the real meaning of his thought is to be found in his relationship with the Communist Party, which sums up all his contradictions. His elementary belief in the historical mission of the proletariat meant that the only political solution he could envisage was joining or supporting the Party. In 'The Communists and Peace' he speaks on behalf of Communism without joining the Party, but relentlessly attacks its enemies in polemical terms. But nothing could be easier than mocking M. Robinet, who wrote editorials for *Le Figaro*, but his criticisms of the journalist Georges Altman are facile. Like many others, Altman followed a trajectory that took him from Left to Right but, more importantly, it led him away from the Communist Party, which he saw as the greatest threat of all.

It is actually a much earlier text dating from 1946 ('Materialism and Revolution') that does most to situate our abiding image of Sartre's thought. Although it is not very political and avoids polemics about contemporary issues, it denounces materialism because it goes against the revolutionary spirit, which cannot exist in the absence of a desire to liberate all human beings, and not just one class. He writes (pp. 228–9): 'No opposition really exists between these two necessities of action, namely that the agent be free and that the world in which he acts be determined ... Freedom is a structure of human action and appears only in commitment; determinism is the law of the world.' I could cite every page of this text: there could not be a clearer assertion of the primacy of a freedom that exists only in an impotent subjectivity.

Sartre's most complex text on the working class and Communism is the 'Reply to Lefort', which was written in 1953. I have no intention of passing judgement on Sartre, and especially on the sympathetic view he takes of the Communist Party, though it sounds strange and irritates a historian-sociologist who learned from Hannah Arendt and Claude Lefort himself what totalitarianism really is. On this essential point, it is Sartre who lost the argument: his subtle comments on the links – and the distance – between class and party ultimately lead to the conclusion that we need the Communist Party if a revolution that is unavoidable but not inevitable is to take place. The text was written in 1953 and republished in *Situations III* in 1956, and those dates make it hard to accept. It is also difficult to accept the pages on the 'passion' of the working class, which is a prisoner of its dehumanized labour; hence the need for the Party to act as the agent of reconstruction. Why is the vision of the working class and its task so negative and so one-sided? At that time, I had already spent years interviewing workers from all categories and all branches, and had reached the conclusion that their class consciousness was most acute at the point when their craft-based autonomy was eroded and penetrated by the principles of so-called scientific management, or in other words the logic of profit. Sartre had a historical awareness of that reality, as he evokes 1903, even though he seems to know nothing about the great strike of 1913. But why speak of the 'masses' when, on the eve of the First World War, more than half of all workers were skilled? The rise in the number of unskilled workers resulted from the transformation of production that took place after the Second World War. It seems that Sartre accepted that Lefort was right to insist that it was the lived experience of the working class that would give a meaning to that action, but claims that its meaning must come from outside, or in other words be defined by the Party. At first, he appears to conclude that only the Party can make the actions of the working class meaningful, and that position was unacceptable after 1936, 1947 and 1948. He does not, of course, completely identify the working class with the

Party; he simply asks us not to see the working class as something that is self-contained. The outcome is, however, perfectly clear: Sartre denies that this class has any capacity for autonomous and liberating action.

Sartre is therefore the great witness to the twilight of the labour movement. He depicts it at the moment when it ceased to be a social movement, but never suspected that it might be the totalitarian grip of the Communist Parties that was to blame for its decadence. Sartre was not writing at the dawn of a new period, but at the end of an old one. The dominant interpretive discourse that emerged during Sartre's last years, and which usually denounced him, was not mistaken when it argued that he was talking about the past, but it was mistaken when it failed to see the often desperate appeals to actors who no longer existed.

Ideological Shadows and Personal Freedom

I have accumulated enough arguments to demonstrate the negative character of the intellectual 'climate' over the last half-century, which began with the decline of Sartre. The field of social thought, and especially of the social sciences, had been sterilized, not by any one theoretical orientation, but by a dominant interpretive discourse that infiltrated everything, closed down many avenues of research and sometimes even exerted a direct pressure that could take the form of violence. I am not referring here to structuralism: structuralism produced some great works, and the dominant interpretive discourse used it only by distorting it. It did the same thing with Marxism, which it used to create the image of a society in which there were no actors and which was subject to strict determinisms, many of them economic, and which imposed its absolute power on non-actors.

The situation was very different – and worse – on the other side of the Iron Curtain, where only Poland never lost contact with the intellectual world to which it belonged. Elsewhere, all that could be taught was a catechism based upon texts that were regarded as sacred. There was no obligation to refer to any particular school of thought in the universities of certain Western countries, but most of them deliberately ignored the findings of research because they were suspicious of research from the outset. In more concrete terms, researchers were not recruited purely on the basis of their professional skills, as there was no real way of assessing the value of their work. These shadowy areas were surrounded by a vast zone of prejudices, taboos and a refusal to understand that blocked the creation of new modes of thought. These pressures worked to the advantage of very different intellectual orientation, and my criticisms are not intended to be one-sided. In the United States, one president of the American Sociological Association stated in his inaugural lecture that we had to stop talking about the structural-functionalist school, because there was no other school and because structural functionalism *was* sociology. I can still remember the shock of attending Talcott Parsons' seminar when I first visited the United States in 1952. He was then at the height of his fame at Harvard. I am certainly not accusing him of having become trapped into his own system, but I still shudder when I think of the immense distance that separated us at that time. The great American universities had almost nothing in common with the badly organized space in which a new European generation, influenced by both Marxism and the experience of totalitarian regimes, was being educated.

Are we to conclude that the world of the social science was, for much of this period, divided into 'schools', in the same way that, when Charlemagne died, his empire shattered into three kingdoms that rapidly disintegrated? Such a conclusion would be more than unacceptable, as it would soon prove to be exaggerated and doctrinaire. I have never felt that I was trapped into *une pensée unique* in any of the countries in which I have worked. I certainly did not feel that in France, Italy or Belgium or, I might add, in the United States or Quebec, or in Chile or Argentina before the military coups. The margins of true freedom, which were not restricted to the acceptance of what was not forbidden, varied from country to country, and from university to university, but it was always possible to analyse the restrictions that placed upon thought without accusing the system of being repressive, even though it was usually very introspective.

I restrict the present analysis to the case of France because I have spent most of my working life here and because the country has had a great influence on me. It is true that the dominant ideologies could not be contained and that they did affect the creativity of many people, but it also true that, on the whole, the majority enjoyed the freedom to speak out and that their freedom of expression was respected.

It was those societies that experienced a high degree of state centralization, often based upon a concept of progress that demanded a complete break with the past, that developed the most integrated conceptions of social life. The earliest capitalist societies were very different. Societies that had been modernized by more or less enlightened despotisms were even more different. In French society, which comes into the first category, the dominance of statist thought did not mean that there were no spaces occupied by value-based behaviours and conflicts over values. There were few checks on intellectual life in France at this time. For a long time, French intellectuals mobilized to support great causes. They had called upon citizens to fight kings and, despite some pointless outbreaks of violence, the secularists forced the clericals to accept the separation of church and state. That eventually had positive effects and led to the creation of a tolerant *laïcité*. It would be paradoxical for a French intellectual such as myself, who has spent his whole life in university institutions, to complain about a lack of freedom. I enjoyed complete freedom. What is more, a number of good fairies guided many intellectuals of my generation, myself included, towards freedom and the creative spirit. Georges Friedman set up the first groups to do research on the sociology of work at the CNRS and invited me to join one of them. But it was really a new institution, the École des Hautes Études, which became the Sixth Section of the École des Hautes Études en Sciences Socials in 1975, that gave the social sciences, together with historical studies, the official existence they had hitherto lacked. Several personalities played a major role in creating that institution, but it was Fernand Braudel, the leading figure in historical studies, who succeeded in arranging this encounter between history and the social sciences, and it was to the great advantage of both. It was also Braudel who brought together a wide range of specialisms, without divorcing them from one another, and who thus created an open space that had a lot in common with the German ideal of the nineteenth century and with the best British and American universities. There is no room here for an autobiography, but my opinion of the half-century that has just ended is sufficiently critical to allow me to express my admiration of and gratitude to the man and the institution that allowed me to develop my work in complete freedom, and in a climate that encouraged the creative spirit. That is the first patch of light I have to signal after this long journey through what seemed to be an endless zone of shadows.

The Return of the Political

I now wish to add a few more patches of light to this panorama. It was the return of the political within social thought that first challenged the dominant interpretive discourse and did most to unsettle it. The oppressive influence of totalitarian regimes made it necessary to give a new priority to the analysis of political power, as no one could seriously defend the thesis that Nazism was primarily designed to promote the interests of German capitalism, even though some did believe that. For a long time, the influence of the Communist Party made it impossible to recognize the pre-eminence of political phenomena in so many situations. As a result of its influence in France, a strong theory of totalitarianism, which put the Communist Party on the side of evil, was replaced by a weak theory of anti-fascism that put it on the side of the defenders of democracy. Claude Lefort, who was the first to revert to a critical form of political thought, did not completely succeed in persuading the French to take an interest in the thought of Hannah Arendt. Raymond Aron was more successful, because he was considered to be on the Right, and because people on the Left were more willing to listen to him without feeling compromised. In terms of political thought, François Furet was the dominant influence, with his new political reading of the French Revolution. The return to political history was spectacular enough to inspire the collaborative work of François Furet, Jacques Le Goff and René Rémond. It was this return to political thought, which was the direct result of the crushing weight of the totalitarianisms, that breached the 'untranscendable horizon' of an impoverished Marxism that had become the language of an intellectual and academic world that could not escape it.

Those who see François Furet as the inspiration behind the French 'neo-cons' are making a big mistake. The renaissance of social thought was not a by-product of a political or even intellectual current, and is inseparable from the general shift that took us from forms of thought and action that were dominated by the search for the laws of a system to the formulation of demands for freedom and justice on the part of those who did not want to have to choose between a Communist or post-Communist Left and a neo-liberalism that was increasingly becoming the servant of markets and transnational companies. All the great Western countries underwent similar transformations, albeit in very different ways.

The new recognition of the autonomy of political action made it a useful weapon in the struggle against totalitarian regimes. In some cases it also led to a defensive republicanism, or one which went so far as to prioritize the problems of the state over those of society.

At a very different level, the new interest in the political also fed into alter-globalization. The defence of the Palestinians and especially the growing mass opposition in Europe to American policies in the Middle East helped to promote anti-globalization. Its importance stems from the fact that it adopts a global stance in response to economic globalization and America's hegemony. Two different tendencies coexist within it. The first is based upon local calls to strengthen what the Americans call 'grassroots democracy', and finds its most forceful expression in the Porto Allegre forums. The second is more visible at the summit than at the base, and its primary target is American hegemony. It is therefore political rather than social. The same spirit inspired the anti-American movement that rose from the ashes of Castroism thanks to Venezuela's President Chávez. Chávez not only won the elections in his own country but also became a major influence as far as away as Buenos Aires, not to mention Bolivia, Ecuador and Nicaragua. In France, the strength of this new ultra-Left became spectacularly obvious with the victory of the 'noes' in the referendum on the proposed European Constitution and especially with the many discourses and initiatives that reproduce the most extreme forms of 'breaking with the capitalist order'.

There is no reason to confuse the two statements made in this chapter, and they are very different. The first, which is the more important of the two, states that the political is an autonomous dimension of social life, and that it is its autonomy that guarantees public freedoms. In totalitarian regimes, in contrast, everything is political, especially economics and the social. The second, and almost antithetical, position we find among 'republicans' is that the preservation of institutions is more important than the struggle for the rights of certain categories. This is the central theme of all forms of Jacobinism.

Field Work

The renaissance of social thought began with the development of field work. The idea that a ruling class or some other system could be globally dominant was undermined both by the recognition of the autonomy of the political and, even more so, by the growing number of human actions that were resisting impersonal forces such as the market or war. After a period of doubt and even despair in the face of our apparent inability to influence a globalized economy, we saw the re-emergence of social movements that challenged the economic order. The first critiques emerged from the environmentalist movement, and they quickly led to earlier models of development being challenged. Our modern societies were organized around rationalization and secularization, but we now recall that the dynamism of capitalist society, which allowed it to conquer the world, could not be divorced from the extreme concentration of resources in the hands of an elite and, therefore, by the transformation of other categories into figures of inferiority. That is why, once the world had been conquered, we saw the beginnings of struggles to liberate the dominated categories. All these victorious struggles had the effect of undermining or even destroying the modernization model that had proved so effective for several hundred years. So much so that some thought that, at any given moment, society was nothing more than an arena for conflicts and negotiations. That schema rejected the form of historical thought that had triumphed with Fernand Braudel, who placed the emphasis on *la longue durée*, or in other words on what is not affected by direct human interventions.

It was the sociology of work that led, at least in Europe, to the rebirth of sociological analysis and to the rejection of both economic determinism and authoritarianism. This discipline demonstrated the error and the lies inherent in pseudo-scientific talk of scientific management of work, from Taylor to Ford, and the presence, even on the shopfloor, of forms of collective control that allowed the exertion of pressure on management to open negotiations over working conditions. These detailed studies can sometimes seem far removed from the realities they observe. They are, however, of great importance because they constantly belie the claim that, because it is 'scientific', the social order cannot be transformed by any kind of opposition. Field work got rid of these baseless ideological discourses. Sociology has succeeded in staying alive because it continues its demands for research and for the analysis of documents. Such demands are less spectacular than radical denunciations of globalization, but they undermine visions that are as arbitrary as they are grandiose. When sociology is forced to abandon its field work, it no longer has the strength to resist the ideological pressures that are brought to bear on it. That is why, after having analysed the May 1968 in France 'on the spot', and then the life and the fall of Popular Unity in Chile (1970–3), I insisted on undertaking a set of field studies of the 'new social movements'. It was to that end that I developed the *sociological intervention* method.

The method consists primarily in ceasing to study actors and situations from afar, and in studying the relationship between the researcher and the actor. Researchers help a group of actors to think about what they are doing, and develop what they see as the most likely hypothesis, or the one that gives most importance to the action they are studying. In most cases, the actors are happy to accept the hypothesis, and see it as proof that their action has been recognized. If the hypothesis is wrong, it results in confusion and leads to a dialogue of the deaf, but if it is correct, it enhances the actors' ability to think and act. As the books summarizing the findings of the interventions I have undertaken with François Dubet, Michel Wieviorka and, over shorter periods, Zsuzsa Hegedus, this is a slow and difficult way of working, but it could not be further removed from the determinist conception that so often frustrates concrete attempts to carry out sociological research. On the other hand, both the words of the researchers and the responses of the actor are impressive. They take us to the heart of the world of actors who regard themselves as actors only because they represent higher values, or in other words the idea that a self-founding subject can break with the discourses that talk so complacently about their lives. It was its least ideological activities, or in other words the compilation and analysis of documentation, that gave sociology the strength to put up an effective resistance to the outpourings of arbitrary ideologies that try to smother us without even troubling to base themselves on anything empirical.

More recently, I was particularly struck by one example. I had read a large number of books and articles, most of them based on objective data, and felt that I was surrounded by very different forms of the same assertion. It was a denunciation; women are the victims of inequality, and we find that the violence they suffer very often begins in the family. This is not a discourse that can be reduced to a vague denunciation; on the contrary, excellent studies have already explored the reasons for this equality, violence and *sexual harassment* [English in the original]. But I was embarrassed to find no mention of any initiative, and no positive response on the part of women to their situation. I then decide to close my books and to listen to individual women and groups of women chosen from various categories talking about their experiences of personal life. I very quickly discovered that what these women were saying was very different from the words that were put into their mouths, and that listening to them completely transforms our image of women. They are certainly not just victims. They are creating a new culture, mainly for themselves, but also for men. The idea that it is impossible to escape male domination, which was the dominant theme of post-Marxist studies, was marginalized.

How can sociologists fail to accord the utmost importance to observations made in the field or to information contained in documents that allow them to think without being poisoned by dominant ideologies? When all is said and done, the dominant interpretive discourse inspired very little research during the last quarter of the twentieth century, and relied on few findings, while studies that deserved to be described as sociological were gaining such ground that they revealed the emptiness and arbitrariness of statements which, at first sight, seemed to reveal more profound truths but which were nothing more than unoriginal reworkings of basic prejudices.

Michel Foucault, the Ferryman

I began by evoking the approach the dominant interpretive discourse tries to force upon us by condemning other ways of thinking or relegating them to the outer darkness. It has, fortunately, never completely succeeded in doing so. Indeed, one is struck by the diversity and the richness of the currents that have resisted it, not to mention those that have always been alien to it. But what we have yet to encounter is a mode of thought that subverts the dominant interpretive discourse from within by giving a central role to the subject it wanted so much to eliminate. Such a mode of thought does exist; witness the work of one of the most important, and perhaps even the most eminent, intellectual figure of this period: Michel Foucault.

I felt encouraged to create a mode of thought that could resist the dominant interpretive discourse when I encountered, as a middle-aged man, the later work of Michel Foucault, which was written between 1976 and 1984. This was the period that produced the last works to be published in Foucault's lifetime: *The Care of the Self* and the *Use of Pleasure*, and then the lectures at the Collège de France, and especially *The Hermeneutics of the Subject*, and the re-publication in the second volume of *Dits et écrits* of texts that were often scattered across journals that were difficult to find. The reader may be surprised to find me referring to the work of Foucault here, or almost at the point where Parts I and II are articulated. Was not Foucault the author of *Discipline and Punish* and, some years before that, of *The Order of Things*, which is still anti-humanism's flagship. But it is precisely because Foucault had such a major role in the dominant discourse that it is important to show that he was also one of its main critics. Long before he began to question the vast project for a history of sexuality that began with *The Will to Know*, he expressed his irritation with those who made him say that knowledge is power. He completely rejected that idea, because it made much of his own work incomprehensible. From that point onwards, he insisted that the main purpose of his life had always been 'truth, truth-telling, *Wahr Sagen*, what it is to tell the truth'. But he was already adding that the relationship between telling and the true is made up of reflections, the self's reflections on the self.

The two things reinforce one another, and it is in his last books that they become most complete. Especially when he insists that, for the Greeks, self-knowledge (*Gnothi Seautou*, to cite the answer the oracle gave Socrates) must be associated with the care of the self (*Epimeleia*

Seatou). Human beings are subjects because, as well as producing knowledge, they think about themselves as the creators of knowledge and, at a deeper level, about the self-to-self relationship. Foucault even finds in Plato the origins of all those schools of thought that, throughout the Hellenistic period and the early centuries of Christianity, put the emphasis on the care of the self, which becomes the central issue in ethics, while Aristotle and his successors, from Aquinas to Descartes, concentrate solely on the central role of knowledge.

Foucault was inspired to accord this central role to self-reflexivity by something that lies at the very heart of his work. He rejected essentialist humanism, and constantly sought to demonstrate how the way the subject is constructed varies from country to country; he then demonstrates that it is not possible to construct a subject without resisting some domination, or rather relations of domination, which raises the issue of subjectivation. Both these themes force him to concentrate on sexuality, or in other words on the way different societies use desire and even pleasure to construct it as the domain of ethics. It is true that, being a disciple of Nietzsche, he was tempted to see that creation as an aesthetic world rather than an ethical world, but his awareness of all forms of repression brought him back to the theme of action-upon-the-self (*askesis*), and to assert that it took precedence over self-knowledge (*mathesis*).

It is sexuality that really allows him to see how modern man is best able to construct himself as a subject.

Even though the last books published in Michel Foucault's lifetime, and the first major book to expound his ideas (Dreyfus and Rabinow 1982) have been widely read and discussed, one wonders whether the last phase of his life, when he abandoned his initial project for a history of sexuality, has received all the attention it deserves. The feeling of distance induced by the return to Greek, Hellenistic and Roman history may have prevented us from seeing that Foucault had inverted the model that was still present in the first phase of his work. He makes a very general critique of that model in the last lectures at the Collège de France and in the many texts he wrote in his last years. Michel Foucault is still the great ferryman. He began by rejecting Sartre, worked through the main themes of the dominant interpretive discourse, and finally elaborated ideas about the subject and subjectivation that free us from the suffocating notion of a society in which there are no actors, no reflexivity and no consciousness. Hence my pilgrimage to, or detour via, the late Foucault before I begin to expound more clearly my views, which intersect with and are backed up or even legitimized by his innovatory efforts.

Part II

A New Way of Looking at Things

6

The Theatre Fills Up

Posthumous Eloquence

The remainder of this book is dedicated to those who were born during this period but, before we leave behind the drabness of its final stages, we must evaluate as accurately as possible the importance and nature of what has been said about it. My hypothesis is that, during that half-century, we witnessed the exhaustion and ghostlike survival of the European model for modernization. We have already evoked this model, and we must now look at its principal logic.

Whereas previous empires were primarily concerned with the preservation of their social order, the West concentrated all its resources in the hands of a conquering elite. That elite mastered nature with science and technologies, conquered space thanks to telecommunications, and territories through wars. It was thus able to accumulate both material resources and well-being. The concentration of resources in an over-armed battle group had the side-effect of giving other categories, including workers, women and children, and the colonized, an inferior status. Those words sum up the history of the West: extreme internal tensions were the price that had to be paid for the conquest of the world. The creation of an absolute monarchy, the beginnings of capitalism, science and the philosophy of law marked the beginning of this period, but it was followed by an age of revolutions. Citizens overthrew kings, wage-earners defeated their all-powerful bosses, the colonized drove out the colonizers, and women won the right to have control over their own bodies. The wealth that had been accumulated was redistributed on a slightly less unequal basis, and the level of tension fell: revolutionary movements were transformed into plans for social reforms. The disintegration of the great European model for the conquest of modernity was complete when the conquering elite handed over power to the market, while new empires were being built outside Europe and in defiance of the European model. In the very heart of Europe, that model was altered and covered in blood by totalitarian regimes that tried to force a racist communitarianism on the whole population and eliminated the 'inferior' enemy within. Hitler's Germany finally killed off the European model, which had been weakened by the blood it lost during the First World War.

It was when this European model had been exhausted and then destroyed, when it had lost its power to conquer, and when the dominated categories had, to some extent, succeeded in freeing themselves from their subjection, that the ideological ghost of that history appeared. Those who were on the side of neither the mighty nor the humiliated, be they intellectuals, politicians or journalists, interpreted this period, in which there were almost no actors, as an epic tale in which there were no real characters. They therefore revived the 'spirit' of European development, looked for signs of an absolute domination, and found them everywhere. But they found neither dominant nor dominated groups at a time when social-democratic or nationalist states were redistributing much of their national income, and when the working class had been torn apart by the split between the socialists who chose the West, and the Communists, who were initially more powerful in several countries but who had chosen the East and the Soviet bloc.

A New Way

Let us take up the argument from the point where we left off at the end of Part I. We can see the ruins piling up all around us. The noble statues that represented the institutions have been toppled; there are no more social controls over violence anywhere. Hunger, deportation and illness are destroying whole populations. Society, defined as a combination of forms of interaction, decision-making systems and agents of acculturation and repression, is in an almost universal state of decay. And the 'body social' has been beaten, decapitated and broken. Evil is biting real societies in the way that fleas bite, and drugs and the lure of easy money are destroying the lives of individuals. As a result, institutions no longer inspire any confidence, and nor do the courts, the schools, the political parties or the trade unions. This pessimistic vision can easily be tempered by those who recall the horrors of the century we have just lived through. But it is still true to say that, after the great totalitarian disasters that are still being replicated here and there, we are witnessing the creation of a completely disoriented world, rather than of a victim of the barbarism of savage leaders.

I am not trying to paint a dark or gloomy picture of the contemporary world. In Part II, I will try, on the contrary, to find new ways of thinking and new forms of social action. I began by removing the obstacles that stood in our way as quickly as possible. I have said it often enough: no matter whether it was described as functionalist or as critical, the sociology of societies has taken a trajectory that must be abandoned. The conceptions of social life evoked in Part I can no longer advance the discipline. The Marxist heritage leads to denunciations of globalization, American hegemony and even new forms of slavery and the domination of women; what I call neo-liberal sociologies are exacerbating the crisis in our societies still further, and believe only in self-interest and pleasure. Utilitarianism blocks all policies for social reconstruction. And finally, we must once again mention the powerful regressive trend that is taking us from society to community, from differentiation to homogeneity, and from *laïcité* to the obsession with identity.

Yes, all the ways forward are blocked – with one exception. But it is so broad that we can easily rediscover the diversity of themes and schools without which sociology is reduced to nothing more than a few message that are broadcast over loudspeakers to the whole population several times a day. I will go down this road as quickly as I can, always remembering that, if I stray from it, I will inevitably fall into a snakepit.

If we get away from representations of social action that are based upon an idea of *society*, which, in my view, no longer serves any purpose, we have to formulate an analytical principle that can serve as the main basis for a contemporary sociology. The new direction in thought and social analysis is what I call the *sociology of the subject*, and the word 'subject' has to be given all the more emphasis in that it has for long been held in contempt and seen as a product of a past that has gone for ever.

Why a sociology of the subject? The first, and probably the most important, reason is the historical reaction against Nazism. Nazism can no longer be seen as a manoeuvre on the part of big German capital, and nor can it be seen simply as an exacerbated form of German nationalism. Those who centred their analysis of Nazism on the persecution of the Jews were right, and they can base their arguments on texts by Hitler and his closest collaborators. But the violence was so great and went so far beyond any social, cultural or political project that it became an expression of evil. When evil is unleashed, it is impossible not to appeal to an elementary feeling of humanity that takes the form of despair, compassion, rebellion and courage. The protests were silent rather than vocal: it is easier to hear the voices of the dead than those of the living, and when we later learned about the scale of the Soviet camps, and when Kolyma became as central to our preoccupations as Auschwitz, how could we not look for ways of evaluating and understanding such things in terms that were neither social, political nor economic? Indeed, it would even be difficult to describe it as cultural, as the point is to defend the most vital thing of all: the assertion that human beings have rights, even if it means defying regimes that refuse to grant human beings any rights at all, and even the right to be human.

We must not, however, allow ourselves to be seduced by a voluntaristic optimism. Looking beyond the breakdown or undermining of institutions, I see the 'end of the social' as a confrontation between the 'objective' world of the market, technologies and war, and the world of the subject. The subject is directly involved in contemporary society. Behind the figure of the citizen or the worker in the societies of the recent past, we find the subject. I am, of course, aware that this discourse is based upon a faith in the liberating action of the subject and social movements, and I believe that faith to be justified and even necessary. It must not, on the other hand, lead us to forget the dark and deadly side of the 'end of the social' trend. That notion introduces the idea that the preconditions for the formation of actors are decaying from within. That is very different from the phenomena of domination, colonization or destruction that we experience so continuously during the European model's classical period, which was primarily concerned with the conquest of the outside world. We have gone from problems that could be defined in terms of domination and exploitation to new problems that must obviously be defined in terms of decay and desocialization, but also in terms of the self-construction of the subject. Those who think we are still living in the old political model, or who believe that all problems ultimately come down to colonial domination or class domination – of which male domination is no more than one partial aspect – are profoundly mistaken. The most dramatic problems arise within our world and our culture, and not from the conflict between our world and those who are subject to its domination. That is why the most visible problem is ecological: the death threat hanging over our environment, and therefore the planet. This is indeed a challenge to a mode of development, a way of life and way of controlling all economic and social activities.

Our representation of the world prevents us from advancing as quickly as we should be. False ideas that are out of step with observable practices, that are based on erroneous information, or that are simply confused, prevent us from looking for, finding and discussing real problems, and therefore from making the right choices. And yet this period did see the publication of some major books, and some of them have become classics. As we enter the twenty-first century, we have succeeded in introducing many new problems and new solutions into our intellectual repertoire. The human sciences have been given a new lease of life by analyses of totalitarianism and globalization, by encounters between cultures, by respect for minorities, by the impossibility of pursuing our present mode of development, and by the need to improve the living standard of the poorest. We have also learned to judge cultures in terms of the roles they give women, and we have got over our illusions about the end of religions. We also have the ability to transport and use rapidly increasing quantities of information. We would therefore be wrong to derive an unhealthy pleasure from describing ourselves as a continent that is in decline, or as a set of countries that can no longer manage their present or plan for their future! Such pessimism is all too easy; it is an excuse for not looking for our real weaknesses. In the intellectual realm, the important thing is to identify the mistakes we have made, and the ideas we have been unable to elaborate or use. We need to name, study and evaluate the greatest inadequacies of the half-century we have just lived though.

The mist is gradually lifting and the clouds are clearing. More and more people are waking up, even if they do have hangovers. No one can escape the need for self-criticism. For my own part, I think I have always pointed out what seems to me to be the right intellectual direction: I have always believed in the freedom of actors, the importance of conflict, and the need to transform our main intellectual instruments. And that is why I also recognize the right to adopt a critical tone when we talk about what is still a recent past. Now that both our great hopes and our great rages have subsided, it is easier to distinguish between what is true and what is false, and between forms of knowledge that will last and those that are doomed to a rapid destruction.

The reconstruction of a social thought that can analyse the contemporary world, and especially the so-called advance of developed countries, must take as its starting point what I call *the end of the social*. This is a very weighty hypothesis, but it does seem to me to be in keeping with the general findings of the best studies. I am trying to avoid a confrontation between modes of thought that appear to be diametrically different. The themes of the end of the social and of a change of *paradigm* seem to be to provide a starting point that everyone can accept.

We then have to choose: do we have to explore the main themes that will establish a new social thought, or not? That is obviously our goal, but not all those themes can be dealt with adequately here. I have therefore decided to introduce the few concepts that are, in my view, indispensable if we are to begin the work of reconstruction. We need to redefine the idea of *modernity* and the idea of the *subject,* and therefore the idea of *social movements.* Even when we have accomplished that task, we are still a very long way from the social realities that I wish to apprehend. First f all, I need two other concepts that sociology cannot do without: *conflict* and *alterity* (rather than difference). If I am to go any further, I will encounter the theme of *institutions* because I begin by defining the subject as a *de jure* being. It will then be possible to deal with more complex themes, and we must put off studying them for as long as we can: religion, politics, family life, relations with time and space, and all the things that have always been the concerns of sociology. For the moment, I will be satisfied if I can at least open the doors that give us access to ways of understanding new behaviours and the new ways in which societies are being transformed.

Dream or Reality?

As I begin Part II of this book, in which I propose to outline a conception of social life that does more to explain the realities of the last century than the modes of thought that have been dominant for so long, I am not thinking of sociologists past or present. I am thinking of the obsessional question bequeathed us by a century that was bloody, fanatical and mendacious: is it still possible, on the shores of these oceans of death, suffering and violence, to think in terms of freedom and individuality, and to understand the struggles that have been waged for political, social and cultural rights? Or is the mode of thought I am trying to elaborate merely pathetic? Does it have any legitimacy in an era of clashes between totalitarian regimes, and the upheavals caused by a brutal capitalism or by Chinese state capitalism? Perhaps those who speak, not without scorn, of my 'petty bourgeois idealism' are right. If I did not have an answer to these humiliating attacks, I would have given up writing books long ago, and I would certainly not be writing Part II of this book. That so many pundits on the ultra-Left in both Europe and the Americas failed to foresee the rise of Nazism, refused to understand the meaning of Vichy's policies, or refused to denounce the Soviet camps, is of no help to me. I am not primarily concerned with denouncing evil and death, but with demonstrating the reality and importance of the creative and conflicting political behaviours to which I wish to devote my full attention. And yet, I am still worried: is there still such a thing as a world?

Before I begin to expound my views, I must therefore once more explain why it is reality, and not a pure product of my imagination, that I am talking about. Aerial views show a planet that is covered in fields and deserts, shopping malls, prisons and deserts. At that altitude, we hear no human voices, and no messages, appeals or protests reach us. In order to get away from this description, which is too general or too superficial, sociologists of all tendencies have, ever since the beginnings of sociology, tried to get as close as possible to those they want to know and understand: in factories, hospitals, suburbs, schools and prisons. And they have long been trying to create protected spaces where they can listen to projects and protests. At the same time, they, like the historians of the present, seek out the written or oral documents that might provide them with information about the place or period they are studying. Some even listen to individuals and, rather than asking them questions, enter into a dialogue with them. A sociologist who wants to be a real researcher must not stand above 'society' but below it, and get close to the people who live in society, think there, and formulate complaints or projects there.

We must not judge the actor in the name of society; we must judge society in the name of the subject. Our goal is to shed light on the experiences, orientations and information we all use to construct our lives. Our lives can no longer be a mere reflection of history, because they are guided by the subjective self-to-self relationship that reflexivity and consciousness helps us to establish. These words are no more vague than the words we use to name industrial society or various political regimes; they are in fact less vague, because what we are constructing is based upon a long listening-process, and on notions that designate not an objective reality, but the situation of the subject. If we wish to discover how and why we act, our priority must be to understand a world in which the subject is constantly confronted with objects and the way they are managed. Those who short-circuit this world of subjectivity establish, at best, vague correlations that explain nothing, even though they are undeniably useful in a descriptive sense.

That is how we have to begin: by listening to the social and cultural actors so many authors and so much of the school curriculum have sentenced to death, and by at last rediscovering the moment when the noises we hear in the morning drown out the litany of those who go on repeating: 'The subject is dying, the subject is dead.'

No, the subject is not dead. The subject invites us to visit a workshop that is much more real than the castles dreamed up by those who believed they could interpret the meaning of history.

7

Modernity

The choice of the four themes discussed in Part II does not mean that I intend to begin writing a treatise on sociology, or a textbook. My guiding principle is a desire to identify the approaches that allow us to construct a new kind of social thought. The theme of *modernity*, especially as defined here, appears to me to deserve priority, primarily because it indicates which battles we should be fighting, and which we should not be fighting. Let me make it clear from the outset that the notion allows us to outflank both the defenders of rationalization and those who preach multi-culturalism. To put it in more positive terms, the theme of modernity automatically produces the distance between the subject and the actor that allows us to understand the very idea of a subject. By asserting that the universal is present in every particular experience, the theme of modernity protects us from all philosophies of history and from even the most powerful of society's attempts to make its mode of thought hegemonic. Divorcing the world of social practices from the idea of a subject who does not belong to that world is essential if we are to adopt fully the approach I am trying to describe here. The importance of the idea of the *subject*, and that of *human rights*, is that it allows us to evaluate social behaviours by referring in either positive or negative terms to the construction of a subject endowed with universal rights, rather than in terms of their social utility.

The theme of *social movements*, which has been weakened by the vague use that has been made of it, regains its strength only when it is associated with the theme of the subject. A social movement is never reducible to a conflict of interests; if we are to justify the use of the term, we have to add that both adversaries must, like the labour movement and industrial capitalism, refer to the same 'issues', resources or values.

It is only when we have covered the first part of this trajectory that we can approach the most hotly debated problem in contemporary sociology: that of *intercultural relations*. I choose that expression because it gets away from both the radical multi-culturalism that blocks all communications between cultures, and the false universalism that ultimately drowns out the specificity of every culture and every social movement. A complete reconstruction of social thought might seem desirable, but in order to do that we would have to pursue things to their logical conclusion and present an overall picture of sociological theory. Doing so would distract us from the book's primary intention of outlining the initial stages of a reconstruction of social thought.

No notion has come under heavier attack than *modernity*. Many insist that is a sign of the West's global dominance: modernity is a way of saying: 'we are modern. Modernity is what we have done, and the way we have done it. As for the rest of the world, you are no more than under-development, an obstacle standing in the way of modernization.' We must reject that definition as vigorously as the apparently quantitative definition that insists that development means nothing more than getting beyond a certain threshold. For a long time, we spoke of developed countries, and underdeveloped or developing countries, but it is difficult to define those expressions, which can be accepted and used only in order to locate the most characteristic thresholds and to draw up a list of those countries that can, at any given moment, be placed in one of the three categories. It is not difficult to see that that there is no strict correspondence between the three categories, and that levels of production and productivity, standards of education, and the degree to which political institutions are democratic are so many criteria that, while they must all be taken into consideration, cannot all be dissolved into a general dimension of development. In the same way, Amartya Sen has already exploded monetary definitions of living standards.

Reason and Rights

Modernity has to be defined in very different terms. Modernity exists when every particular situation and every functional element in a society can be considered and defined in general, or even *universal*, terms that go beyond the particular conditions of the action under consideration. To take the most obvious example, we can accept that, while it certainly has local economic, political or cultural causes, scientific developments in certain countries in the world, did, over a period of two to three centuries, reveal scientific laws, productive methods and modes of calculation that have a universal value. It is absurd to speak of Western physics, or North American or European biology. We must, on the other hand, make a very clear distinction between the characteristics of universality, and the historically concrete and particular conditions that explain why modernity emerged in a given place and at a given time.

What are the component elements of the great inversion that led every individual and every particular group to recognize that he or it not only used reason and universalist principles, but also embodied a universalist individualism, or in other words asserted the rights of all, and asserted that those rights were the same for all, and therefore universal?

It cannot be said too often that there are a number of components to modernity, because it is dangerous to see universals everywhere. Bearing that in mind, we can state that there are two basic principles behind the universalism that defines modernity.

The first is a belief in *reason* and *scientific and technical rationality* because, just as customs, traditions and even technologies are closely associated with particular periods and particular forms of cultural organization and cultural orientation, so only scientific and technological reason, which has no *a priori* reason to reject traditional technologies and customs, can appeal to the universal nature of scientific proof, and therefore to the possibility of reproducing experiments and formulating laws that are valid all over the world and for all cultures. Let us begin by ruling out certain objections that should not be made here. The appeal to reason and belief in scientific rationality do not mean that scientific knowledge is fully or exclusively defined by its universalism. Many people, from Popper to Merton and Khun, have outlined a more modest conception of science. The fact remains that existing scientific knowledge does go beyond the framework of social and cultural differences. It might be further objected that human experience cannot be reduced to its rational components. To invoke the universal nature of reason is certainly not equivalent to saying that human experience is exclusively rational; it really would be irrational to defend that thesis.

The other component, which is of more direct concern to historical knowledge and the human sciences, is the assertion of *individual rights* that are independent of all attributes and any social, economic or other particuliarity. The famous text of the Declaration of the Rights of Man and the Citizen of 1789 states: 'Men are born and live equal, with equal rights.' That is the important point, and it is obviously not an empirical observation; it is an assertion that, over and beyond the obvious differences that exist between individuals in terms of their capacities and behaviours, there is a universal definition of the human being that goes beyond all forms of social organization or political power. Once again, it would be very rash to criticize this grandiose position on the grounds that it forgets the content of human experiences and imagines that individuals who have been reduced to their pure individuality can be equal, regardless of their political positions, social relations or cultural loyalties.

Many people assert that these two components of modernism form a whole: the task of science is to destroy all social thought's 'holistic' temptations and to force all individuals to regard themselves as particular individuals who are not part of a whole.

That interpretation is unacceptable. While it is true that science divorces knowledge from the objects it studies, the accumulation of resources in itself leads to a sharp social polarization; categories that are regarded as inferior must therefore renounce both their subjectivity and their capacity for initiative. They can only derive their subjectivity from a *religious* conception that sees subjectivity as the grace of God. Religion can reinforce the interdependence of a system's elements, and therefore its immobility, but it can also create an individualism that sees all individuals as the creatures of God. They can therefore all establish a relationship with God. These two interpretations of religion are complementary, and not contradictory. Religion guarantees the established order to such a degree that it aspires to being its central power, but it also offers a *defence* against political, military and economic power. In Christianity, the martyrdom of Jesus, who is the Son of God, gives the assertion of the individual and his neighbour an unparalleled strength. That can deliver us from the globalizing temptation that is so loved by philosophies of history, which claim that all the elements of historical evolution – politics, economics and forms of religious life – are marching in the same direction.

The assertion of all rights, and therefore of the universalism of rights in every concrete area of life, be they political, social or cultural rights, is such an 'unnatural' stance that it could only be the product of a long history punctuated by battles, victories and defeats. The assertion of human rights can never be guaranteed; both systems of power and the communitarian spirit strive to deny a universalism that appears to them to negate their central role. We therefore have to look at the hypothesis that we may see the emergence of societies that *reject* modernity. There is nothing artificial about such a hypothesis; our modern and contemporary history is full of such societies. All communitarianisms, from closed cults to Nazism, have rejected modernity. Nazism did so quite consciously when it defined itself as *völkisch* or 'popular' – and gave the world 'people' the meaning it has in the Germanic tradition, which defines it in terms of the historical, cultural and biological unity of a human group. As we know, that conception was for a long time contrasted with the so-called French conception of *civilization*, which claims to have a universalist meaning. (I will refrain from entering into a debate that deserves to be conducted in more nuanced terms so as to avoid making a radical contrast between a so-called French conception and a so-called German conception. That contrast is not in keeping with reality.)

The image of a possible future in which there is *no* modernity is more disturbing. Those worries are now more real than ever, as China's rapid rise to power seems to be taking place within the framework of a state capitalism in which there is no freedom, and no social or cultural policy. No one doubts that China will, probably very rapidly, take on economic, technological and military dimensions that will allow it to defy any other power in the world. I introduce this hypothesis briefly, and purely in order to recall that there is nothing necessary or natural about the existence of modernity. Modernity is a human creation of a social and cultural nature, but that observation must not introduce a note of relativism. The importance of the historical link between the Europe of the seventeenth and eighteenth centuries and universalism does not mean that universalism cannot exist in its own right, or that it cannot assert itself in very different historical situations.

If we define modernity in terms of a combination of rational thought and the human rights of all individuals, we remain, however, at a superficial level. Although it is assumed that they will merge into one, the two components always tend to become divorced from one another.

The history and nature of modernity are defined primarily by the growing divorce between the objective world and the world of subjectivity, between our knowledge of the world and our self-knowledge. In the modern world, the relations that are meant to bind things together have almost nothing to do with the meaning they take on for consumers. The social sciences were born of this dualism. Their goal is not the same as that of the natural sciences; it is to understand behaviours that imply a *normative orientation* towards the other. The autonomy of the world of the subject is becoming ever-greater. It had little autonomy at the time of the great revolutions, when the language of necessity fused with that of freedom; it became more autonomous when the first sociologists taught us that the meaning inherent in a situation and what it means to the actors are complementary, and that the only way to understand behaviours is to define them in social terms, with society defined as either an institution or a system of domination. It became more autonomous still when classical sociology fell into decay, and it is now threatened with extinction. All that remains is a clash between communications networks and self-consciousness.

The constructs we call societies, which are made up of activities and laws, or hierarchies and solidarities, are dissolving, rather as though the monuments we thought were made of marble and cement were no more than castles made of sand that looked solid but which are falling apart as the wind dries them out. The wind, which has become a storm, is the accelerated movement of financial, economic and media exchanges. It is blowing across the whole planet, and setting everything in motion. Where once there were territories, there are nothing but flows; where there were clearly defined frontiers, the economy is becoming more and more globalized. And our institutions, laws and political wishes no longer have any influence on these global flows. We find it difficult to accept that what we call the economy and what we call society, which were for so long two sides of the same coin, are becoming divorced, rather as though the inscriptions on the obverse and the reverse were written in different languages. Society is dying because no institution and no collective has any hold on the global economy. We have long been accustomed to defining the major domains of social life in terms of their role in the activity and survival of the whole; that idea is no longer acceptable. This raises a question to which no seer has an overall answer. But we must find enough elements of a solution to ensure that the question has a meaning and that our actions are not demented.

The social sciences have been trying for too long to reconstruct totalities that are decaying, or even to deny that they are decaying. I suggest a different answer: the meaning no longer lies in the situation or the system; it lies in the actor, in the actor's self-consciousness and demand to become a self-constructing actor. And it is at this point that a word that has been taboo for so long has been driven out from our vocabulary and collective action: for today's actor, the 'good' is defined in terms of what allows him to be a *subject*, to construct and assert himself as a being who enjoys both rights and freedom. The subject is the direct and unmediated encounter between the empirical being and his self-image. The subject is his own value and has no need of religious, historical or social intermediaries. This face-to-face encounter is hard to tolerate, but no one can avoid it without descending into a hell in which objects have lost all meaning.

Practices have become divorced from their symbolic meaning: this observation, which lies at the heart of our problems, sheds light upon the complete divorce between a global or integrated vision of society, and therefore the individual, and a representation that sometimes completely divorces the objective reality of situations from the subjective meanings of behaviours.

It would be dangerous to regard the integration of these two points of view as 'normal'. In our type of society in particular, it is futile to try to integrate individuals, and especially young people, and we would do much better to recognize that these individuals have the right to assert themselves as they see fit, and in terms that are non-social but not purely individual. They have a right to assert themselves as men and women who are free and responsible for themselves. What we should be looking for is the correspondence between the level of practices and that of rights. For human rights do not always have the same basis: that depends primarily upon society's ability to intervene in its own affairs and the degree to which it produces itself, or what, in my first books, I called its level of *historicity*. Our representation of our capacity to create and transform ourselves depends upon our society's level of historicity. If its level of historicity is low, our image of our creativity recedes. We project it (*entaüssert*) into transcendentals that are far removed from lived experience. When, in contrast, out ability to act upon ourselves – thanks to technology or thought – is at its greatest, we can directly apprehend ourselves as our own creators. But the relationship of dependency between the representation of the subject's rights and our ability to create a rational technological and administrative world cannot be divorced from the opposite relationship. The level of practices itself depends upon the level of rights to the extent that we no longer evaluate a society in terms of its functionality as a social system; it must be evaluated in terms of the subject's freedom and must measure our ability to produce our own lives in freedom. The way we judge a society can no longer depend solely upon its organization, degree of integration and ability to manage internal changes. It depends upon the degree to which a society respects basic 'human rights' or, conversely, refuses to do so. Only the first type of society deserves to be called modern. We therefore cannot describe as 'modern' a society that does not grant women the same rights as men, or that does not give them control over their own bodies.

To sum up, and to talk in historical terms, we can speak of a more or less uncoordinated sequence of figures of the subject, each of them closely bound up with the degree to which society is capable of acting upon itself and the form that action takes. After the upheavals of the Reformation and the Renaissance, it took centuries to construct the image of the subject as citizen. That image found its most powerful expression in the work of Jean-Jacques Rousseau in the late eighteenth century; it can still be found in that of Alexis de Tocqueville. It then began to decay as the paradigm changed: money replaced reason, and religion or romanticism distracted our attention away from the defence of citizenship. The rapid development of industrial society then gave birth to a new figure of the subject. Rationalism triumphed thanks to the development of science and industry, but the labour movement introduced the idea of social rights, and the struggle to defend them was as bitter as the struggles that allowed the citizen to be liberated. During the twentieth century – beginning in 1917 and ending in 1989 – we witnessed a whole series of crises that drenched the world in blood and camps, attacked scientific reason and attempted to abolish everyone's rights, be they civil, social or cultural. The idea of democracy was drained of meaning; social rights retreated in the face of the inevitable mobility of productive factors and the triumph of markets. Cultural rights were threatened with extinction as they were crushed by racisms and eroded by communitarianisms.

And yet, now that those years of misfortune are over, new efforts are being made to understand human beings. Witness, in particular, the growing importance of the defence of women's rights and the protection of a planet that we ourselves have put at risk. The figure of the subject now has to be redefined as the new banner under which we fight to preserve the continuity of the heritage of the citizen and the worker.

Whenever a figure of the subject is destroyed or harmed, someone will attempt to eliminate it by reducing social life to a logic that is characteristic of natural phenomena. Structures attempt to take the place of the subject, even though we are under no obligation to regard the two as incompatible. And yet suffering and injustice, exclusion and discrimination, and the violence that is spreading everywhere force us in our turn to answer the question the sphinx asks every age: what is good, and what is evil?

Before leaving the notion of modernity in order to explore its implications and preconditions, I must explain why I do not use the word in its usual sense. Modernity has long been defined in terms of the rapidity of change, the absence of social organization, and therefore by the disappearance of frames of reference and systems of enduring norms. Baudelaire provided the extreme form of this definition from the start when, in his *Salons*, he defined as 'modern' the presence of the universal in the instantaneous rather than in stability. I am quite happy to accept the negative side of that definition: modernity is indeed the opposite of an established order that is capable of reproducing itself. But the existence of more or less rapid change leads to an impasse or a nonsense: changes of all kinds are now occurring much more rapidly than in the mid-nineteenth century, but that does not allow us to say what is and what is not modern, because what now appears to be changing rapidly will soon come to be seen as part of a relatively stable past. Similarly, when we now look at the nineteenth century, we find that it displayed a surprising stability compared with the upheavals of the following century. That is why, while we are right to dismiss the idea that a stable order has disappeared, we cannot be content with talk of rapid and incessant changes: we must find a defining element that goes beyond pure change and turns its back on the quest for a stable, traditional order. That is why it seems to me that the idea of *universalism*, which has been there since the beginning of Enlightenment philosophy, is indispensable. That this provides a useful definition of modernity is clearly demonstrated by the negative examples I have given. There are, in other words, such things as contemporary societies with a high rate of growth that are anti-modern to the extent that they are reconstructing a communitarian vision of society.

My goal is to shed light on the experience, orientations and information that allow all of us to construct our own lives. Our lives are not just a reflection of history. They are guided by the subjective self-to-self relationship that is created by speech, reflexivity and self-consciousness. These words are often rejected on the grounds that they are too vague, but they are no more vague than 'politics' or 'family'. Indeed, they are less vague because what is being constructed is based upon important notions that refer, not to an objective reality, but to the situation of the subject. Modernity is the most important of those notions, but class consciousness, rights and freedom are important too. It is by entering the world of a subject who is constantly confronted with a world of objects that we can begin to understand how and why we act. Those who short-circuit this world of subjectivity establish, at best, vague correlations, but they cannot explain or understand anything. That is, at least, the way things stand in the era in which we live. In the past, there were worlds that were neither objective nor subjective: the world of 'society' was an end in itself, and it defined good and evil with reference to itself. Such situations are part of a past that has gone.

Modernity does not Belong to Anyone

We therefore cannot divorce the assertion of the idea of modernity, defined in the most general and even universal sense, from the critique that has to be made of all those – and they usually live in the most advanced and powerful countries – who identify with modernity but at the same times contrast *their* modernity and development with the backwardness or underdevelopment of others, or with the bankruptcy of some representation of history. The fact that some countries are, in economic and even social terms, more advanced than others has nothing to do with the idea that the most advanced countries should be completely identified with modernity. If we make that mistake, the concept of modernity immediately loses its universal character. It can retain it only if we accept that no country, no personage, no company and no region can identify with modernity, which remains a general evaluative principle.

Even so, that answer has to be complemented by a response to the criticism that rationalism and individualism reject every other dimension of the collective and individual experience of human beings. Some accuse them of ignoring the affective life that develops mainly outside consciousness, while others criticize 'rationalism' for its failure to recognize that human beings are social beings who live by their work, and who therefore live within social systems and, to be more specific, with particular forms of authority. Others, finally – and they are now the most eloquent – see rationalism as a negation of religious beliefs, traditional cultural ways of life, and the historical consciousness of nations, not to mention minorities. All these attacks are so wide-ranging that it is impossible to imagine how serious thinkers could be so blind to human experience. It is just a short step from this to accusing this rationalism of being the ideology of the ruling elites.

Those who voice these criticisms have to be reminded of the history of our thought and our society over the last few centuries. The notion of modernity, I repeat, cuts us adrift from our loyalties and duties. But there is also a positive side to it: it postulates that every individual has the right to conquer his or her rights and choices, and to defend them against established powers. The assertion of the human rights of every man and every woman has always been made in the context of collective struggles against authority. Citizens asserted themselves by overthrowing absolute monarchies; collective action won workers the right to have a labour contract and to be indemnified for the risks they ran; women have won the recognition of their rights, even though they have neither won complete equality nor put an end to the violence that is used against them. In all these fields, we have seen the development of an image of the individual that grows richer as power tightens its hold on him. That hold is not the effect of reason, but of the instruments that tighten their hold on individuals and at the same time make their domination take a less obviously brutal form.

Modernity and Modernization

Even before we begin to devote our attention to the huge problem of cultural and historical diversity, we have to write in capital letters that there is ONLY ONE MODERNITY but that there are MANY MODES OF MODERNIZATION, and then add that none of those modes is reducible to the mere implementation of modernity. No image could be more false than – the one that depicts all countries as a caravan led by the most advanced countries, while those who lag behind follow in the footsteps or the tyre tracks of those who went before them. There are many roads to modernization. The example of Europe easily convinces us of that: the Dutch and British mode of modernization, which was based upon the role of the bourgeoisie, was very different from the French mode, which attached great importance to the state, and even more different from the German mode, which was based upon a very different conception of the state. If we go beyond the borders of Europe, we find still greater differences, if only between the United States and most countries in Western Europe. If we do not divorce modernity in the singular from modernizations in the plural, we create such confusion that we can have no helpful debate, as everyone accuses everyone else of making mistakes that we can only avoid by making a distinction between societies' modes of transformation and modernization, and a concept of modernity that never completely coincides with any national or local situation.

The most common mistake is to define modernity in the same terms as modernization, and to see it as a step towards some ideal-type or ultimate society. It is to look at the life of a society, to identify its mode of modernization and at the same time to find within it elements of non-modernity or even anti-modernity. The theme of the *reinterpretation* of elements of traditional societies in countries that are undergoing a rapid modernization helps us to avoid most mistakes. The important point is that we should not be talking about 'modern' or 'traditional' societies, and, above all, that we must not think that the fact that, because all its elements are eminently modern, a given society or culture is therefore modern. Many elements of the most highly modernized societies are not modern, or even anti-modern.

Can a society that rejects the rule of rational thought and does not respect human rights be modern? It may acquire power, and especially military power, may accumulate resources in the hands of the state or a ruling category, and may even encourage the development of the sciences and technology. None of that prevents it from turning its back on modernity, because it does not apply a universalist approach to human rights, even though it does apply that approach to its system of production. We can say that there can be no modernization without a reference to modernity, but that there are many modes of modernization that do not take modernity as a goal, and that use it only as a means.

Is There Anything Beyond Modernity?

Entering a new type of society and culture means primarily that we enter a new paradigm in which cultural categories replace socio-economic categories when it comes to the analysis and organization of that society and that culture. Such a transition is neither continuous nor clear-cut. We have to emphasize at least the two main aspects of this mutation.

It began with an eruption in Berkeley in 1964, and then in Nanterre, Paris, in New York, in Trento in Italy, in Berlin and in Tokyo in 1968, to mention only the most visible events. The eruption represented a break with the society that had been reconstructed after the war. It had given priority to the infrastructure but, because it changed neither social life nor family life, it created a widening gulf between young people and the authorities. In France, this led to a rejection of the Pompidou government, which was proud of its economic achievements but blind to student demands. Its rejection, which was symbolized by the barricades and the huge demonstrations, led to the occupation of many university buildings and industrial sites. But the students and their supporters expressed themselves in the only language they all understood: that of the labour movement and, above all of the Trotskyist and Maoist Left. Hence the students' appeal to the workers, and hence their error of judgement. They thought that their hands were weak, and wanted to pass the banner of the revolution on to the strong hands of the workers. And yet the great strike of May got nowhere, while the student movement transformed the whole of French society.

The primary meaning of May 1968 is that cultural problems had taken over the political stage, but the students brought about this major change by looking to the past and not the future. After 1968, many of them flung themselves into revolutionary action, so much so that they flirted with or supported terrorism. Fortunately, the new Socialist Party created by François Mitterrand in alliance with the Communist Party, convinced the *gauchistes* that the situation was what Trotsky defined as 'permanent revolution', or in other words a direct transition from bourgeois revolution to proletarian revolution. In that sense, France did not go down the same road as Italy.

Hence the time-lag that left analysis out of step with action. This explains the success of a Marxism that – especially in the period 1969–74 in France – rejected the Hegelian aspect of the young Marx and claimed that an epistemological break divided the young Marx from the mature Marx and the purely economic analysis made in *Capital*. Sensing that the demise of Marxist discourse and of all philosophies of history was imminent, thinkers like Jean-François Lyotard adopted a post-modern conception that broke with the basic principles of modern thought. Lyotard proclaimed the death of all central organizational principles and of social thought. The reference to progress was eliminated, and huge importance was accorded to difference, while the shattering of the integrated and self-controlled personality gave rise to the idea of a 'fragmented' ego.

This current of thought, which was vigorous but not very consistent, was widely accepted. Indeed it was so widely accepted, especially in the United States, that our entry into a post-modern society was seen as a *fait accompli*. Teachers in the social sciences quickly spread the idea that modern society had been replaced by post-modernity. That idea was reinforced by earlier architectural critiques of the modernism that had inspired the contemporary architecture of Le Corbusier on the one hand and Gropius and the Bauhaus on the other. The skylines of New York and Chicago had become its triumphant symbols. That movement's influence had lasted for over a generation. I am talking about it with hindsight, and many authors, like Zygmunt Bauman, broke with it. It was becoming increasingly clear that we had entered, not the phase of modernism's decay, but an era in which a *new modernity* was emerging. The dominance of cultural categories within new social movements such as political ecology and the new feminism demonstrated the success of this new modernity. As we enter the twenty-first century, that long transition, which was confused but vigorous, seems to be over, or at least to be running out of steam.

We must now devote our efforts to understanding a new modernity that remains true to the general principles of modernity but finally breaks with all forms of historicism, Marxist or not.

If we accept the definition of modernity proposed here – the appeal to universalist criteria that applies both to our understanding of nature and to the way we think about human beings – the idea of post-modernity is hard to accept, unless, as I have already suggested, we accept the idea of an authoritarian state. Reducing the world to a clash between reason and freedom on the one hand, and religious fanaticism on the other, is still less acceptable. It is, however, true that we are seeing a growing conflict between an increasingly global economic system that seeks a political hegemony, and a defence of lived experience that can easily come to mean respect for the powers that be. Those who speak of a technocracy or techno-bureaucracy are mistaken if they believe that those categories define those who hold power. Power is almost always in the hands of individuals or groups who are not primarily concerned with technicity and rationality. And human rights are certainly not their highest or most constant concern. Those we call techno-bureaucrats are in fact often people who have a broader understanding of modernity in both the technological and the social domains. It is therefore a mistake to believe that we have moved from a world of princes and party leaders to a world of bureaucrats. We would like that to be true, and we would like to think that our leaders are now more concerned with rationalization. But the reverse is also true: contemporary technologies make much more allowance for political or religious choices that are independent of their country's scientific and technological structures.

Just as we must not define modernity solely at the level of concrete historical structures, it would be paradoxical to believe that those structures are in a complete state of decay. We also have a duty to imagine a world in which the modernity model no longer exists. Its civilization would be anti-modern rather than post-modern. It would be based upon a rejection of reason and individual rights on the part of both its leaders and its population. It would eliminate – much of what has been called civil society, and would subordinate it to an absolute state: a religious, military or bureaucratic state, or an Orwellian state in which all reference to individuality is banned. It is not absurd to imagine that what has been called the 'Western' model might lose its dominance, or that an authoritarian state capitalism based upon a great military power might come to play a major role in world affairs. Many other catastrophic scenarios can be imagined, from war and genocide to mass acts of terrorism that lead to chaos.

Why do I evoke these possibilities? Because they help us to understand that there is nothing 'natural' about the importance we attach to individuals and therefore democracy. That is not the final goal on which all roads to modernization converge. And they help us to understand that we must do all we can to create the social conditions that favour a respect for the individual.

I am certainly not suggesting that we surrender to a destructive social relativism, rather as though every country had its own conception of modernity. On the contrary, it is because I have chosen *one* definition of modernity that I can envisage the emergence, and even the dominance, of societies for which that category is meaningless. This helps us to understand that we live in institutions in which a belief in reason and respect for human rights has to take pride of place. The main implication of my position is not that the rich world must be defended but, on the contrary, we must look to *all* parts of the world to find the elements we need to build a democratic society. That is what many intellectuals, politicians and activists of all kinds have refused to do for the last fifty years because they rejected this notion of modernity. Revolutionary or terrorist groups such as the Red Brigades in Italy and their like in France and Germany believed only in revolution and many of them in France and Italy applied the slogan 'Revolution: the only solution'. The existence of such political groups is not worrying so long as they do not have a certain capacity for action, but intellectuals and semi-intellectuals who claim they are creating a true 'democracy' by preventing the 'enemies of the people' from taking part in political life are going down a road that turns its back on democracy. We also have to stress that such false ideas cannot result in solid research and intellectual constructs that will last, and remain aware of the weakness or emptiness of these discourses, some of which have had a lasting influence. The first professional duty of intellectuals is to refuse to let anyone pull the wool over their eyes.

Individuation

For those who understand modernity in the usual sense of change and differentiation, and therefore the destruction of an immobile bloc that looks down on society, it is self-evident that this theme goes hand-in-hand with that of individualism. While some complain complacently about our cities because they foster anonymity and violence, others see a wide range of opportunities, a labour market that is much more diversified, and emancipation from the authority of the family and the gossip of neighbours. The two discourses are complementary: the weakening of primary ties with families, schools, a neighbourhood or a group of friends is liberating for individuals if they are in pursuit of a goal, which may be professional or, more generally, social but which is usually very individual. Many of today's young people therefore go off to try their luck elsewhere.

The negative side of individualism is the loneliness and the loss of any feeling of belonging that goes hand-in-hand with the absence of any project or the abandoning of earlier projects. Many of the lonely turn to drugs or become involved in delinquent communities that cut themselves off from society.

A perception of these very different types of individualism does not lead to any great discoveries because group loyalties, to say nothing of identifications, are obstacles that stand in the way of individuation. We can reduce the gap between these two situations if we interpose an idea that Danilo Martucelli formulates in highly sophisticated form in his case studies. Individuation results from the way we resist the *ordeals* we encounter in various areas of life, rather than from isolation or integration into a group. The great advantage of this formula is that it centres the analysis on *individuation* rather than on the individual or individuals; it therefore combines the individual and social points of view. Martucelli disagrees with those who say that it is by becoming citizens that we become individuals. That idea is dangerous because it has a positive meaning only when citizenship is defined as a set of rights and not a series of obligations. It is all the more dangerous in that the meaning of citizenship, which we must defend and strengthen as much as we can, is being undermined everywhere as nation states lose some of their capacity for autonomous action. Indeed, many individuals all over the world are now denied their civil rights, and even the right to work.

I am not trying here to defend the extreme individualism that sees social non-belonging as a value in itself and that extols negativity. The theme of individuation, as defined here, is a first step towards the approach we must adopt if we are to escape an increasingly pointless dichotomy between the world of the individual and that of society. We can no more accept a reciprocity of perspective here than we can accept a complete divorce between the two spheres.

The notion of individuation can, however, have very different meanings, and we have to opt for the general version of the notion because it is more in keeping with the analyses we wish to make.

Individualism, defined as the rejection of social loyalties and determinisms, can easily coexist with a mass society, and can even break the bonds with an established, law-governed society. Individuals can become part of a different milieu defined by a marginality that often takes the form of delinquency. In less extreme cases, the assertion of individualism can be identified with membership of a group of minority community. Religious believers are deeply individualist, as they perceive a divine presence in the messages that are sent to them as individuals. Even forms of possession can be highly individualized, as one believer can be 'ridden' by an Orisha when his neighbour feels nothing.

This great variety of examples leads us to at least one preliminary conclusion: the assertion of individuality and the process of individuation are not reducible to the rejection of a life that is ruled by institutions. Individuation is certainly a rebellion against many aspects of society, especially when society is in ruins, but it is also a way of defending rights in every domain of social and cultural life, and not outside them.

No Positive Freedom Without Negative Freedom

We are no longer attached to the idea of natural law, which was an extension of a religious tradition and guaranteed that we were born and lived free, and with equal rights. We have inverted that formulation, and say that in a disorganized social environment, or in a bureaucratic and authoritarian environment, individuals can construct their own lives and embark upon a successful process of individuation only if they demand their own legitimacy by going against the social order and only, therefore, if they evaluate and judge situations in terms of their own demands for individuation. This inversion has already been defined: actors and individuals no longer define themselves with respect to a situation; the creative freedom an individual is given provides the best definition of the situation.

We constantly use this kind of argument when we talk about our families, schools or companies. This new orientation can take very different forms ranging from a withdrawal into oneself, to the assertion of the principle of individual rights, or even actions designed to transform the social order so as to find within it a support or some protection we can use to create ourselves.

This idea has to be given as a great an extension as possible. Just as the idea of socialization represented society's conception of how its new members should be integrated, individuation has to be the ultimate goal of social policies, as opposed to the norms that force individuals to submit to some authority.

Everyday language has given a very favourable welcome to this new definition of relations between individual and society. We increasingly speak of the rights of the individual in concrete and complete terms, not just to ensure that the right to citizenship is recognized but also to ensure that the rights of the individual are respected in the workplace, and in the individual's cultural milieu, and especially his linguistic and religious milieu. Demanding the right to be an individual who is recognized as such would be meaningless in a universalism that is far removed from concrete social situations.

Individuals assert their civil and political rights very strongly, but feel threatened by the contradiction between their right to remain free with respect to all external authorities, and their duty to cooperate with their communities, or even their comrades. That cooperation can be exploited by authorities that are not interested in enhancing their individual autonomy. The usual solution is the one found by industrial society when collective action made it possible to win the right to work for everyone. Collective action in all domains overthrew the authoritarian tendencies of the ruling milieus. Those milieus used violence or mass meetings to impose a group cohesion or homogeneity that posed a direct threat to the proletariat's hopes for emancipation. The leaders of social movements call for a dictatorship of the proletariat, but we know that it inevitably leads to dictatorship over the proletariat.

What does the right to be an individual mean? What is the man or woman who claims that right asking for? Does that individual exist outside society, his working or family environment, his sports team or his loving relationship? We can all sense that there is a danger that we will lapse into absurdity. Why defend the right not to belong, rather than the right to belong? Why defend isolation rather than participation? So let us dismiss these formulae, whose only purpose is to make a mockery of the question I have just asked.

The right not to belong, not to be integrated and not to be identified with some category is in fact not something vague. It is the negative freedom that British thought talks about so much. We must not contrast it with the positive freedom to which we refer when we speak of cultural rights. But can there be such a thing as positive freedom if negative freedom does not already exist? Let us take the most common example.

The demand for religious freedom has to be supported. The state must not place any restrictions on religious practices, and public opinion must not be unleashed against minorities. But does the assertion of the right to religious freedom have the same meaning, depending on whether we add or do not add that everyone must be able to follow the religion of their choice or to cease to follow it, to convert to a different church or faith, and to marry a partner who does not belong to the same church? The freedom not to believe, to have no religious loyalties, to convert and to leave a church is not just as important as positive practices: it takes us to the very heart of freedom. There can be no religious freedom if we are *not* free not to believe and *not* to integrate.

These comments are not just a stylistic exercise. Many countries have not just a state religion, but a religion which is identified with a nation and a civilization. Many religious communities deny their members the right to convert to a different religion or to marry a man or woman who does not follow their religion. Cultural rights, which must be granted to everyone, can be transformed into duties, religious obligations and a complete absence of choice, unless the individual concerned leaves his or her social and national community when he or she leaves the church. The freedom not to believe is the only safeguard against this deviation. For similar reasons, social rights, and especially those of workers, cannot be used to further the goals of parties or unions that seek to impose their power on all members of the social class or professional group by arguing that they are its sole legitimate representative.

No problem could be more important than this because so many societies are or have been dominated by one church or party that makes membership obligatory. It is impossible to recognize cultural rights if we cannot fight the inversion that turns them into instruments of power. The only possible safeguard is to ensure that individual freedom takes priority over the freedom to belong to a community. This is a key aspect of what the French call *laïcité*.

Respect for the individual is a precondition for respect for social and cultural rights, and therefore a precondition for democracy. This brings us back to the more classic formulae that are so often mentioned: the equality of citizens presupposes that every individual has the same equality of opportunity as everyone else, irrespective of their wealth, nationality, religion or gender. At one time, many people liked to say that only concrete rights mattered, and that so-called 'formal' political rights served only to conceal economic and social dependency. That type of discourse led to disaster, because respect for the universal nature of individual rights is an essential component not only of modernity, but also of democracy. Do we have to go so far as to say that we should respect only those political or religious organizations that respect *all* individual rights and accept that men and women, and young and old, have equal rights? The answer to that question has to be no. The state does not have the right to intervene in private activities. Equality, and especially equality between men and women, is so important that everyone must be free to criticize their party, union or church if it does not respect his or her right and causes them offence, which may be illegal. A state certainly does not have the right to intervene in, for example, the organizational forms of religious practice, but must ensure that individuals can appeal against any party, union or church that infringes his or her rights. This is tantamount to saying that the law or, better still, the constitution, must take precedence over all the regulations that determine how particular organizations function. This is an argument against compulsory union membership or the closed shop system that has been accepted and is considered democratic in many countries, but not against forcing companies to sign agreements with the majority union. Respect for the rights of the individual cannot be divorced from respect for collective social and cultural rights; rights and behaviours cannot be divorced, which means that any organization's freedom of expression and freedom to organize must be restricted to some extent. A non-democratic revolution cannot respect the rights of the individual, but we know that support for revolution is an intellectual challenge to democracy.

Hatred of the Individual

The individual I have been describing so far is a *de jure* being, and therefore a basic element in the construction of a social organization that must be evaluated primarily on the basis of its respects for the rights of men and women. Respect for the individual and individual choices is the number one test of a democracy.

I can scarcely be accused of dissolving the problems of society into those of the individual, but I have often been criticized for doing the opposite. The individual I am talking about is not, I have been told, a real individual because I say nothing about the emergence of subjectivity or about individuation. I have also been criticized for deliberately distancing myself from psychoanalysis; the reality of the unconscious is never mentioned here, and a reader who is in a hurry might conclude that my comments apply to an individual who is identified with individual consciousness, and therefore with the norms of society.

I have spent many years studying work, working-class consciousness and the labour movement, and I have never restricted my analysis to looking at the effects of the state of capitalism or any other deep economic structure. In an attempt to understand the liberation movements that emerged from the world of work, I looked at production, work, technologies and attacks on the autonomy of the workers. The goal of the schema I have rapidly recalled was to replace the analysis of an economic system with an understanding of actors, and the central logic behind their action was to retain or regain control over that was being produced. This industrial society was based upon an effort to invest in both labour and capital, and therefore upon an ethics of 'deferred gratification': we must not consume what we have, and must save it in order to improve our future lives. In this society, the human personality was defined primarily by the conflict between the law and the drives, many of which were incompatible with the construction of a society based upon productive investment. Some drives were therefore repressed. This society was still illuminated from without by progress, development, the abolition of privileges and the triumph of reason.

What happens when that construct collapses? The European model for modernization was defined by an extreme concentration of resources, and therefore by very high levels of internal tension: it produced both forms of domination and forms of protest, which the dominated categories used in an attempt to liberate themselves. They succeed in doing so. Like the king's subjects before them, wage-earners, colonized countries, women and, to some extent, children have broken the chains that held them prisoner. They have won a certain freedom, and sometimes a certain well-being; contemporary individuals feel that they are defined by others, and define themselves as consumers and communicators. The reservoir of repressed drives has been drained. Desire is spreading everywhere, and sexuality has taken the place of work. I have developed these themes on more than one occasion. But the individual, defined as a demand for and a will to individuation, cannot find freedom in the market, or only in the market.

The same remarks can be applied to interpersonal relations and group activities. The individual is always swamped by group identities, competitive relations and the quest for collective pleasures that are as immediate as possible. Are we to conclude that the individual is vanishing at the very time when he is becoming his own end, that he is being dissolved into his actions and relationships, and that there is no longer any central core in his individual and collective life?

The answer towards which we are heading is that, far from disappearing, the individual is growing ever strong, or at least strong enough to resist the rise in consumption and exchanges. The individual can offer enough resistance to prevent his own destruction, but that resistance does not prevent the demand for individuation and self-construction is not being repressed. We are surrounded by an imaginary world made up of novels, works of science fiction and new mythologies that have been hastily cobbled together. But to stay with our almost direct experience of what is forbidden or repressed, there are forms of individuation that resist this imaginary world's assaults and the consumption schema that is forced upon us by powerful advertising media. On the one hand, we never feel that our individual choices are completely determined by the policies of states and companies; that is the case only when there is a monopoly on decision-making and power. When that is the case, on the other hand, withdrawal is an effective defence against the discourses we can no longer hear, just as it was for television viewers when Eastern Europe was under the Communist regime.

In order to reach a better understanding of the individual's capacity for resistance, we have to look at the things that are destroying the individual. How can we fail to understand that, on the battlefield, in the deportation camps, on the slave ships and in the fields where the slaves picked cotton and corn, the primary, obsessional goal of those who destroyed, tortured and humiliated so many individuals was and is to take away their individuality, to destroy a subjectivity that never disappears completely, even when human beings are nothing more than the numbers tattooed on their forearms? And what makes Nazism a monster beyond compare is its stated desire to dehumanize individuals, to reduce them to ashes or soap. It has been asked if the individual the SS wanted to reduce to something non-human before throwing him into the muddy ditch or the gas oven was a man. We have to maintain that he was a man, and that the SS were not men. We cannot prevent certain critics from claiming that the defence of the individual is a luxury to be enjoyed by the 'Western petty bourgeoisie' at a time when the sub-proletarians of the poorest countries are dying, worn out by work and ill-treatment and unaware of any crisis. But that objection is in reality put forward by individuals living in the very heart of the countries whose dehumanizing tendencies they are denouncing. In order to justify their hatred of their own society, they deny the individual all individuality, and all human attributes.

It is here that we must sense the presence of an individual being: in the midst of the rage of destruction and in the violence of the taboos that prevent most of the destroyed from looking at themselves and from speaking their own name, or even the name of a loved one. Individualism is not a flower that an aristocrat puts in a buttonhole, and nor is a quest for the spectacular on the part of a man or a woman who wants to start a fashion with his or provocative statements. What

I am talking about here has nothing to do, in either positive or negative terms, with those images. I evoke the hatred of the individuals because the awareness that one is an individual can be blocked both by those who hold power, and by us, if it seems to stand in the way of our pursuit of pleasure, success or even knowledge. Our individuality was once masked by our loyalties and beliefs; increasingly, it is masked by drives that encounter nothing but taboos. Individuality is not revealed by the clear gaze of consciousness; the trimmings of consumerism can hide it as easily as the catechism of religions.

The approach I am using to try to define myself as an individual is similar to the one I adopted in *L'Intervention sociologique*. It differs from a survey in every respect. It is based upon the intervention of a researcher who presents a group with hypotheses about the meaning of its action and observes how the adoption of a hypothesis changes, in either a positive or a negative sense, the group's ability to think and act. This is not so much a matter of individuality as of a collective attempt at individuation. The sociologist's intervention refers the group back to itself, and helps it to acquire a self-image. This brief excursion into the domain of individual psychology suggests that self-knowledge is neither spontaneous nor purely reflexive. It is the critical examination of a situation that allows the actor to become conscious of his commitments. Individuality is not a settled feature of consciousness; it is often driven out of consciousness, perhaps more often than desire, which defies taboos and is free to express itself through immediate consumption.

The main themes of this chapter – *modernity, modernization, individuation* – have been the target of so many attacks and criticisms that it comes as a surprise to see that they are still alive and can still be used. These notions were rejected because they were thought to be problems internal to the capitalist system that defined the situations in which the class struggle took place. It was supposedly futile to judge capitalist societies in terms of their modernity. That criticism does apply to the idea of modernity if we understand it as a further advance down the road to a progress that is primarily defined by rationalization and secularization. But it has no impact on my definition, which sees modernity in terms of support for rational thought and respect for individual rights.

There is no denying that, in the 1960s, the Soviet Union made a difficult economic recovery, thanks in part to the successes of Soviet science. The USSR was modern in that sense, and the great research institutes it had inherited from the ancient regime were remarkable examples of scientific creativity, especially in mathematics and physics. But where human rights were concerned, the verdict could only be summary and negative. That made it impossible to see the Soviet Union as a modern society. That verdict was unacceptable to the fellow-travellers, for whom loyalty to the Soviet Union was an article of faith. The idea of modernity played an important role by allowing us to break with the notion that there was a complete dichotomy between the capitalist world and the socialist world. Similar comments could be applied to the unconditional devotees of the market economy, for whom the principles laid down by the 'Washington Consensus' guarantee economic success, which implies that we do not need to look at the political nature of the countries in question. All attempts to reduce social analysis to economic data must be resisted, but we cannot lapse into purely legal or political analyses that pay no attention to economic or social problems. We cannot over-emphasize the difference between these pseudo-explanations, which are based on *a prioris*, and the construction of real analyses.

Why begin the indispensable reconstruction of the social sciences with the idea of modernity? Because, after the portentous proclamations and complete failure of a conception that gave society's 'economic base' a central explanatory role, social thought moved from that quasi-theological vision to the extreme fluidity of explanations that restrict themselves to 'readings' and construct narratives that do as much to eliminate actors as determine sociologies.

My reaction to both these ways of destroying historical and social knowledge is to construct a notion that can block them. At first, I did so in fairly classical terms by defining *modernity* in terms of the universalist judgements that safeguard us from all historical and cultural relativism. *Rational* knowledge transcends all particular ways of explaining phenomena; similarly, the idea of *human rights* applies to all individuals, whatever their loyalties or characteristics.

It is not difficult to clear up the misunderstandings that might be created by these formulations. But they must be complemented by an answer to a question that has dominated the history of the last two centuries: What is this 'man'? Or rather, what is this human being who has rights? Man in general? If so, his rights are very abstract, and they are far removed from his concrete social situation. And if we replace this human being in a society, a culture or a gender, how can he retain his universal characteristics?

We cannot give an immediate answer to this question, which has such major implications for our personal and collective lives. We must first – and this is an essential step – solidly establish the one notion that directly and necessarily complements that of modernity: the notion of the *subject*.

8
The Subject

The Inner Gaze

We have always lived under the gaze of an other. The other is one more figure of ourselves, but not our shadow; indeed, we often feel that we are its shadow. The other is never a stranger but, should the other disappear, we too would cease to exist as human beings. We have all known, or know, men and women who have lost their shadows and who can no longer speak or control their bodies. Although the other is always present, our relationship with it constantly changes. When we were walking by night, our gaze could scarcely see through the darkness but, high above us, there was a bright light that helped us to find our way. As we gradually emerged from the darkness, it faded, like the light of the moon, but we could see further. At high noon, the one light was as bright as the other, and it seemed that they were about to merge, and that we would become the other, and that the other would become us. This was a moment of exaltation and fear: surely there was only one world. We called what appeared to be inevitable moment of fusion secularization, rationalization or positive knowledge.

What actually happened – this was so long ago – was quite different. We ceased to see an image similar to our own image high above us, but felt its presence within us, either viscerally or intellectually. The two of us were inseparable, but we were divided, in the way that societies were divided into classes and parties. With difficulty, and not always successfully, we limited the impact of these crises and the suffering they caused us. We succeeded in living by dominating the image that had dominated us for so long.

As our self-confidence grew, we were able to rid ourselves of these internal problems. We discovered and accepted that the other is not us; the other is our double, and we cannot live without our double. Whenever we try to do so, disaster ensues, the prisons fill up and bodies swing from the gallows. It is tempting to say that we are an other, but that expression has in fact a different meaning. The fact of the matter is that we ourselves are two figures and one commands the other, even though control passed from one to the other overnight. Now that we have grown wiser and have learned from the disasters, we must give up all our attempts to be just one or to be, like Jupiter, one figure with two faces. We have accepted that our lives harness together one who speaks and one who listens, between one who approves or disapproves, and one who pursues his interests or pleasure. Losing sight, even for one instant, sight of our double, who is neither a distant cousin nor our clone, would destroy us. It is only when we succeed in accepting our duality that we can understand that wisdom and happiness are possible, even though they are not guaranteed.

A Double Being

The opening lines of this chapter are meant to emphasize that defining beings in terms of their relationships with themselves is more important than defining them in terms of their position within society. Defining them in terms of their social position allows us to predict behaviours that are determined by the actor's position, and to discover that people who enjoy greater security are more conservative than people who are exposed to insecurity. These hypotheses can be given a concrete form, and they are by no means tautological. But these correlations in themselves tell us nothing about the moral behaviours that actually explain most of our acts. We cannot explain religious behaviours by relating them to the social position of the people who adopt them. When we begin to be able to explain the meaning of the beliefs of people who define themselves as Muslims or Christians, we begin to see the import of the obligations and rules they accept. In a society in which religious institutions are weak and control nothing but beliefs, it becomes even more necessary to define beliefs in terms of what they mean to believers, and they do not mean the same thing to everyone.

My hypothesis is that the way an individual or group experiences a situation depends upon how that situation strengthens or weakens the bond between the real individual and his or her ego-ideal. The ego-ideal is not a superego but, on the contrary, a being with rights, and especially the right to be recognized as an autonomous actor. That formulation is easily understandable when we are talking about bioethics or respect for the individual. Many of us respect certain moral principles because they guarantee our freedom. The analysis becomes more difficult when institutions intervene between the actor and the principle that dictates his action. In countries with a Christian culture, we readily accept that Jesus Christ's most important teachings are 'love thy neighbour' and 'separate temporal and spiritual powers'. We expand on this by saying and writing that individual rights are universal, and that every individual is also the whole of humanity. We have an equally clear understanding of the opening sentence of the Declaration of the Rights of Man and the Citizen (26 August 1789): 'Men are born and live free, with equal rights.' The two formulations are strikingly similar, as neither refers to particular individuals, with their attributes and loyalties, but to all individuals, who are equal because they all have universal rights. And it will be recalled that, in the previous chapter, I recognized that respect for the universal rights of every individual is one of the two main dimensions of modernity.

It is this relationship between the social being, as identified by his identities and loyalties, and the *de jure* being, that I wanted to bring out in the introduction to this chapter. That introduction can no more explain religious behaviours than it can explain social movements, because the institutional forces behind concrete religious or political actions have considerable density and power; on the other hand, nothing can detract from the need to see that the self-to-self-relationship is the basis of the moral judgements that are present in any religion or social movement. Talk of God, progress, the working class or the nation is always an appeal to the human rights in which we recognize the presence of the subject. The rights–duties couplet is the expression of a doubling of the individual, whose id is defined both by his loyalties and his self-consciousness. And human rights as a whole are nothing more than the right to self-consciousness or, to put it more simply, the right to speak, because this doubling can only exist thanks to speech and our capacity for symbolic expression. This also means that an individual or group is more than what he or it is as an empirical being. Human beings recognize each other to the extent that they create a self-image and a self-consciousness. Their ability to name themselves allows both groups and individuals to transcend themselves; it gives them the right to say 'I' or 'we', and above all the right to establish and maintain a relationship with the self that transcends the empirical self because it is a form of self-consciousness. It is the *logos* or speech that creates the world of rights, and their immediate correlates, namely duties. When we speak of interiority, consciousness, prayer or commitment, we are acknowledging our capacity to create ourselves through the act of giving ourselves names, of drawing our image or placing limitations on our loyalties and identities. Nothing could be more basic than the distance between the self and the self, and speech is both its instrument and its cause. The world of rights and duties exists only when it is spoken or 'declared'.

We cannot speak of the subject without using the word *consciousness*. The word is obviously present, or at least implicit, when I speak of doubles and doubling, or of society's hold on itself. This raises some inevitable objections, and not everyone will agree with me. Most human beings, it is objected, do not have any capacity for reflexivity, or the ability to say in clear, conscious terms what they feel and want. I am accused of being naïve and fanatical when I assume that all human beings think and live in the same way that an English, French or German teacher lives! That reaction seems unacceptable to me, but it does hit home: when I speak of consciousness, I am certainly not referring to some capacity for sophisticated analysis and expression. But surely no one believed that working-class consciousness, which I studied in such detail, was an intellectual, explanatory or reflexive discourse. As for the language of Christianity, it too uses the word consciousness in a sense that is not purely intellectual. We therefore have to specify the meaning of a word that is so easy to pronounce and so difficult to define.

I understand 'consciousness' as meaning that an individual or a group of individuals have a self-image that implies the ability to make moral value judgements about their behaviours. It might be more accurate to speak of a moral consciousness or conscience [*conscience*], provided that we understand that expression as meaning not a recognition of a society's values and norms, but a recognition that we have a responsibility to ourselves, and that we therefore have rights within society. We cannot speak of human rights unless we believe that human rights act in the name of basic rights that must be defended against all forms of authority. When I say that all human beings must be respected and recognized because they have beliefs and not because they respect laws, I mean that consciousness is the human capacity for thinking about ourselves in terms of rights, rather than defining ourselves in terms other than what we do, our professional abilities, our position in society or our level of education. When Robert Badinter, acting in accordance with François Mitterrand's stated wish to abolish the death penalty in France, convinced the National Assembly and the Senate that it should be abrogated, he did not invoke the possibility of juridical error, or the fact that Blacks and Whites get unequal treatment; he convinced parliament that society cannot take a human life because it recognizes a higher principle of equality that transcends all inequalities and all social situations. That principle can only be understood by the consciousness or conscience I am talking about and which, more importantly, the Declarations of the Rights of Man talk about.

The notion is not difficult to understand: it recognizes that human beings are beings who are endowed with consciousness. The word introduces modern society to something that is as important as reason. In the past, this consciousness was not self-sufficient and had to take on the mantle of religious faith, the honour of princes and warriors, or the belief that the triumphant bourgeoisie, and then revolutionary workers, were the agents of progress. Consciousness had to shed all these social forms before the human subject could appear as such. When we speak of consciousness, we immediately enter the realm of universalism. We assert that an individual human being is also a universal being, and cannot claim to be an individual human being unless, thanks to that speech-act, he is divorced from himself *qua* a particular being and become as a universal being who is divorced from the empirical individual by the speech and action that create him.

Defenders of the determinist conception of human actors see them as mere social beings who are defined, and therefore determined, by situations, functions, power relations and evolution. They ignore and therefore hide or attempt to destroy the other side of human experience, namely the self-to-self relationship, which is of a different nature from relations with institutions and even other people.

The three constituent elements of *individuation*, and therefore of its reflexive form – a subject with a sense of values – are, therefore: doubling thanks to speech and the creation of symbolic expressions; the recognition that the presence of the body is not merely social; and the active divorce between the individual and society, which is more commonly observed among minorities. Gays, for example, have played an important role in involving our societies in the general trend towards subjectivation.

This analysis leads to a conclusion that may lead to its rejection. I can understand that, but the rejection is based on a misunderstanding. It in fact seems to me that we have to say that the relationship with the self is more important than the relationship with the other. That attitude was clearly expressed by the women whose testimony I introduced in *Le Monde des femmes* (2006). Sexuality transcends mere sexual activity and becomes an essential element in the construction of the female personality when it is enriched by a relationship with the other, and especially by a loving relationship, yet the construction of the self as woman is still the most important thing of all. The misunderstanding occurs when that phrase is interpreted as giving projects, desire and personal life priority over relations with one or more individuals, when it is in fact the individual's openness to the other that elevates him to the status of a subject. I am obviously not referring to a self-to-self relation within a self-enclosed life, but to the self's attempts to create itself, and therefore to subjectivation, or the discovery of the subject within the empirical individual. The self-to-self relationship has a universalist content that transcends the relationship with the other, which is always restricted by the particular nature of our partner. The ideas I am outlining here must not be seen as a withdrawal into individual life; on the contrary, I hope that the 'grand narratives' of public life and history will be replaced by the 'grand narratives' of the subject, and the creation and defence of the subject against all forms of the 'we'.

The decay of the social affects social actors as well as institutions. Can we still say that there is a distance between the individual and the subject when there are no actors left? In theory, we cannot, because the two notions are inseparable: the subject is the actor's self-reflexivity to, to put it more simply, the individual's (or group's) will to become a subject. Globalization is shattering the whole of social reality as it penetrates all levels of organization and decision-making. Yet while it is difficult to conceive of a society in which there are no actors, perhaps we have to force ourselves to do just that. If we take the idea of the end of the social (which I regard as playing an essential role in our understanding of the contemporary world) to its logical conclusion, perhaps we have to give up defending the subject, and admit that the only important social actors are those who wage wars and those who denounce the economic order, namely the soldiers who loot and the populists who preach revolution. The answer has to lie in the divorce between the *social* actor and the *personal* subject. This has often been suggested, but it has to be formulated with greater clarity. The subject is defined neither by social roles nor social relations, even if they are inter-subjective. That break *necessitates* the idea of a subject who can oppose existing forms of power only by becoming dissociated from all social mechanisms, and even from interpersonal relations. Given that we are experiencing the end of the social and the demise of societies, we can define the subject only in relation to the self, self-reflexivity and self-legitimation.

What initially looked like a threat to the subject provides the most solid definition of a subject who can no longer be described as 'social' and who must be defined as a self-reflexive citizen worker or soldier.

Attacks

In the course of the century that has just ended, the idea or notion of the *subject* came under more virulent attack than any other. It is difficult to find coherent accounts of the reasons why it was rejected, but we must attempt to formulate them.

The first is that the word 'subject' suggests the very 'enlightened' image of an individual who is identified with reason, who is devoid of all particular qualities and who is not defined as a worker, a member of a family or a citizen of a country. My answer to this objection is that the subject, who is not defined by his social attributes and who possesses universal rights, has to be seen for what he is, or in other words as a subject embodied in a worker, citizen, believer, and so on. Human rights, which were originally conceived in political terms –citizenship – have been extended to all domains in the form of social rights and then cultural rights. But it is true that, the more we take into consideration actual beings who are involved in actual social and political relations, the greater the danger that we will use human rights to justify violence or even a civil war that will give power to a new ruling elite that speaks in the name of the dominated and undermines human rights. This does not lead us into a blind alley, but it does mean that the universalist dimension of human rights must always be associated with the cause we are defending, and that cause is socially determined. This is not a matter of details or subtleties; these are the problems that dominated the entire twentieth century. The Germans and the British, followed by the Scandinavian countries in particular, asserted that social rights were an extension of citizenship. This notion gave birth to social-democracy, which gave Europeans and others a guarantee that political, economic and social rights would be respected for at least half a century. If this combination of the universalism of human rights and the rights of particular social or cultural categories is not present, there is a danger that those who speak in the name of human rights will be destroyed in the name of a class, nation or religion, and that human rights will be destroyed at the same time. The historical realities involved are so huge that it is impossible to believe that those who claim that bourgeois freedoms are an obstacle to the conquest of real social and cultural freedoms are speaking in good faith. It is therefore unacceptable to see such hugely important notions being eliminated from the field of sociological thought in the name of arguments that are so obviously weak that they can only be supported in bad faith.

The second objection we have to overcome comes from those who have always distrusted the theme of subjectivity, who take up the defence of objectivity and attempt to explain behaviours in terms of objective factors such as levels of social involvement or exclusion. My answer to this objection is that sociology does not have to choose between objective and subjective explanations. Its hypotheses can be verified in both objective and subjective terms: we must 'explain' behaviours in terms of the actors' positions, and 'understand' what actions mean to their actors by using arguments similar to the one I am using here.

All this allows us to conclude in categorical terms that, when so many intellectuals of all levels denounce the notion of the subject, their objections are meaningless: they are either tilting at windmills, or do not respect the elementary requirements of sociological proof.

The rejection of the idea of the subject is sometimes so extreme that we have to explain it in historical terms. In the case of France, we find the apparently indelible marks left by the struggle against the Catholic Church. It is here that we have to seek the reasons for French thought's pronounced tendency to reject anything that goes by the name of 'subject' or 'consciousness'. It is feared that it will lead to the return of the priests. Those who denounce this or that type of domination take their enemies so seriously that they believe that there are no actors because they have been destroyed by human forces. They readily take their enemies' side because this representation of social life is the only one that allows them to be both the enemy of the dominant forces and the adversary of all forms of subjectivity. This is also why 'advanced thinkers' refused to give women the right to vote for so long: they feared that the influence of the priests would put the Republic in danger. It would therefore be better for women not to enter public life.

Let us assume that the ground has been cleared, and that we can reconstruct a sociology that has at last rid itself of these ideological prejudices. We must not get beyond these prejudiced criticisms and demonstrate that the idea of the subject is essential if we are to understand collective actions, and especially social movements.

The difference between a *social movement* and a pressure group, popular feeling or a current of opinion is that only a social movement takes as its primary goal the defence of the freedom of the individual subject, and therefore of basic rights. A social movement goes beyond the defence of interests or ideas. The words 'basic rights' are a clear indication that what is at stake transcends the social, and concerns the very humanity of human beings. What gives rise to a social movement is primarily an awareness of not being recognized and respected, an awareness of being humiliated or, as we used to say, *alienated*, or in other words deprived of that direct relationship with the self without which no rights can have any solid basis.

The twentieth century taught us a brutal lesson about the differences between social movements and the revolutionary regimes that speak in their name and give them the opportunity to take power in order to change society. The sailors at Cronstadt twice played an important role in the Soviet Revolution, but they became a social movement when they attacked Lenin's government and painted an outline picture of what a democratic society could and should look like. 'Democracy' is a complex word and is full of historical meanings that are at once complementary and contradictory. It refers primarily to a political regime that respects basic rights, places restrictions on all powers, and especially state power, and prepare the 'emancipation' of categories that are dominated, or in other words deprived of subjectivity. Eyewitnesses and actors are better than analysts at recognizing that there is more to a social movement than strategies and ideology, and that social movements call for the 'recognition' of the freedom and self-determination of those who inspire them and who speak so often of their trampled *dignity*.

It is not difficult to move from a definition of self-consciousness to an understanding of social movements. It is even easier to turn to the horrors of evil. The century that has just ended taught us that repression does not end with fighting and war: it becomes debasement and extermination. As Michel Wieviorka rightly says, cruelty goes beyond violence because it wants to destroy the humanity of its adversaries, and not just their interests, social existence or culture. We have spent our lives living in the horror of places that were places of dehumanization, and not just death camps. How can we reduce such crimes to political actions or economic interests, when we rightly speak of crimes against humanity to which no statue of limitations applies? We have seen hell, not the power of ruling groups. And we have seen individuals risking their lives to assert the dignity and freedom of all human beings. In what sense do these expressions have less explanatory power than the economic situation or wage scales?

The Emergence of the Subject

We are now in a position to understand the emergence of the idea of the subject as a concrete reality, and to get beyond all the figures that once represented it. We are therefore able to grant it its field of application, by taking stock of both the novelty of the contemporary world in which the idea of the subject reappears, and of the kinship between the unveiled and fully visible figure of the subject, and all its other figures, which wore a wide variety of historical costumes – religious, political, revolutionary, and so on – without ceasing to be figures of the subject we now see as a conscious presence. In order to do so, we have to stop speaking of the subject as a distant being who is divorced from us and that exists beyond the social. The subject is not something we can call God or Progress. We have to be suspicious of the 'civil' religions that create even more opacity by forcing a hierarchical and impersonal discourse on the subject. This positivism is explained solely in terms of the social in an attempt to eliminate every figure of the subject. The subject's presence is more visible in the religious figures that locate it beyond the human world, but the subject is still dominated in such situations, and is exploited by the self-proclaimed representatives of the sacred. The subject is truly present in a divine figure only when the individual can still communicate with him directly. God's presence within me is a side-effect of the human creation of a God who transcends the human world. Modernity begins with social life's capacity for self-creation. It begins when we claim for ourselves the creative force that can lead to the discoveries of science, the creation of works of art or institutions, but also to our direct awareness of the subject as we contemplate the origins of good and evil.

This modernity does not destroy the subject for the benefit of instrumental reason; on the contrary, it ensures that instrumental reason is internalized by all the individuals to whom it gives a consciousness rather than a soul, and a capacity for inner speech. The subject allows us to go in search of ourselves by constructing the states and societies without which there would no historicity and no possibility of constructing and transforming our living conditions. At the same time, states and societies stand in the way of the subject's immediate relationship with himself. This contradiction is even more pronounced with the religious figure of the subject; the discourse of the sacred intervenes between human speech and the divine word, and so do the domination of priests and the higher interests of direct or indirect religious powers. The subject is threatened by powerful forces in every type of society, but with the religious world those forces take on a non-social form, and especially the form of sin, whereas the obstacles were truly social and political throughout the modernity that preceded our entry into our contemporary hypermodernity. The masters of the state, the economy and the ideological world are strongly opposed to the conscious subject. The subject therefore has to take a more militant form. The subject is present when peoples rise up against kings and privileges, and liberate themselves; the subject is at the heart of the labour movement, in the true sense of that term, and at the heart of the consciousness of the working class as it fights the masters of the economy in order to emancipate the workers and the whole people, thanks to technology, labour and progress. It is when power dominates economic and social life and becomes a totalitarian power, that the subject, whose militants have either been killed or corrupted, falls back on himself and sees a radical but lethal dichotomy between a world of rights, and a world of instruments, calculation, machines, plans and the propaganda of social and political powers.

The subject manifests his presence in private life as well as public life, but is threatened on all sides. In private life, the sacrifices the weak and the dependent are forced to make and which they agree to make, often without actually saying so, prevent us from recognizing the subject at the very point where he is ready to run the greatest risks in order to assert himself. In public life, the subject, although present in social movements, is reduced to silence, hidden behind the great mobilizations that respond to the people's political leaders' call to rise up against their enemies. As we already know, the idea of 'the people' refers to the way the state perceives society, and therefore takes us back to the social order and its integration and defence. The idea of the people is bound up with that of revolution, just as the idea of a social movement is associated with that of the subject, and there is a great difference between these two ways of thinking and acting. But this is not the place to discuss the role conflict plays in the shaping of the subject, as we must first identify the presence of the subject in both social and personal life. And in order to do that, we must keep a certain distance between ourselves and all organized or controlled forms of collective action.

What has to be recognized is the constant appeal to a *non-social* argument, which we can describe as humanist or whatever else we wish to call it, that determines our social choices and means that there can be no 'overall' solution to our social or personal problems. It is tempting but dangerous to believe that the subject can be seen only in periods of crisis, transition or invention, or only when values become deinstitutionalized, as was so obviously the case in the history of Christianity and the other great religions. This idea is dangerous because it associates the subject with a different social order, whereas the subject comes to life only when there is a certain distance between him and all social practices. The subject is always, or always demands to be, at a distance from the social order. The best indication that the subject is present is the perceived distance between him and the identities and norms that are imposed upon our social environment, or the demand to be distanced from them. This is not a matter of trapping the subject in his loneliness, but of recognizing that the subject needs an autonomous space to make his demands heard and seen. We have to assert the need for that distance before we go back to looking for the subject wherever calls for action ring out.

What I mean by the subject is not the quasi-secularized image of God proposed by the theism of the eighteenth century, the religion of the Supreme Being, or even the Convention's Religion of Reason. The subject is not the Reason that guides Progress towards well-being. The subject is neither a theological actor nor a historical actor, and still less a moralizing principle that promotes the interests of society, or enhances its integration or capacity for change. Indeed, that latter definition could not be further removed from what I mean by the subject. In my view, the subject is, I repeat, the self-to-self relationship, the distance and doubling that are created by speech. The subject is a consciousness that gives rise to the moral judgement that describes anything that heightens self-consciousness as 'good', and anything that destroys or dissolves it as 'evil'. The notion of the subject therefore has the same *raison d'être* as the society to which it is opposed.

The idea of society has defined good and evil in terms of social functionality and dysfunctionality. In the contemporary world, the subject looks increasingly as though a protest against the world is being invaded by instrumental reason, profit, and powers that are very remote from our individual experience and that can be seen in workings of the markets, and the concentration of power in the hands of oligarchies, monarchies, parties and especially all-powerful party-states. Closer to home, the subject also protects us from management, administrative rules and the school curriculum. The subject is a positive experience, and especially an assertion of rights, before becoming a critique of the social order or of the individuals who hold power. The subject is the individual's encounter with himself or herself, and that individual's self-consciousness. The subject's basis is the tension and union between the 'I' [*je*] that names and the 'me' [*moi*] that is named. Rather than accepting that the *moi* is constituted only through its insertion into social life, life at work, economic life or any other life, the subject speaks loudly of 'I and me' [*moi et je*].

This is why the subject is defined so well by the idea of *reflexivity*, which was introduced by Anthony Giddens and which is widely accepted in contemporary thought. The subject goes in search of the road that will take him back to himself; he sees and touches himself, and listens to himself before embarking upon the great adventure of recognizing another as a subject, and then creating categories that are defined by their struggle against apparatuses and conjunctures, which he will wage until he finds a self-definition that extends to the whole historical field.

This self-to-self-relationship and these words that are addressed to the self appear only when human action is able to create a completely 'artificial' world of calculations, machines and communications networks that dissolve the subject into the oeuvres of collective activity. In that situation, the subject, if he does not vanish, can only live if he asserts himself, demands to be his own creator and demands the right to take responsibility for himself.

The Discovery of the Subject

There is no 'natural' correspondence between the meaning of a situation, and especially an economic situation, and the consciousness of men and women, who are not just actors but usually 'people' who experience that situation by adapting to it and protecting their personal interests, but also by giving it a meaning other than the meaning society would like to impose upon them. Stories about wars and concentration camps, or about debacles and the looting that comes after triumphs, always tend to suggest that men and women are leaves blown by the winds in different directions. Human beings are not in fact dead leaves: they use language to describe their situation. Conversely, it is helpful to invoke that image, incorrect as it may be, in order to stress the dangers inherent in seeing history as an epic, a dream or an adventure whose meaning is experienced by every human being in the course of his or her own life and personal reactions. There is nothing immediately perceptible about notions such as the subject, subjectivation or even the actor. While an analysis looks closely at the facts in order to study, say, the workings of an organization or the application of a law, the discrepancy is reduced, but it never disappears. Interpreting a situation is not a collective undertaking; those who are capable of giving their experience a meaning find that the majority of people do not agree with them.

How are these interpretations shaped? How do they attempt to get their pertinence recognized, and how do they convince others that they are true?

They are not based upon consciousness or a sophisticated analysis of the situation. Various actors speak to each other, answer one another and discuss their exchanges. It is in this fragmented text, which contains more replies than reflections, that we find issues, proposals and demands, but we find them 'in little pieces'.

In our day-to-day lives, there is a considerable discrepancy between the meaning we ascribe to a situation and the way in which we experience it. We comment upon our own acts and those of others, judge them, try to make ourselves understood, and try to understand ourselves. We do not know the deepest meaning of our words and acts, but we do know that a tragedy is being played out, that a choice is being offered or refused. The more we repeat or reread this dialogue, which is full of gaps, discontinuities, hesitations, demands and rejections, the more we distance ourselves from a confused text that seems to conceal its own meaning, and the closer we get to giving our behaviours a meaning that was present but concealed by the constraints of the law, by the pressure to organize trade and production, and by the resistance of other people. Beckett and Ionesco glimpsed the permanent presence, not of non-meaning, but of obstacles to meaning that depersonalize, and which correspond quite closely to what sociology used to call 'roles' and 'norms'. The analyst has to intervene to reveal the hidden meaning, which has been repressed or even destroyed, of behaviours that try to conceal their own meaning and to conform to 'common sense', which is a product of public opinion, and to categories that have been constructed by the social order.

Rather than having to represent our psychic lives as the law's repression of our drives, we can try to find what it is that gives a meaning to demands that are stronger than those of the law, received ideas and the criteria of normality. These are the demands of a subject who is always present but always hidden. The point is to break the glass of consumerist behaviour in order to discover that it is what we achieve that makes us the creators of meaning. In the midst of all the external solicitations and signals, we have to turn in on ourselves and look at our most intimate and personal feelings, as well as at our commitments and what is at stake in them. The conversations the researchers and I had with women, either one-to-one or in groups, brought out, with astonishing ease, their ability to assert and create themselves. That ability remained invisible so long as we spoke the language of society, and of society's inequalities and systems of justification and repression. The more we think about it, the more we release a subjectivity that everything in our immediate lives hides or rejects.

We cannot find the meaning we are looking for unless a researcher intervenes and creates an unusual and privileged bond. The researcher appeals to what is most meaningful to us, and that has both moral and intellectual implications; it lies beyond the screen on which we project a 'social' that can be described without making any reference to the demands of the subject. There is then a danger that we will be deceived by a semblance of choice, and by what appear to be moral judgements, demands and projects. Some would have us believe that the meaning of our behaviours lies in organizational systems, decision-making systems and action systems that supposedly produce some objective meaning. The main task of those who hold power is to convince and persuade us that we are not subjects, or even actors, but just the 'agents' of determinations that find their *raison d'être* only in nature and 'reality'. We have to go in quite the opposite direction if we wish to find the meaning of our behaviours and situations. We must turn away from lived experience and go back to the meaning of life, from experience to the ways we create and construct ourselves.

Interpretations must remain as far removed from lived experience, needs, desires and opinions as from the logic of determinations and the strength of the determinants of social, personal and collective behaviours. The subject is a growing self-consciousness, to employ the simple expression Germaine Dieterlin uses in her *Essai sur la religion bambara* to describe the '*tered*' of the Dogons of Mali. The notion is distinct from both 'soul' (*nid*) and 'double' (*dya*), which define more tightly knit forms of social organization. This does not mean that *tered* can be defined without any reference to society; what is more important, for my purposes, is that it is a capacity for self-transforming activity rather than a transcription of a social role.

The Day-to-Day Presence of the Subject

We must break off this investigation into the figures of the subject for a moment because, the closer we get to recognizing the subject, the closer we get to gods and wise men. It becomes more difficult to detect the presence of the subject, who is at once so creative and so distant, in actual individuals or groups. Where can I see and touch the subject? Is the subject present in the military parades of totalitarian regimes, or in the wretched poverty of the homeless and the jobless? Is the subject present in industrial, administrative or agricultural work? Is the subject present in the midst of populations that are killing one another or, far, far away, in the meeting of bankers who think of nothing but money, be it the money of their companies or their personal fortunes? The list is endless. The lives of human beings are made up of routines, great suffering and minor joys, but also of great passions and deep-rooted hatreds. If we define the subject as an assertion of the right to have an individual life, to enjoy the respect of others, and to be protected from the power of organizations and governments, what space is left for the subject in all this everyday existence, in all these efforts to survive or to improve ourselves, in the problems we encounter at work, and which are our sole topic of conversation, both in the café and at home?

The question is so basic and so overwhelming that it is tempting to avoid it by moving to higher ground and restricting our search for the subject to projects that transform the social order that can be elaborated and implemented only through collective actions. If that were the case, would it not be easier and safer to use a different vocabulary: that of the economics or sociology of organization, or of political sociology? Wouldn't it be easier to talk about the defence of interests, attempts to form alliances, about the creation of ideologies, and about the definition of objectives?

These few lines sum up all the objections, which may or not be formulated as such, that come to everyone's mind when we hear talk of the subject, rights and individuation. Our answer to such crushing objections and misgivings has to be vigorous and categorical. Wherever you see interests, jealousy, love or hate, power and authority, you must learn to see the subject, subjectivation and their enemies. For the life and death of the subject is always being played out everywhere, in both individual lives and social movements, in both free societies and societies that live under a tyranny.

What is so surprising about this answer? You have heard priests saying that sin and grace are everywhere for hundreds of years. Didn't you realize that the revolutions that overthrew absolute monarchies and undermined colonial powers were so many demands that were put forward in the name of freedom and of everyone's right to both freedom of opinion and free trade? We have just lived though a century that was greatly influenced by the ideas of class struggle, exploitation and workers' rights, and we are still accustomed to using those words to understand all life's circumstances, from unemployment to bans on using national languages, from money's dominance over men to men's dominance over women and, in many cases, men and women's dominance over children.

It will be objected that we could turn to the widely accepted idea of a reversion to the idea of individualization; only the dogmatists of what used to be the Left think that it promotes capitalism and personal egotism. The answer to that is that, while individualism appears to be a simple notion, it is in fact difficult to define and has little real coherence. For many people, individualism means the development of multiple, intersecting loyalties, and the break down of the vision that saw class relations as having a very general import. For others, it means the weakening of social relations, as opposed to relations with machines, games, musical equipment or communications over the Internet. Still others see it as a form of introversion: we explore ourselves and replace social analysis with a psychological exploration that takes the form of an expanding range of therapies, while psychoanalysis goes on managing a much greater intellectual capital. Individualism can also mean increasingly vigorous competition within market economies where there are fewer and fewer statutory guarantees. I could easily go on. Individualism can also be seen as leading to communitarian-style loyalties, membership of cults or even a classic economism.

If we are to define the importance of the return to individualization, and it is indeed of crucial importance, we must move to the higher level of analysis where individuality becomes a 'value' or a basic moral principle; individualization cannot be reduced to meaning a rejection of analyses that are constructed in terms of groups or groupings. Individualism must be interpreted as meaning the right to an individual existence, and the right to construct it on the basis of a demand for individuation. It is at this level that we encounter the notion of the subject. This is the only notion that allows us to understand the true meaning of individualism, and to rescue it from the most base or even dangerous interpretations. But the meaning of the transformation of ideals, projects and demands, which is implicit in the theme of individualism, can only be understood if we reinterpret individualism as an expression, both concrete and indirect, of the idea of the *subject*, which must take the central role once played by the workers, and by the citizen before him, in the history of earlier centuries.

The only difference is that, in those societies that have most power over themselves, the subject now emerges in his own right, whereas we used to encounter him dressed up as God, a nation, a worker or a democrat. None of those words has lost its role as a figure of the subject. But many of us increasingly recognize that these collective figures embody the subject, and we recognize it more directly: we understand that they are exploited or repressed, rewarded or punished because they are subjects. There is no more and no less awareness of the subject today than there was in the past or in other places, but it has become more direct, because we now have greater responsibilities when we look at ourselves. That reflexivity could not be directly organized around the idea of the subject if that idea were not present *everywhere* in the same way that class relations, the right to freedom, and respect for both others and ourselves are present everywhere.

This also means that the enemies of the subject are everywhere, as are all forms of the anti-subject, no matter whether they speak in the name of a science-based positivism, an appeal to the irrational, a reference to a divine message to which we must submit, or a common good that forces us to do our duty. The battle is being fought everywhere. No matter where we find ourselves, there are no neutral or ambivalent zones; there is only the fear and cowardice of those who dare not openly attack the freedom and dignity of everyone, just as we find anti-Semites or Arabophobes who refrain from insulting Jews and Arabs in public, but still think of them with hatred and scorn.

I am not asking the reader to endorse an unaccustomed language from the outset; I am speaking at the level of the most concrete and most common lived experiences. We make value judgements in our everyday lives, as well as through our laws. We cannot do without words like justice, freedom and rights. The only problem I come up against is that we do not often ask ourselves about the origin of these 'values'. In our part of the world, we have reached the conclusion that the teachings of Athens and Rome, of Christianity and the French Revolution merge into a generalized humanism. We know that it is not applied, but it is present in the minds of most people. The problem with this soft consensus is that, although we use these big words, we are only too happy to accept a tolerance that implies an acceptance of the intolerable. Wouldn't it be more stimulating to formulate this humanism in more sophisticated and demanding terms, at a time when we see the cemeteries and camps filling up everywhere, and when humanists are being hunted down and massacred?

For a long time we were easily satisfied with a revolutionary voluntarism that also referred to the great texts about human rights. We repeated that we had been taught by great men and emotionally proclaimed our resolve to defend sacred values. It is high time that we stopped talking like that. We must refuse to be swept away by these currents, because we know where they will take us. And above all, we must avoid the mistakes that made modernity the ultimate value-judgement, and reject the triumph of empiricism, positivism and a psychology that was dominated by self-interest. The idea of the subject gives a strong meaning to behaviours that are oriented by demands that go beyond instrumental rationality and the self-interest of those who have lost their faith. It is therefore quite natural that I should see the subject everywhere, just as religious believers saw the will of God in everything, and just as believers in progress saw the meaning of history everywhere.

Reinterpreting Figures of the Subject

Given that the primary meaning of modernity is that we can act upon ourselves by having recourse to the universalist principle of reason and individual rights, it is unacceptable to describe modern societies as barbarous, or to say that they are manipulated by the media, have been reduced to markets and eroded by the materialism of interests and emotions, or are incapable of thinking about the great options available to human life and nature. It is also unacceptable to think that such societies dismiss the great religious or ethical answers on which we have always sought to rely, or that they can no longer supply any response to our great problems.

Once we have dismissed those ideas, one question remains. It is asked more and more often, and has to do with the objections I have just answered. Is not the subject, as defined in our times, threatened by the triumph of capitalism, of a mass society and the pursuit of self-interest, and does not the subject therefore have to rely upon older figures of the subject that are trapped within other systems of thought? Isn't the current figure of the subject forced to turn away from the present and find itself involved in a dialogue with the other great figures that represented him in earlier societies?

We can accept that argument, as it is essential not to put all our trust in the progress, rationalization and efficiency that create a 'secular' quasi-religion which does away with the past. Let us accept that we need to find a unitary subject in all the figures that were and are hidden by the tools that are used by forms of domination.

Reviving the beliefs or the thought of a distant past is, however, quite out of the question. We must do precisely the opposite, and reinterpret the religions, wisdom and political thought of the past as so many *veiled figures* on a subject who can become self-conscious only in modernity. At the same time, there is a danger that the subject will become lost as the pace of contemporary life speeds up; if the subject is to survive, he must have a unitary form throughout his history and the repeated transformations that the figures of the subject have undergone. This reinterpretation of the past is essential. If we cannot reinterpret the past, it will be replaced by a brutal return to the most obscure aspects of subjectivation, and by the dangerous quest for a hidden world order that can be revealed by prophecies or, worse still, by the creation of new powers that will recognize only the equality that subjects us all to the same domination.

There can be no subject unless we distance ourselves from the social order to some extent. That distance can be created and maintained only by those who reject the most simplistic forms of rationalist evolutionism, and who look to non-modern cultures and societies, or even the oldest cultures and societies, to find other distancing mechanisms. I am not thinking only of the many calls emanating from religious beliefs and rites; I would like to revive the inspiration behind the labour movement and 1789, before one was overtaken by scientific socialism, and the other by state terror. As for the Christianity that has left so many marks on our civilization, its message is the complete antithesis of the secularization I reject because it is so artificial.

It is more difficult to find links between our contemporary image of the subject and Islam or other schools of religious thought within or on the margins of monotheism. Modernity leads to a reinterpretation of religious, moral, political and social movement; none of them can be identified with the subject, but they all represent figures of the subject. It was only with modernity that the full self-presence emerged, but there are aspects of modernity that are hostile to subjectivation. Those figures of the subject that come to us from afar allow us to discover and criticize them. The 'modern' insistence on the central role of reason in modernity is seen as an act of aggression by the defenders of religions, who wish to give religious thought an absolute pre-eminence. This seems to be a twofold error: as we well know, the appeal to reason, which is so important in Christian theology, and especially for Aristotle's disciple Thomas Aquinas, can easily be reconciled with faith. This does not mean that faith and reason are of the same order, but simply that reason has to be applied to the domain of faith if religion is not to lapse into the irrational, magic or mere emotionalism. Secondly, religion cannot establish links with modernity through reason alone; as I have stressed on a number of occasions, it must also do so through the rights of the individual. In societies that have little self-understanding, the subject has indirect, 'externalized' figures that are projected into a transcendent world. We therefore have to work back from these indirect, earlier forms to the idea of the subject. Belief in progress, in citizenship and in a God both brings us close to the subject and prevents us from approaching the subject because it creates a sacred space. That is the other side of religion, and it is closely bound up with the power of institutions.

We find both these aspects of the religious in social and cultural movements. This is especially true of the labour movement. Its central aspect, or the struggle waged by the working-class unions, was a figure of the subject, but it was usually dominated by political actors. In the Scandinavian countries and Great Britain, trade-unionism had a lasting influence on socialism; in France, in contrast, the political very quickly took control of the trade unions. We could take the parallel still further: some class struggles are similar in nature to the wars of religion that were associated with the struggle for political power. We always have to recall that the link that exists between the idea of the subject and the religious field, or other fields of the same type, is not based upon reason alone; it can also be based upon individualism, conscience or individual destiny.

The Subject Challenged

The conception of the subject that I have just introduced goes against what would appear to be the most widespread ideas. We now ask what the idea of a subject who talks to himself in the way that characters in classical plays soliloquize can mean in a world in which the powers of communications are absolute. How can the idea of the subject mean anything in a communications society? How, to extend the argument, can this subject be introspective in a mass society? Hasn't the subject been replaced by characters on television? Hasn't the subject been plunged into urban life, and exposed to all kinds of stimulation and to the turmoil of feelings and drives?

The arguments that are put forward with such force, and believe that they can simply dismiss what I am saying, were already being put forward over a hundred years ago, when machines were becoming more common in industry, communications and even the administration. Did the idea of the subject mean anything in *Metropolis*, or in the factory where Charlie Chaplin works himself to exhaustion? Hadn't the subject already become as pathetic as a man wearing aristocratic dress on the production line or at a big sporting event? These objections are powerful and many people find them convincing. But the more I am called to order and told to look at modern thought and modern *realities*, the more I cling to this discourse. Ever since we began to talk about modernity, we have also talked about machines, systems, languages, the fragmentation of existence, and the growing complexity of the world of knowledge. But there is nothing in all these exhilarating or depressing advances to suggest that there is no introspective subject in this increasingly artificial world. As the networks of machines and as communications become further and further removed from natural language, the more we discover zones of nature that our senses cannot penetrate. The gap between the world of the subject and the world of objects becomes wider. Isn't that what Weber meant when he coined the wonderful expression 'the *disenchantment* of the world'? There are no spirits in the technological world, and dreaming is not allowed during working hours. But does that mean that there is no more enchantment, or that it is just madness or an adolescent crisis? This may well be one aspect of modernization, but it is not the most important aspect. Its most important aspect is the liberating development of reflexivity. Rather than looking to heaven or hell, we look into ourselves, like Montaigne in his tower, like Descartes, who has such a poor reputation these days, and like Rousseau, who still gets a favourable reception. The awareness of being exploited or of having made some gain increases the distance between the personal subject and the social actor, and the fragmented logics of social and other systems. To say that the subject who is liberating himself and becoming self-reflexive may be tempted by the comforts of more utilitarian and optimistic modes of thought is bad faith. The subject is not just a bourgeois or a civil servant. The subject is also the man of the Enlightenment, of the Revolution and of liberation struggles of all kinds. Why reduce him to his most mediocre aspects, when he can so often be generous and heroic? The scientific and technological world does put us to the test, but it also gives us control over our environment. We protest against the obstacles that divorce us from ourselves, but we are also producing technologies that help to reveal us to ourselves.

Women as Subject

The subject emerges directly in those societies that are most able to transform themselves. But, in that situation, there is a great danger that the subject will disappear into his own achievements and drown in purely instrumental rationality. The answer to that contradiction is that the subject is most likely to emerge in the form of a dominated category that is rejected by the powerful, who deny it any subjectivity, even in the most highly modernized societies. The category that now best represents the subject is that of women. More so than any other category, women were for a long time denied the right to subjectivity (and especially political rights). In the course of some recent research about Muslim women in France, I listened to a young woman who had just being telling the group about the difficulties she was having with a family she loved but could no longer stand, and who had just burst into tears. She fell silent for a moment, and then said: 'I've just realized that, for the first time in my life, I have said "I", and I've said it in front of all of you (other Muslim women) who have said "I".' The refusal of men and institutions to recognize the subjectivity of women makes them privileged embodiments of the subject. The research I am referring to forcefully demonstrated that women define themselves primarily as women, and that their main goal is to construct their lives as the lives of women. It also demonstrated that they believe that their success or failure will be decided in the field of sexuality.

The notion of the subject must of course apply to all members of society, and women are aware of that, but it was they who took the initiative. As for men, they can easily accept that it is women who are bringing about the great cultural transformation that is taking us from a culture of world conquest to a culture that can recognize and construct the self. The men and women I listened to were aware of the historical importance of the changes that men are denouncing or that women are announcing. Constructing ourselves as subjects is indeed our culture's primary goal, and it is women who launched that conception who are showing the way. The main conclusion we have to draw from this is that we no longer live in a society of men. We are not entering a unisex society in which men and women are completely equal; we are entering, and have already entered, a society of women. It is true that it is men who have the power, the money and the guns. But women have begun to speak, and it is women who discovered the meaning of the changes that are taking place, and those changes have now gone so far that everyone is aware of the breaks that have been made.

There can be no subject without conflicts, or even defeats. Indeed, it is at such moments that the women or men who have not been 'recognized' by others assert themselves. The example of women is once more the most important. Feminists have won some rights, and done away with some inequalities. Above all, they have won the right to contraception and abortion. Those measures were difficult to accept, and they were adopted only because women asserted themselves with a slogan that was so extreme and so shocking, but which was quite rightly seen to be a much more radical self-assertion than the progress they had made in the workplace. 'A child if I want it and when I want it' does away with the genitor or relegates him to second place. Even today, the formula shows that the relationships between father and child and mother and child are not symmetrical, and that women play the main role in relations with children.

The main purpose of these remarks, which summarize the content of a recently published book, is to demonstrate that the sociology of women and feminism is not a separate chapter within sociology; it is central to any sociology that is reconstructed around the notion of the subject.

The Subject as Freedom

How does the subject live? How do we detect the presence of the subject? Is the subject domineering or liberating? All these questions relate to the theme that runs through these pages. The subject appears to be very similar to the individual ego, but does not display those aspects of the personality that the ego uses to defend its interests or to express its doubts. At this point, a comparison with religious beliefs or with other hidden figures of the subject, such as progress or equality, has to be made. Any attempt to elevate the debate to the level of the subject is associated with the attempt to escape the forms of social organization into which the individual is integrated. It is not true that we live in a world that has been crushed by the media and mass consumerism, or in what David Riesman calls a 'lonely crowd'. The subject rises above the network of social roles; it asserts ideals and condemns the intolerable.

There is a danger that, like so many religious figures and wise men, the subject who insists on being at the centre of everything that gives his life a meaning or takes away its meaning will become prophetic. We can therefore say that this idea of the subject defines that part of us that rises above even the most important problems of everyday life. We cannot make any social progress if we fail to recognize that some issues in our societies transcend the social. Those who urged us to fight Hitler and Nazism were not just asking us to make a political choice; they were speaking in the name of freedoms and the respect that is owed to all human beings. Even though we know that many of them turned into corrupt, authoritarian leaders, those who fought colonialism transposed their desire for independence, which was the most impassioned form of their subjectivation, into their action. There is much more to the feminist struggle than a demand for laws against inequality. Nothing could do more to define public freedoms than the capacity to make room in the public space for that which transcends it: debates and conflicts that manifest a demand for freedom, equality and justice, but also for individuation and respect for other cultures. In both private and public life, men and women have rejected the intolerable and have sacrificed themselves for causes and human beings because they would be ashamed if they did not try to save them. They still do so. Resistance fighters and dissidents are not typical figures of the subject, but no definition of the subject is acceptable if it fails to take into account behaviours that go beyond courage and that recognize that we have a duty to the victims of violence or injustice, even when our laws and customs do not demand such great sacrifices.

It is just as important to note that, in all social categories, private life is at least as full of subjectivity as public life, and that most of the acts that reveal the existence of the subject remain secret. There is more grandeur, more sacrifice and a greater effort to create the self and the other in day-to-day life than in the great tragedies reported by a press that reduces everything to either anecdotal news or horror stories. We are so carried away by the flow of events that the subject can only be found in exceptional situations, but the subject is everywhere. Yet the idea of the subject has no divine or epic connotations. The idea of the subject is not an image of death or society: it introduces debate where others see only necessity.

Thinking in terms of the subject is quite different from thinking in terms of *nature*. Nothing could be more ideological than the idea of a set into which components have to be integrated as a matter of priority. The idea of the subject is often contrasted with that image, as it is based upon self-creation and self-transformation, but also upon the struggles that are associated with the great capacity both societies and individuals have for transforming themselves.

While no one would deny that abortion is a serious issue or that euthanasia has its dangers, it is more important to defend the freedom of women who find themselves in a situation in which they might become trapped, just as we must respect the freedom of consciousness of men and women who decide to put an end to their own lives. Once very controversial, these themes are now widely accepted, and the positions of the Catholic Church, which are in keeping with its traditional teachings, have less and less effect on public opinion.

Similarly, political ecology is acquiring a primordial importance, and has to be put on the same level – or even a higher level – as the post-feminist movement. What I do object to is the ecologism that rejects all human intervention in the name of nature. Ideologies such as the Gaia theory give serious cause for worry. That is not, however, the main orientation of the ecology movement, and especially not of moves to protect the environment that demand a broader and more responsible vision of development that goes beyond economic activity. This political ecology is the most important example of the transition from a 'progressive' and evolutionist conception to a more critical or even *ambivalent* conception of progress, and the most innovative attempts to find a way of reconciling the two rather than contrasting them. The economists have taught us that both economic development and respect for the environment must be combined with the fight against inequality and exclusion.

These are two of the direct implications of the thought whose general principles I have outlined. As we can see, it does not become lost in the mists of an over-general approach. It tries to take account of the new awareness and the new struggles that are shaping both new issues and new social actors.

To close, let us look at things from a historical perspective. The power to create has come down from heaven to earth and, after having been embodied in the figures of the citizen, class consciousness and the 'liberated' woman, has gradually entered the individual or the personal subject. While this is a source on inspiration for the individual, it also has certain negative effects. The distant divine subject was certainly controlled by the churches or by other guardians of the sacred who were anxious to sanctify their own power, but that threat was reduced because societies had so little ability to act upon themselves. As their ability to act upon themselves increased, and as the figure and action of the subject grew stronger, the power of the sacred world increased, as did that of its armed guards. The triumph of creative individualism cannot be divorced from that revival. It is crushed, on the one hand, by the power of the new clerics and ideologues and, on the other, by drives that have been freed from any word from the father. They are spreading like a rising tide, and are drowning the individual. Now that the subject has been freed from the weakness that kept him safe from a distance, the subject's only strength is his self-consciousness. That self-consciousness has no more power for action and self-defence than humanitarian organizations or reliance upon a few well-chosen therapies. Like the setting sun, the subject glows red in all its splendour on the horizon, but it quickly vanishes as the darkness takes possession of the lands and seas it once warmed and lit up. The subject has often been threatened and imprisoned by distant or collective gods, some in heaven and some on earth, and for a long time we were separated from the subject by a 'superego' imposed by the social order. That situation has now been reversed: the subject is no longer crushed by the superego, but is being dissolved into the id that has taken control of speech. It has become even more difficult to find the subject in this *fun culture* [English in the original] than it was when fortified temples dominated the lowlands. We fought to revive our double and to free it from the immortality that kept it apart from us. The subject is no longer the prisoner of the knight-priests; he is a prisoner of the soulless merchants whose money colours and discolours everything that passes through their hands. Seeking self-consciousness and the will to be oneself, within ourselves and in the milieus where we live, is already our main task, and it will help us to see and hear the subject. And it will become more and more important.

The world of the merchants is so often invaded by the hordes of violence and marked by the shattering of the personality that there will be no shortage of opportunities. We must rediscover transcendence, but we must rediscover it within ourselves. It is claimed that certain techniques can help us to do that. Defending private life – sexuality, emotional relationships, the family – frees vast territories from the domination of interests, and creates room for desires and pleasures. The subject sometimes gets lost there, but it is difficult to speak out against the triumph of desire and pleasure. I could easily be mistaken for a reactionary who wants to go back to the taboos of the past. I am not suggesting that we have to create a space that is protected by the sacred or by self-interest. To send the subject off in search of himself and the double he needs, no matter whether it is sacred or profane, is an exalting task. We can no longer discover the subject and bring him closer to us looking to heaven. Increasingly, we have to look inside ourselves to find the subject without whom we will be unable to resist the armed priests and the merchants. The subject has at last become the subject's search for himself.

The Subject is not Alone

All my efforts have been devoted to criticizing the scientistic and determinist conceptions that thought they could drive the social actor, and above all the self-referential subject, from the field of social thought. I wanted to contrast the dominant interpretive discourse that has so often spoken in the name of revolutionary movements and parties that degenerated or vanished, with the image of a self-creating subject capable of making moral demands that are more forceful than interests or loyalties. It is becoming clearer and clearer to me that the subject is a force for liberation, a force that says no and a force that fights.

I am aware of the reasons why I have constructed, or want to construct, an image of a subject who is both independent and burdened with all the symbols and instruments of the struggle for freedom and for all rights, but I would like to recall briefly that the subject is also generous, and involved in situations, struggles and loyalties. The subject is not one individual: the subject is present in individuals and groups that are aware that they belong to a people, a culture and a history. Because I have fought all communitarianisms, especially when they succeed in fusing into a culture, a political power, an ethnic or linguistic group, I must, if I am to avoid the mistakes that lead to unacceptable accusations, make a distinction between community spirit and communitarianism, and between the collective defence of nationalism and destructive ethnocentrisms. The forces of freedom, from the greatest armies to the smallest partisan bands, fought in the name of the subject or some figure of the subject. The strongest friendships and the greatest sacrifices were made in the name of a commitment to the rights of all.

I am a fighting a permanent battle against the drift into a 'collective consciousness' that quickly proves to be a negation of the subject or that subordinates the subject to a society in which he must keep his distance from power, its interference and its cruelties. But warning of those dangers would be futile if it prevented us from recognizing in the existence of the subject the pulsation of friendship, of love, self-sacrifice, of solidarity and the call to arms to defend freedom and drive out the enemy.

I hope that these words do not create confusion by giving the impression that we must fight on all fronts at once. They are intended to reveal experiences and actions whose meaning is as clear to their authors as it is to their enemies. The subject is always very aware of belonging to a community, to a people that constantly defends itself against all attacks. The Shoah itself cannot be dissociated from the Jews' ceaseless efforts to act in such a way as to respect a message or even a prophecy that gives them the strength to fight, but which also prevents them from seeing power or wealth as the main objectives of their action.

Finding the presence of the subject in his *closest* relations and not just in communities is now both more difficult and a matter of urgency. I will not surrender to the temptation to seek the subject only on mountain peaks or on the top of monuments. The subject is present in families of all kinds, in the largely unknown world of relations between parents and children, in the world of love and hate, in the construction of personal identities, and in the awareness of belonging to a lineage, a tradition, a community and a history. I at least want to avoid the crude misunderstanding that insists that the subject is a solitary creature with no ties. The subject only really exists when he is capable of experiencing the tension that exists between the awareness of being part of a group or a history, and self-consciousness. It is impossible to describe rapidly the relations that exist between the world of the subject and the world of the lived experience of groups and communities. Just as social thought cannot be divorced from forms of collective action, everything in sociological analysis and even in the themes of novels reveals the presence of world history, the history of every individual, and the history that historians reconstruct.

My task is to reveal the reference to the subject in a world in which structuring reference to society and the state are disappearing. The actions of the subject can never be found outside the behaviours, organized or not, that bear within them both the meaning of creativity and of protests, as well as a continued loyalty to a heritage. It is hoped that these brief remarks will be taken for what they are: they are intended to be a reminder that, while the subject and his figures never vanish into the fabric of social relations of the development of the economy, they are not statues that loom over the *polis*. The subject is the movement that helps us find the way that leads to ourselves, through all the disorder and confusion of social situations, ideologies and discourses.

9
Conflicts and Movements

The dichotomy between what I have called the dominant interpretive discourse and the ideas developed here in Part II is so complete as to be clearly visible. On the one hand, we have a determinist vision that gives little room for manoeuvre to actors who hide their dependency beneath a false consciousness and the illusion of freedom. Major schools of thought – Marxism, structuralism and the linguistic revolution – did away with all reference to the subject, while the militant *gauchistes* accused it of being a bourgeois notion that simply protected privileges and did nothing to defend the concrete interests of those who faced the greatest threats in the workplace, as a result of their national and linguistic origins, or because of certain forms of family life. Their point of arrival is my starting point: social systems are breaking down and being shattered, and what we call the social world is being fragmented and losing its coherence. Capitalist globalization and clashes between civilizations dominate from on high the social life of populations that have no control over them. Deprived of all support, social beings appear to be retreating into an uncritical and consumerist individualism or, at the opposite extreme, becoming trapped into obsessive identities, and are prepared to eliminate all minorities and all differences. There is, however, a third solution: individuals can discover the subject who exists within them, and legitimize their *de facto* existence in terms of a *de jure* existence. The divorce between the 'I' that legitimizes, and the 'me' that is legitimized, is exacerbated in modernity: respect for individual rights with a universalist import is one of its components, and the other is a respect for the rational thought bequeathed us by the philosophy of the Enlightenment.

This desire to be a subject, which so many rationalists regard as a pretentious illusion, is, however, better equipped than any collective awareness of belonging to a community to resist the pressure of impersonal and depersonalizing systems, and especially of the machines and totalitarian ideologies that are using both authoritarian modes of thought and extermination camps to destroy the human world.

Conflicts at the Heart of Society

While the idea of conflict has to be re-examined critically, it must be recalled that it has done a great deal to enrich sociological thought. It has destroyed all those images that depict society as an integrated whole and tell us that we must take it or leave it. It is therefore rejected by two schools of thought which, while they are very different, agree about one thing. The absolute defenders of social integration and the interdependency of all elements of social life believe that conflict is pathological and must therefore be eliminated if we are to have social peace and promote both individual and collective well-being. This position can be examined with interest, but it is of little import because day-to-day observation of these actors who are supposedly perfectly integrated into their society reveals that they are in fact ideological. The second position is more interesting. Revolutionary thought also believes in the internal unity of society, and it is precisely because its unity is so strong that only a break can bring about social change. That is the *raison d'être* behind revolutionary politics: overthrowing the past presupposes or creates a post-revolutionary centralism and seeks to create a high level of integration in both institutions and the ruling group.

Both these positions are far too extreme. If, on the other hand, we regard conflict as a central element in all social ensembles from the family to the state and the nation, we do away with the 'all or nothing' conceptions of both the defenders of the abuse of order and the fanatical believers in change. The idea of conflict is the antithesis of all plans for an ideal *Polis*.

The idea of social conflict is strongest in industrial society, because the idea of the complete integration of social life and political life meets with great resistance in capitalist industrial societies. How can we speak of trade-union action, the labour movement, or even of social laws and collective agreements, if we do not start out from the idea that conflict is deeply rooted in social life, but must be limited either by social movements or by the state and its laws?

Conflict then becomes something that strengthens society rather than weakening it.

The contrasting utopias of complete social integration and the revolutionary break both lost ground as the West began to modernize fully from the end of the nineteenth century onwards, or when union organizations began to emerge and when social laws were first passed. As self-defence groups, protests and, at a higher level, social movements began to be organized, conflicts increasingly extended to the whole of society. The most complex societies might be described as societies that are being fragmented by a great number of conflicts that emerge and develop, and that are resolutely independent of one another. In certain countries, such as France, overall conceptions of social integration, both conservative and revolutionary, have always resisted the idea of conflict, which implies that the various parts of society are relatively autonomous, and results in the conviction that reforms can be successfully implemented, and that unjust and intolerable situations can be remedied. The idea of conflict and that of 'social partners' therefore complement one another, as do the ideas of the state and social integration. Their complementarity is even greater in social-democratic countries or countries with an industrial democracy.

The socially disruptive element is always present, but *gauchisme* offers only a poor or extreme interpretation of history, and cannot transform itself into a force for sustained action. This has been the case in many countries, from the Italy of the 1970s to the France of the post-1968 period, and from guerrilla campaigns in Columbia to the armed struggle in Bengal. Terrorism is often an exacerbated form of *gauchisme* that emerges in situations where extreme struggle appears necessary and where the ability to modify or destroy the ruling order is weak. When that point is reached, there are no valid grounds for regarding acts of terrorism as Leftist, as they may have quite the opposite effect.

Between the extremes of well-tempered conflict and waves that break against social fortifications, we can easily detect the existence of a certain type of collective action. The crucial point is that it is not mid-way between the two; it is of a different nature.

Power and the Subject

To recall that the presence of conflict can be seen everywhere is too facile. All individuals and all groups find themselves in various relations of power or domination. All groups and individuals encounter obstacles that prevent them from asserting themselves and defending their interests. They always have either to submit or negotiate, or in other words accept a logic that is not really the logic of the subject. These banal formulae mask an even more banal reality: social life and social relations are based upon a plurality of dominations and conflicts. That assertion is unacceptable unless we appeal to the idea of the subject. It is precisely because the idea of conflict is ubiquitous that it is easy to write a history of conflicts without basing it on any specific interpretation. The notion of conflict is so general that it does not correspond to any one type of action; it corresponds to all actions. It therefore refers to the state of the social system, and not a category of actors.

A *social movement*, in contrast, is defined by the actors who bring it to life and who want to change the way a society's main resources are used. Such movements can appear at any level of the social organization, but they always correspond to the same type of action. A social movement is more complete than a conflict because it introduces positive orientations, but it is also more complex than a revolutionary break. That is why I have always defined social movements as a combination of social conflict and an identification with the most prestigious cultural resources of any given country.

The subject's inner conflicts are more central than those that come from outside. The subject comes into being by distancing himself from the 'man' or 'woman', and therefore from an individual life that is governed by the pursuit of self-interest or the quest for pleasure. It is the subject, or rather the process of subjectivation, that comes into conflict with the empirical aspect of the ego [*moi*]. The conflict does not arise simply because someone is dominating me, but because one part of me rejects another part, and that turns me into a subject. These formulae may look far removed from observable social realities, but that is not the case; the part of me that I abandon is adopted by a system of organization and production that seeks to destroy the subject. I work, follow the instructions I am given, and use ready-made categories to define and judge my behaviour; I too go in pursuit of pleasure and profit, and I know that the idea of the subject would be of very little interest if it referred only to the choices that are made by anchorites or prophets. I can only assert myself as a subject if I am exploited to make the social organization work, and both the social organization's means and ends are alien to anything to do with subjectivation. Neither the subject who becomes detached from the life of the individual that supports him, nor the rationalization of powers that rule the world takes priority, as they are two sides of the same primal reality, namely the self's action on the self. This is not a divorce, as it leads to subjectivation and can even transform it into a protest against all systems.

The same argument can be expressed in different terms. The world of profit and power seeks to eliminate the world of the subject because it sees it as a dangerous threat. In order to get rid of it, it creates ideals and symbols with which individuals are called upon or forced to identify. We are all invited to live our lives by respecting scientifically based social norms or administrative rules. Is not the modern world a world of action, whereas the traditional world was one of belonging and heritages? Our belief that the modern world no longer has any depth and has to abandon, in both painting and economic life, the fixed gaze and figurative representation has had many far-reaching effects. We were exhorted to invent forms, movements and communications networks. Communities, traditions and cultural particularities continue to resist those networks. But is this a conflict? It is more like a bipolarity, as the forces of change have no interest in destroying traditional structures, and those structures can survive only if they accept new forms of organization, or in other words the protection that is offered by existing structures. The most serious conflicts, or those that give birth to new social or cultural movements, are conflicts between two different ways of using the resources that are available within the same territory: one thinks in terms of trade, and the other in terms of symbolic meanings and non-commercial values. Religious forces, in particular, come into violent conflict with economic forces, but they create new forms of power. When religions are weak, as they are in Europe, it is communitarian forces that provoke the most extreme conflicts, especially if they have an ethnic or racial basis. In other situations, it is new capitalist economic forces that destroy the old social and political order. In all these cases, we are dealing with conflicts between different domains of social life, and they go far beyond the conflicts that are inherent in the political or moral order.

Self-consciousness means more than the construction of a self; it also means abandoning part of the self. Religions, social and political movements, and utopias knew this, and called for 'sacrifices' to be made, just as Jesus called upon his disciples to abandon everything, from their loved ones to their material good and their loyalties. How can a truly economic world not come into conflict with the world of politics or that of belief? Doesn't the logic of social organization come into conflict with that of the personal subject? That is why I do not use the expression *the social subject*. We must avoid anything that might take us back to the image of an integrated society in which all institutions reinforce one another, and remember that there is a discrepancy between the workings of the social system and the demands of the subject. Those who speak of a reciprocity of perspective between system and actor are making a very serious mistake.

What I have just said takes us from a very general notion of conflict to the much more specific and powerful notion of a *social movement*. I have already criticized the vague use that is sometimes made of the notion of a social movement: some use the term to refer to any collective mobilization and, in order to compensate for the weakness of their definition, restrict themselves to studying how 'resources are mobilized' because they do not ask themselves why these movements exist. How do people mobilize, and what is the role of the political apparatuses? What kind of alliances do these movements need to form if they are to succeed? Those who adopt this type of analysis take no interest in the goals that mobilize people because they believe that social behaviours are economically determined. Neo-liberals and Marxists are similar in that respect. But not everyone can be a Charles Tilly, and start out with a Marxist approach and then produce some remarkable studies of history. Once we have ruled out this false solution, the real problem remains: we have to find a specific and explicit definition of social movements. Introverted societies, such as some Mediterranean-style rural communities, and the ghettos and *quartiers* that have grown up in our city centres or on the edges of our conurbations, are conflicted societies. Here, conflict can even have a structural role, as we can see from the vendettas or inter-neighbourhood struggles that have played such a major role in Italy. In societies, both big and small, that are dominated by poverty, unemployment, discrimination and in which there is no integrative force, permanent and predictable conflicts supply at least a negative integrative principle. This has often been noted in prisons, where conflicts, gang warfare and personal clashes take extreme forms that often result in the death of the weakest participants. There is nothing exceptional about these situations; the world of 'poverty' is based upon this logic of conflict.

There are many conflicts that do not produce social movements, and many social movements which, even though there is always an element of conflict, give cultural issues, rather than conflict in the strict sense, the power to mobilize, either because those conflicts are projected into the future, or because they are identified with a past that is deemed to have been destroyed by some invasion.

Do Social Movements Still Exist?

If we see them only as combat units that are defined by the adversaries they bring into conflict because they are always mixed up with political and even ideological interventions, social movements are more resistant than any other component of social life to the inverted sociological analysis that, as I am trying to demonstrate, we require in all domains.

The studies that are devoted to them are still centred on the system rather than the actor; they rely upon data derived from economic and social history, even though that history calls for a different type of analysis. And above all, they are still influenced by the obsession with absolute forms of domination such as slavery, serfdom, the exploitation of wage-earners and so on. This vision denies the movement's actors' ability to produce meaning, and makes that the prerogative of masters. This is particularly obvious in Christian thought. Only the creator-God, who has been betrayed by man's lapse into sin, can save men thanks to His Grace, with the help of the church and by asking sinners to make sacrifices.

We need to find new forms of social action, and even new social movements that are identified not with the victims' reactions, but with the priority they accord to self-reflexivity. To that extent, it is easier to give a historical rather than a truly theoretical definition of social movements. To do so, we can go back to the idea of a European – or, more broadly, Western – model of modernization. That theme is so important that it is worth recalling its content.

The extreme concentration of resources led to an extremely high level of tension and conflict between the ruling categories and those categories that were trapped into an inferior status. This very specific characteristic of 'Western modernization' gave 'liberation movements' a central importance in the political and social history of the most highly industrialized countries from the nineteenth century onwards, and especially in the first part of the twentieth century. The labour movement in all its forms, decolonization movements and feminism strove to overturn the extreme forms of discrimination and inequality that affected wage-earners, the colonized and women; so much so that social and political struggles created the impression that they were so many 'particular fronts' within the same broad struggle. This gave rise to and imposed a representation of a society that was governed by one central conflict whose manifestations would be seen in every domain of collective life. That conclusion is acceptable if the central conflict is not reduced to a struggle between economic interests, or even a class struggle.

The almost universal success of these three types of movement helped to 'relax' the European model for modernization, and that in turn undermined the social movements themselves as they turned from brutal confrontations to negotiations, or even to mechanisms that incorporated parties, unions and other forms of organized actions into a social politics that then became a component element within politics in general.

This brief historical recapitulation brings us face-to-face with a question: can we still speak of social movement, now that the European model for modernization has been undermined, now that other modes of modernization are becoming increasingly powerful, and now that the state is playing a more central role than antagonistic classes? How can we define social movements? We have to base our definition on transformations within the collective conflicts that have just been evoked. If the central conflict is that between the subject and the power of a 'global' and impersonal system, we would do better to speak of *cultural movements* rather than social movements, as it is a model for culture and the personality that feels threatened by the instrumentalization of reason and by the transformation of religious belief into a form of state power. If we endorse such formulae, how can we not speak of *cultural movements* whose goal is to defend the local against the global, the predictability of our working lives against flexibility at work, and the diversity of cultural creativity against the over-centralized production of mass culture? On the whole, the continuity between the old social movements and the new is more important than the difference between their contents.

Is it possible to imagine that this increasingly globalized world will eradicate the weakest and most fragmented cultural movements, and that all that will remain is an immense central mass surrounded by isolated pockets of resistance that are both conflicted and full of hope? The importance of the movement born in Porto Allegre, which led to anti-globalization forums and huge gatherings almost everywhere in the world, is that it is self-centred and not focused on its adversary. Self-assertion and exercises designed to enhance our ability to understand, communicate and act are no longer preparatory stages that will lead to the emergence of a social movement. They are the main component of that movement. They *are* a social movement because they are creating an imaginary space and time. The main goal of some of the movements that emerged in the United States, and then Europe, in the 1960s appeared to be symbolic gestures. They included sit-ins, agit-prop theatre and even new kinds of open meetings that gradually began to attract growing numbers of women. The women's movement itself generated emotionally charged gatherings which freed women from the inferior status that trapped them into so many constraints.

The increasingly impersonal and distant character of the power that bears down on social life is coming into conflict with an increasingly open desire to ensure that we all have a personal future. It is impossible to imagine an anti-globalization movement that is not aware that those involved are strangers to one another. The more the dominant powers surround the actor on all sides and attempt to silence him, the more the actor must use his whole personality to fight it: the fight is as physical as it is intellectual.

We are still the prisoners of a vertical vision of political and social history, and we must find a new point of view. Curiously enough, it is, perhaps, in the religious domain that this change has been most successful: the institutionalized churches are in retreat, but expressions of a shared personal faith are becoming much more common, as are mass gatherings of the faithful. Increasingly, conflicts are centred upon the actors, and not only on the actors' right, but on ways of ensuring that they are respected. They are therefore becoming more closely bound up the actors' awareness of what they perceive to be direct threats, whereas the old social movements were inspired by quasi-military mobilizations against class enemies who were also seen as the enemies of society as a whole.

The explanation for the decline in involvement in politics and union activity is that the defenders of the people and the workers are using a strategy and a language that are alien to the motivations and attitudes of the categories concerned. In 'classic' conflicts and social movements, there was a close correlation between conflict and involvement or integration. There is now a danger that a purely combative radicalism will lead to ruptures, or even a revolution, rather than conflicts or social movements. In today's context, no conflict or social movement can emerge or develop unless it can interpret subjective data as well as economic information.

Projecting Conflict on to the Individual

One of sociology's earliest and most important discoveries was that the upheavals in traditional societies that resulted from industrialization and globalization were both undermining norms and making it difficult to internalize them. The twin aspects of what Emile Durkheim called *anomie* reinforce each other to such an extent that references to the social system, its norms and its capacities have gradually disappeared. What I call the 'end of the social' is no more than the final stage of a process that was broadly associated with the rise of capitalism, but also with the accelerating rate of social change and innovation. So much so that institutions are no longer capable of protecting individuals, while individuals are collapsing under the burden of the freedom they have been granted, but which is no longer protected by social institutions. The most serious conflicts are no longer social conflicts: they have been displaced into our personal lives. Intrafamilial conflict becomes a rejection of the family; resistance to authority becomes a rejection of school.

There is a general tendency to project 'social problems' on to individuals. A growing number of adults, young people and even pre-adolescents are rejecting society, often in violent ways. Their behaviour can no longer be explained in terms of their personal problems, not least because those responsible for the violence find it difficult to talk about their personal problems. The categories that are most affected by the decay of the social are not those that are most exposed to its effects; it is those categories that have the most direct experience of the contradictions between their strong attachments, especially to primary groups (families, gangs, peer groups, etc.), and their failure to deal with their problems in social terms. That is why the most effective methods of rehabilitation are those that the delinquents or pre-delinquents find in their own environment, though there will also have been close support from youth workers. This can lead to the formation of groups defined by individual motivations, and not by the repressive measures that gradually steer the delinquent in the direction of prison, often with no hope of recovery.

I am not suggesting that we replace sociological explanations with psychological explanations. I am in fact suggesting almost the opposite: increasingly, individual problems arise because social conflicts that have become insoluble are projected on to individuals who are constantly concerned about their capacity for resistance. It is therefore pointless to try to reconstruct authority at all cost; on the contrary, the 'social' must be weakened and its resources must be transferred to individuals so as to identify and make use of their ability to take the initiative and to reject dependency.

Constructive Individualism

The changes that are taking place in social and political life are much more far-reaching. It is no longer possible to take one side in a debate or conflict in an absolute sense. This is not because our problems are so complex that everyone is partly right, but because we are experiencing the end of the belief in progress. The breakdown of an evolutionist vision of history is destroying the foundations of the ideological clashes that stubbornly contrast progress with reaction, and movement with order. We are gradually discovering that our multiple and accelerated modernizations offer us some impossible choices: how can we choose between the *unity* of rational thought and a *plurality* of cultures? How can we choose between the general and the local, between the increased productivity we need to improve the situation of the world population, and the need to control a productivity that poses a threat to nature? In an attempt to get out of these impossible choices, some adopt an extremist attitude. This can lead to a *clash of civilizations*, just as the actions of extremist minorities can lead to violence, but while these behaviours can have spectacular effects, they merely underline the fact that no one can impose a unilateral solution on everyone. We are discovering that we face many problems that do not allow us to choose between two different alternatives. They may well be contradictory, but we cannot divorce one from the other. We have to stop trying to bring about the triumph of progress, and reconcile progress with the fight against its negative effects.

What is the meaning of this transformation, which has nothing to do with a taste for compromise and half-way solutions, as we all know that they can be as pernicious as any others? It is inevitable because, rather than dominating nature or increasing our control over nature, we know that we need sciences and technologies but we also know that there is a danger that our own mistakes will destroy us. There is nothing new about this idea, and many people have long believed that progress is ambiguous. What is new is the need to transform contradictions into component elements of decisions that can reconcile what appear to be antagonistic elements. The main difficulty with such combinations of alternatives is that they prevent actors from devoting themselves to one alternative, and that they find this frustrating. That is in the very nature of *ambivalence*. The example of women who want to earn a living and look after their children at the same time is well known. If they combine their two roles – as the vast majority of women in France do – they are dissatisfied with both their working lives, because they cannot be a complete success, and with their family life, because they feel that they are not devoting enough time to their children. But their ambivalence does not lead them to choose between the two. The frustrating solution that they do adopt is the lesser of two evils, and they reject all other solutions.

Ambivalent reactions to the dangers inherent in all polarizations are becoming more significant. Indeed, they are the only reactions that can resolve real conflicts and get us out of their ever-present contradictions. Political life is still structured around pairs of opposites: right or left, unity or diversity. Such polarizations will not lead to the transformations we require. Organizations or associations that are closer to the grassroots, and less identified with one general principle of action, may play a more positive role. Above all, intellectuals must popularize their new way of thinking, and schools must realize that changing our general methodology can have an effect on both our understanding of the past and our analysis of the choices we have to make now and in the future.

The idea of ambivalence already has a long history. Simonetta Tabboni's work has formulated it in very satisfactory terms, and it is destined to play a very important role in all the social sciences. These methodological considerations aside, we cannot yet gauge the importance of the changes that are now taking place. The idea of conflict, and even of social movements, was so closely associated with philosophies of history that the great themes of macro-history often seemed to be no more than reflections of a philosophy of history based upon the ideas of rationalization and progress, and therefore the idea that the forces of the past were resistant to change, and deflected the present away from the future. That made the analyses I am outlining here impossible. Under such conditions, it becomes difficult to use the notions of historical actors and of the formation of a personal subject. We must, on the contrary, break the link, which we have accepted for far too long, between studying situations and studying behaviours, especially when we are looking at social movements. Social movements are not an expression of the contradictions of the capitalist economy, or of the increase in trade or the rapid growth of trade. If we are to understand them we have to speak of domination and freedom, and of liberation and centralized power. By doing so, we can create a space where we can develop a social science of actors and subjects that can no longer be identified with either progress or resistance to progress, a space in which we learn to reconcile positive and negative judgements.

Violence

We must stick to this conclusion in the face of all attacks from schools of thought that still see conflict everywhere, and that do not see social or cultural movements anywhere. This is to some extent excusable, as we cannot further the study of cultural movements if that notion is not closely associated with the notion of the subject and with all the analyses I have outlined so far, even if we do have to give them a different form. As the notion of conflict loses ground, the rather different notion of *violence* is gaining ground everywhere, as Michel Wieviorka, in particular, has clearly demonstrated. The institutional crisis affects the state even more badly than it affects industrial relations, and globalization is undermining or destroying the ability of many countries, and especially the poorest, to build a state. Violence is taking over the spaces where conflicts should be resolved by institutional means. This is violence on a mass scale, and it can take the form of genocide or the imprisonment of captive populations in camps ruled by murder, rape and torture. Central Africa, from the Great Lakes region to the Democratic Republic of Congo and, more recently, Ivory Coast, has been affected by this violence, as have all places where the state has been destroyed or undermined. Violence also rules in those rural areas where ethnic or regional conflicts can no longer be contained by state power. The phenomenon is especially obvious in urban zones that have been ravaged by both unemployment, racial or social discrimination, and governments that cannot communicate. Neither the notion of social movements nor that of conflict is applicable here. Violence is not even a social phenomenon in the strict sense of that term. But nor is it reducible to a mere process of decay. Violence is characterized by a desire to dehumanize and humiliate, and it cannot be explained in economic or social terms, or even in political terms. We need the idea of the subject, not only because of the positive contribution it can make, but also because of the prevalence of its antithesis, which can be defined as the desire to destroy human beings *qua* subjects.

The undermining of the notion of conflict and the growing importance of that of violence are good illustrations of why we require a new analysis. Conflicts emerge and can be managed within an institutional framework; violence and the cruelty that is associated with it, in contrast, are spreading everywhere, far beyond the specific domain of the state. Because of this institutional crisis, violence in general is taking the place of conflict, just as terrorism is taking the place of war. It is as though the state no longer existed, and as though terrifying the enemy were enough to make him capitulate. Despite the differences between them, all these examples have one common feature: violence, just like conflict and even social movements, is outside the social field, and poses a direct threat to the subject. All these anti-subject forces make it essential to make positive use of the idea of a subject.

New Social Movements

After 1968, I used the expression *new social movements* – which subsequently passed into the language – to describe collective actions to defend cultural rights. Such movements are led by cultural categories such as women, sexual minorities, immigrant works, national or religious minorities and the disabled. For a few years, I thought that the trade unions – and especially France's CFDT – would hoist them on to their shoulders to make them more visible. History went in a different direction: these movements had a new cultural content but went on using the sectarian language of the old revolutionary labour movement. That language quickly swallowed up the message it was supposed to be transmitting. François Mitterrand then came to power and lent his generous support to the traditional Left, which was calling for nationalizations and a break with the globalized market economy. The new social movements broke up, and when François Mitterrand disappeared from the political scene where he had been the dominant figure on the Left for so long, the Left restricted itself to a management programme that took advantage of the temporary improvement in the world economy and then did nothing until the disaster of 2002. There was no great reaction to the Right's return to power, and the presidential election marked the triumph of the Right.

New means of communication such as the Internet and blogs are, however, shaping trends, many of them radical, that are beginning to challenge the political and economic system rather than a dominant category which, for its part, is coming under attack from the alter-globalists at the international level. They are defending a subject whose basic rights – and especially the right to housing – are being ignored. There are two aspects to what Pierre Rosanvallon calls *counter-democracy*, which is based upon an eminently democratic suspicion of institutions, and he makes a clear distinction between the two. One is liberal and goes back, in France, to Montesquieu and Benjamin Constant. It wants a weak government and is afraid of coalitions of interests. Both the Left and the far Left now display the same liberal-inspired distrust of institutions. The other tendency can be observed at a higher level of political life. As the definition of social classes has become more confused than it was under the old system, the subject, defined in terms of rights rather than self-interest, is becoming the main value to be defended.

It would be a mistake to think that politics has become ethical and no longer has a social or conflicted dimension. That dimension does exist, but governments are the primary targets because it is govern-ments that are refusing to implement the new policies inspired by NGOs. NGOs do sometimes succeed in launching campaigns against governments, and movements with few resources can enjoy consider-able success. The movement that protested about the situation of the homeless in Paris in 2006 outflanked the administrative structures that were supposed to resolve such problems within a matter of days. The message is now more important than the discourse; these *new* new social movements are an extension of what began to emerge after 1968. They are now taking on their full meaning, as they call more directly for the defence of human rights, which have to be recognized in the same way that workers' rights began to be recognized in Britain and Germany at the end of the nineteenth century, and then in the United States and France.

Increasingly, the idea of the subject is becoming the basis for struggles that are as impassioned as the class struggle that mobilized the emotions and protests of the working class in industrial society. The idea of the subject is not a way of avoiding social problems and political struggles; on the contrary, it is bringing them back to life after a long period of confusion in which social struggles were increasingly subordinated to the strategies of political parties. The new struggles continue to refer to human rights, and new social movements are now being organized to defend them.

Do I have to repeat that the *subject* I am talking about has nothing in common with the principle of authority to which so many human beings have been forced to submit? When the images that have come down to us from monarchies, from the patriarchal family and from the teachings of the monotheistic religions were destroyed, the principle of authority began to fall into decay. It is now in such an advanced state of decomposition that a principle that once applied to the state has been displaced on to 'society', and has now merged into a broadly anti-authoritarian, permissive or transgressive mood that is intent on satisfying desires that are less and less repressed by taboos.

The subject allows individuals and social actors to assert themselves in the strongest possible terms, provided that we are not content with passive resistance to the dominance of apparatuses of production, consumption and management. While the subject can manifest himself just as forcefully as all the veiled figures that came before him, we must not forget that the subject can also be corrupted and transformed into his opposite. Once again, the parallel with religious faith and clericalism is self-evident. Many obscure, persecuted militants lose confidence in their own action, just as some believers lose their faith. What happens to the figures of the subject that are suffocated by the authorities and forms of social organization they supposedly control? Even the subject can be perverted when he is embodied in a figure that is his antithesis, just as the looting crusaders were the antithesis of what the Gospel preached. Similarly, revolutionary militants can become the antithesis of what they once were, and can be transformed into political leaders or even police officers.

Given that I cannot put forward the hypothesis in more sophisticated terms, how can we avoid evoking the idea that the subject, who has been driven out, repressed and banned by the forces that dominate us, which often have to do with the impersonality of the market, has been *repressed* into our personal unconscious, or into the fears that paralyse our collective unconscious? How could the pressures brought to bear by the majority and the market not condemn those who are looking for a self-to-self relationship that is more intimate than anything most of us can find in our day-to-day lives of loneliness, or even self-sacrifice? It is perfectly reasonable to argue that there is a disturbing urgency about this search for the other, who may be – though this is far from always being the case – a form of headlong flight away from the self, so powerful is the taboo on the self-to-self relationship.

These words do no more than evoke the fragile image of a situational reversal that may have repressed into the unconscious what was, in a different world, the power of the law. At the same time, we are increasingly free to express directly desires that were once forbidden, and those very desires strive to repress the things they feel are furthest removed from them. These brief remarks have the more limited goal of warding off all submissive images of the subject: the subject is freedom of conscience and not a will to power. The subject will sacrifice his own life, but is no nationalist warrior. Let us stop clinging to an image of society and the personality that cannot take into account either our day-to-day experiences or the new debates we now see within public opinion.

From Culture to Cultural Action

Society and culture were once complementary: culture traced boundaries that social actors must not cross. In return, both behaviours and forms of cultural life were regarded as the effects of a general system of social inequality. Discussions of education were reduced to debates about inequality of access to various levels of education. Women were seen solely as the victims of men's power; they were men's 'proletarians', just like the colonized peoples who were defending their popular culture from the rationalism or spiritualism of colonial powers. Mass culture, of course, was an instrument that money used to destroy the independence of intellectuals and creative people in general, and to destroy the people's taste for independence by offering them more bread and circuses.

None of this is false: inequality is present everywhere, and those who devote their lives to making money are rarely defenders of 'high culture'. Both public and private television channels have descended into mediocrity in the name of 'audience ratings' that simply calculate the profits they can expect to make.

All these observations are so accurate, and the need to denounce the lies or hypocrisy of those who talk of culture without referring to the actual workings of modes of production and consumption is so great, as to justify all the discourses of unveiling and denunciation. Indeed, it is easy to be seduced by the double talk, and to speak of the ubiquity of inequality, and of the specificity of every national or local culture, and to claim, in other words, that culture and society are basically one and the same. Society has cultural foundations, and culture has social functions. How can we resist such a balanced and irreproachable discourse? Why not go on supplying new proof that society and culture are interdependent?

Because it is simply impossible to do so, for *two main reasons*.

The *first* is that the correspondence has collapsed. As a result of what I call the 'end of the social', the cultural field has been invaded both by technologies that are ill-defined in social terms, and by contents that are either the property of some dominant culture, or sets of practices that derive their strength from their 'mass' nature. The first reason is easier to identify than the second. Cultural productions have long been created by technologies, and for even longer they have been defined by the way they refer to a non-social world, from the language of music or other cultural sign-systems to religious beliefs, to romantic individualism and a rejection of all the signs of the established order. The liberation of desires and pleasures that frees us from painful tensions or brutally repressive mechanisms is a more recent phenomenon. Given what happened in the twentieth century, we might add that the mass dispensation of death destroyed societies and cultures alike, but surely the contradiction between the death that destroys everything and multiple forms of creativity and social and cultural organization is a feature of all periods. Perhaps we would do better to turn away from Thanatos, and feel the stirrings of Eros, both within us and around us.

All the mutations I have briefly evoked, and with which everyone is already familiar, simply mean that the alliance between society and culture has been replaced by a divorce between technologies and forms, and between the masses and thought. There are no longer any norms or social bonds to bind them together. There is no longer anything to connect the world where forms are created with the world of lived experience. Some forms of knowledge and some technologies do have their uses, but they are not enough to bridge the gap. The example of medicine is often cited; we find that there is a growing gap between medicine and the patient, or between *cure* and *care* [English in the original].

At this point, an old theme reappears. When need and desire are the only things that exist, profit becomes the main goal. This is what we call the 'world of consumption'. It extends to complex productions, but does not always take the production of ordinary objects into account.

Let us go one step further: mass consumerism, and especially the mass media, is defined by the elimination of real actors, together with their intentions, goals and feelings. It has become necessary to eliminate them because money is the only thing that has to survive. The games in which the winners are given sums of money that far exceed anything their lived experience can offer are a grim example of how the logic of non-meaning has become a precondition for the triumph of profit.

Forms, on the other hand, are no longer social, no matter whether they are technological or scientific, and no matter whether they form structures or the rules that govern the world. This rupture makes things that seemed so simple difficult; it is now difficult to associate the rejection of inequality and exclusion with the liberation of cultural creativity. There are almost no cultural policies now, and nor are there many cultural protests. Are we to conclude that there can be no more cultural movements, and that nothing can replace the social movements that disappeared along with the social paradigm to which they belonged?

We now have to pursue a second line of inquiry if we are to understand why the association between society and culture no longer exists. Not all the effects of the end of the social and of the fragmentation of cultural fields are negative. They at last tear away the veils that gave the subject a social appearance, and allow the subject to emerge as such. The subject is directly visible and present only when his social figures disappear, or when it becomes impossible for them to exist. The divorce between lived experience and forms, between consumption and the structures of the imaginary, sweeps away the obstacles that prevented the subject from becoming fully self-conscious and from making that self-consciousness the principle that governs behaviours and transcends the world of practices and forms.

At this point, we could not be further removed from society and culture because, now that they have been freed from one another, it is among the ruins of their complementarily that we see the emergence of a self-creating subject who promotes the rights that turn individuals and groups into beings that can demand their rights in the face of the unbridled desires and money that promote non-meaning and the immediacy of needs.

The subject I am revealing here is not a *deus ex machina*, and nor is he a newcomer or the perfect embodiment of humanity. On the contrary, the subject is always present in every moment of history and in all parts of the world, because no society and no culture is simply what it is. A culture or a society cannot, as classical sociology would have us believe, be reduced to what it does, to the mechanics of its working, its norms, its forms of authority or to a network of statuses and roles. There is, within any human group, a double of the human. This double is not a superego that lays down the law and represses drives; on the contrary, it is a representation of the self that creates rights and, more generally, value-judgements. Modernity has not done away with the 'enchanted' world; it has made something that was superhuman human. What we call humanism is the assertion that it is human beings that give human beings their value, and thus enable them to defend and extend their ideals and rights.

Nothing could be more central to our attempt to reconstruct social thought than this break between the subject and a social and cultural organization that has been broken in two by the divorce between the world of consumption, desire and death on the one hand and, on the other, the world of technologies and structures that are, to a greater or lesser extent, under the control of the state. The subject is on neither side, and this can put him in danger or relegate him to the misty realm of some utopia, but it also reveals his true face by tearing away the veils and masks that forced him to live in disguise, as though the subject's *raison d'être* could be found in society, and as though society could therefore be the source of value-judgements about social reality.

If we accept this general analysis, can we still speak of culture? The word has many different meanings. The meaning we derive from social anthropology refers to all relations between a society and the nature – in both the human and non-human senses – it controls. That definition is now almost meaningless, for the reasons I have given, and which mark the real boundary between the modern societies studied by sociology and the societies studied by social anthropology. As for the meaning that defined 'high culture', it served mainly to divide cultured people from the rest, or those who were highly educated from those who did not go to school or left school early to find jobs. I do not see what use can be made of the word 'culture' in that sense. We therefore have to find a new meaning for it. It in fact refers to an important process that is at work everywhere: movement whereby the subject dominates and reunites the world of consumption and the world of forms. This in turn gives the subject a concrete existence. And that gives every kind of practice an ethical meaning; the meaning is internalized and leaves the mark of its demands on all human actions.

The subject's great task consists in recreating, within him and around him, a unity that has vanished. The strongest figures of the subject are now political ecology, which is trying to reconcile nature and culture, which have been contrasted for so long, and then the action – which does not just take the form of an organized movement – of the women who are overcoming the hierarchical dichotomy between men and women, body and mind, and rich and poor. And the most ambitious form of cultural action is, finally, the attempt to reconcile the universalist idea of modernity with the diversity of social and cultural interests.

There is no longer any such thing as 'culture' in the sense of an institutionalized whole. But the conflict between the shattering of the socio-cultural whole, which leads to a divorce between practices and forms, and the subject who, thanks to his ability to introduce value-judgements into both personal and collective life, and to reunite what has been divided and divorced, is being played out everywhere.

10

The Subject, the Other and Others

Doubling

Any approach that takes the individual as its starting point comes up against an objection, even if it does see the individual as a social actor or a personal subject. It will be objected that human beings do not live alone, and that their living conditions depend upon those of others. It may also meet with an accusation: your approach encourages egoism and the pursuit of individual self-interest, and our society already does enough to encourage that, now that collective solidarities are being undermined at the very time when we should be strengthening them. I share that view, and have shared it throughout my life, much of which has been devoted to trying to understand social movements. But I fail to see why defending the human, social and cultural rights of every individual should imply a lack of interest in the situation of others, given that individual rights obviously have to be defended on a collective basis. To respond quickly to a wrong-headed criticism, let me make it clear that, as always, the defence of personal rights sustains collective action against all the privileged, including those who turn other human beings into serfs or wage-slaves. I see no reason to depart from the centuries-old tradition that finds a link between respect for the individual and struggles for all collective freedoms.

The theme of the *other*, for its part, is bound up with that of the personal subject. The other is not our fellow or our neighbour. The other is a being who is perceived and understood by another being who acts as a *subject* and who recognizes the other as such. The otherness of the other is much more than a difference. To speak of the other is an indirect way of saying that the subject within me cannot be perceived directly, and that it is by looking through the other than I perceive within me the presence or absence of a subject who cannot easily be seen in a world that was created by the powerful. Some will object that the subject lies beyond our grasp, that we only perceive the subject through obstacles and screens, or only fleetingly. I quite understand that objection, but why say that it is impossible to perceive the subject? We constantly see individuals and groups acting on the basis of their self-image. We are all aware of our rights, but we know that it is not because we are individuals that we have rights; it is our *double* who has rights. It is the ideal which, for so long, took forms that were alien to human life because they were so far removed from it. As we gained a better collective understanding of ourselves, those forms actually became part of each one of us.

We now have to recognize ourselves as subjects. Doing so will enable us to identify, in his many different forms, the subject who exists within beings or groups that are different from us. It is because our experience of our double becomes more and more direct, and because we live in a world of consciousness and reflexivity, and not a world of gods and guilt, that we have not been driven away from ourselves. When we look at ourselves, we do not see a surplus; we see a void and a silence. We do not see an accumulation of orders and taboos, and our project is to discover our double. And it is only because we discover the subject within ourselves that we can discover the subject in the other. Recognition of the other cannot but be a recognition of the subject within the other, because mere differences make communication impossible, as, for example, when the parties concerned speak different languages. The barriers can be overcome only if they are barriers between beings who can communicate with one another thanks to their reason and their respect for the universal nature of individual rights.

The women I listened to spoke of constructing themselves as women; they are the very image of a subject because their individuals' double transforms them into *de jure* beings who can also defend the rights of others so as to ensure that all can experience their own creative abilities. The subject *as double* is much more central to the analysis and to behaviours than the *other*, even though the other plays a vital role by inviting us to distance ourselves from our *ego* [*moi*], which is changeable and dependent, and thus opens up the road that leads to subjectivation.

Fragmentation of the Ego and Subjectivation

The first precondition for the emergence of a subject is that the actor concerned must destroy the cultural and philosophical ensembles that force an identity upon him. The idea of a free and responsible individual is a defence against all systems of power and against the unacceptable idea that the markets will automatically choose the most rational solutions. After a century of horrors during which death triumphed, I would like to hear the voice of the subject speaking out against the markets, the ideologies or domination and the calls for war. I would like to reveal the face of the *subject* within us, who has been hidden behind so many masks, but in whose name we have the right and the duty to demand freedom.

I am trying to find the demand for subjectivation everywhere, even in religion. It is that demand that inspires all social movements, it demands that the dignity of every human being be respected. The research I carried out on Muslim women showed me that they were not experiencing a 'clash of civilizations' but both an attachment to and a rejection of French society, Muslim society and their own families. Received wisdom notwithstanding, these women are trying to come to terms with a very complex situation and to enhance their own ability to manage the tensions inherent in it. This presupposes that their own personalities are 'weakened' and that their components are broken down. Highly integrated personalities are more likely to become involved in a clash with adversaries than to find a way to survive cultural changes that are always difficult to come to terms with.

The most interesting notion in post-modern thought is that of the *divided self*. Julia Kristeva elaborates it in very sophisticated terms by speaking of the stranger within us. It is when we feel that we are 'strangers to ourselves' that we can accept and recognize strangers. While this line of thought seems to go against what I call the subject, it is in fact its essential complement. What we have to get as far away as possible from is the idea that there is some correspondence between the actor and the system. All varieties of communitarianism and the notion of a society that is based upon a so-called 'general will' are the most dangerous expressions of that idea.

The more we dissociate the things that social thought tried, sometimes in a spirit of revolutionary democracy, to associate, the more the ego breaks up because it loses its principle of unity, namely the society in which it was inscribed. This provides tolerance with its most solid basis, both as a theory (*tolerance*) and as a practice (*toleration*).

As the subject frees itself from both the ego and the self, it becomes a protest against the social order and the increasingly repressive techniques it uses to subordinate individuals to its interests and its power. This fragmentation indicates that an *ego* is plunging deeper and deeper into the unconscious, and being differentiated both from a *self* that is multiple, as are its loyalties and solidarities, and from the *subject*, as defined here and my other works. And this is the opposite of an aggressive voluntarism.

Extreme multi-culturalism, in contrast, destroys all principles of unity, and can only lead to segregation or open conflict.

This approach seems far removed from the analyses one might expect from a sociologist, given that sociologists are supposed to explain behaviours in terms of the actor's position within society. That is why its importance has to be underlined: it exemplifies the reversal of attitude and approach that sociology must effect and perfect if it wishes to demonstrate its creativity. Sociology will receive no attention if it simply goes on with its traditional research into the social determinants of behaviours, as though 'society' and 'the social' were still well-preserved monuments. It was always necessary to construct the notions of modernity, the subject, rights and now otherness; it is essential to do so now that so-called classical sociology's frame of reference has collapsed. How can we use the social order and symbolic systems to explain behaviours, when no one belongs to a social order or a symbolic system?

The other solution, or the 'clash of civilizations', is becoming more and more threatening. Religious and political clashes are gaining ground, and the number of terrorist attacks is increasing, as is the number of people who are attracted to suicidal behaviours. We are coming closer and closer to a clash between the resistance of populations that are defined by their religion or nationality, and those that are defined by their support for the actions of foreign powers, and those actions are primarily political and military. Both tendencies are gaining ground. We can say that, for some Westerners, Islam represents an outside world that is both inferior and aggressive, but we can also say quite the opposite: Islam has entered Europe because large numbers of Muslims have settled here, and because religious rituals such as Ramadan are being observed more and more frequently. We have to do more to understand this penetration, on the one hand because a European Islam can play a dynamic and modernizing role within the Islamic world as a whole, and on the other and more importantly, because the Muslim presence is once more revealing the religious foundations of European societies where faith, defined as an institutional practice, is on the decline and where Catholics, in particular, no longer submit to their church's positions when it comes to abortion, artificial insemination, stem cell research or euthanasia. The dangerous image that identifies modernity with the decline of religion notwithstanding, we are seeing, not the growing strength of religious institutions, which are in decline everywhere, but a growing demand for spirituality and answers to questions about the meaning of life. The community of the faithful is also growing.

It is not unrealistic to imagine that Muslims should be seen as the other. As the gulf between Muslim and non-Muslim populations grows wider, recognizing the otherness of that population is a matter of urgency, not because a clash is inevitable, but because, on the contrary, we have to recognize the effort the other is making to become a subject. Those efforts are anything but xenophobic. The task is all the more essential, now that inter-communal and even inter-group hostility is growing. The age of social reforms and revolutions is over, as is the reign of the affluent society. Class struggles have been replaced by the appearance of communities or defensive cultural fronts, and they are so many obstacles to subjectivation.

The Subject Embodied in the Other

The weakness of the points of view that clash so constantly in debates about the contemporary world stems from their insistence on defining social actors in terms of the groups to which they belong. Social and cultural movements have to be defined as constructing a new figure of the subject, and this brings about a radical transformation within contemporary culture. The only way to overcome the hostilities and the many misunderstandings that have occurred in this domain is to stop defining social beings in terms of their social situation, or in other words in terms of their relations with other individuals and other groups. The notion of a personal subject would have no content and no importance if transcending conflicts did not help us discover the universalism of the subject, whatever form he takes as he produces himself in new social and historical conditions.

We now have to introduce two more elements into our analysis.

The first, and by far the more important, is that the individual cannot aspire to being a subject unless the *other* is recognized as a subject: it is because I recognize the other as a subject that I can recognize myself as a subject. Recognizing the other as a subject means recognizing that everyone has a universal capacity for becoming a subject. This central argument allows us to escape the isolation the theme of the subject might trap us into by making communication with other social actors impossible. The hopeful formula 'Let us live together with our differences' meets with a positive response as soon as we move to a higher level of analysis: the subject's recognition of other subjects. This is the theme of *recognition*, which Charles Taylor has analysed in such depth.

The problem is that this relationship seems to become more difficult as it becomes more inter-personal. That is obvious from the everpresent and attractive image of two or more merging into one. It is this that gives friendship its strength and elevates love, meaning the fusion of desires or the creation of a couple, above everything else. The most elevated forms of thought make the same point when they see loving as the most noble of all human behaviours: love is a movement that draws us to others. But that movement loses its power when it does not lead to the formation of a completely new mixed being that is gradually defined by rules, limitations, hopes and disappointments. That is what we are always being told by those who observe how love grows cold, and how a couple can be reduced to nothing more than a family cell confronted with economic, social or cultural problems that have nothing to do with the formation of desire, love and couples. This quest for the one that emerges from the fusion of two or more is creative only within a truly religious vision, as it implies the existence of a subject who exists apart from individuals and transcends individuals. A loving relationship with the other can only exist through a shared love of God, even though love does seem to dwell in the hearts of those who use it as a sort of religious metaphor. That is why I go back to the disturbing but spontaneous comments of the women I listened to: the self-to-self relationship must transcend the relationship with the other. It is the self-to-selfrelationship that makes the encounter with the other such a powerful experience: the other is both our double and a combination of a 'me' [*moi*] and an 'I' [*je*]. The 'thou' is the best way of creating this selfto-self presence, and the highest form of interpersonal relationship is one that allows both the subject and the other to become selfreflexive; everyone knows that this would be impossible unless the other did the same.

The ultimate moment in a relationship of otherness is the death of the other. We do not experience our own death, but that statement is meaningless as it is part of the definition of death. We do, on the other hand, experience the death of others, sometimes with an intensity that makes us feel that we ourselves are dying. The stronger the relationship with the other, and the more we recognize the other, the greater the intensity of our experience of the breakdown of communications, the estrangement and suffering. Parents experience the death of a child as their own death and, comforting words about the period of mourning that allows them to return to the bosom of the community notwithstanding, the experience of the other's death does not go away. But while it is painful, it also urges us to love at the level of relationships between subjects, and not as corks that bob on waves of desires, stimuli and manipulations. The presence within us of the death of the other is the most visible presence of the element within us that resists the external determinisms that make us lose our heads.

Women: Dependency, Equality or Domination?

No one would deny that the theme of the situation of women is now of central importance to sociological analysis. The way we judge a country is now influenced by the situation of its workers less than by the position of women, the rights they are granted or the violence they suffer. The men and women who are most distrustful of systematic Islamophobia are, quite rightly, the first to protest when a woman in an Islamic country is stoned or killed by her father for having had pre-marital sex. The law and customs conspire to put woman in a position of inferiority and dependency. In a country such as France women finally won political rights after a long struggle that began much later than in Great Britain. The feminist movement then began to organize around the theme of a woman's right to have control over her own body. The Neuwirth law on contraception, the Veil law on abortion, Simone de Beauvoir's *The Second Sex*, which is feminism's founding text, and, more recently, the writings of Luce Irigaray and the initiatives of Antoinette Fouque have made France a source of new ideas and orientations. But within the space of a few decades, the situation changed, and feminism has become less active. This is mainly because a new feminism has emerged, especially in the United States, where themes relating to women are now central to moral philosophy and political philosophy. It is also because, in France as in many other countries, the feminism that won so many victories now devotes much of its energy to denouncing the inequalities suffered by women, and especially the violence they are forced to endure. The battered wife is now the dominant image of women. This is part of a general trend to replace the theme of conflict with that of the *victim*.

It is not difficult to conclude that the great feminist struggle for equality is perfectly justified and must be supported and broadened wherever women are still subject to taboos and inequalities. There is an intolerable contradiction between their position and the principle that individual rights are universal. It is clear that liberation struggles must be prioritized, especially when they come up against religious taboos. The priority that is increasingly given to these problems thanks to a brave campaign to defend women from violence, and especially sexual violence, and discrimination in Asia, Africa and many other parts of the world – including Western Europe, where excision is practised in secret – does not justify the silence that still surrounds some very important issues. Firstly, must the struggle against inequality lead to the disappearance of differences, to a unisex society, as Simone de Beauvoir wished, or even to a deconstruction of gender categories? The most innovative and sophisticated ideas in this domain have come from a second-generation American feminism.

According to the *queer* movement [English in the original], we have to get beyond the quest for equality; we have to explode the male–female duality, which it regards as a product of male domination, recognize that sexuality takes many different forms, and therefore encourage a plurality of the sexual behaviours on the part of every individual or group. That position seems to some people to be extreme, but it becomes very important when it attacks the notion of gender, which is social and not biological. There are other lessons to be learned from the queer movement, which had had the effect of divorcing sexuality from the image society forces upon women. The critique of notions that are all too easily accepted encourages research – which encounters a lot of resistance – into multi-sexuality and everything else that blurs the distinction between men and women by according a special importance to the transsexuals who are treated with such contempt and brutality in most countries.

Unlike this extreme movement, other feminisms are reintroducing the theme of *difference*, but they are radicalizing it. Major figures, such as Antoinette Fouque in France, have always maintained that there really are two sexes, and that the differences between them are both biological and psychological. But they also stress the inadequacy of the notion of difference, and the need to go beyond it by creating a culture that must be defined as female but which has new meanings for men as well as women. All the activities that have been organized around women's liberation in various countries are successful examples of women's efforts, as both women and feminists, to transform the culture of all human beings. I am attempting to follow their lead by getting away from the idea of equalization and by viewing women, especially in the post-feminist era, as the creators of a new culture. Only a long-term historical analysis can allow us to apprehend that idea. Because they have been deprived not only of power but also, at a deeper level, of subjectivity, women are the harbingers of a new culture that is no longer oriented towards the conquest of the outside world, but towards their self-production as women, especially through their sexuality, which now plays the central role that belonged to labour in industrial society. Even though we know that men still have most of the money, power, guns and technologies, women have already taken *speech* away from men, who have been silenced because they have been slower than women to discover the meaning of the new culture that is spreading throughout society.

If we listen to all kinds of women, whatever their age or social background, it is striking to see that they are thinking positively: women want to define themselves as women, and to invent femininity as a way of life, as a culture that must revitalize culture as a whole. The women I listened to behaved as social actresses, and as women who were redefining their life-goals and everyone's life-goals. We quickly discover that far from merely defending their own interests, or in other words looking for safeguards against the attacks and inequalities of which they are the victims, they are very much aware that they are creating a new culture. But the world that begins to emerge as we try to listen to women is always concealed by purely critical discourses. Attacks on the men who dominate women end up as an embarrassed way of not listening to what women are actually saying. One would like to see a reconciliation between the very rich and daring analyses made by American women and what I am evoking here, namely women's invention of a new culture in which men can, without encountering any particular resistance, also share.

No matter which of these paths we take, we have already come a long way from the routine approach that restricts studies and observations of women to their sufferings, rather as though suffering was the only thing they could do.

I am very much afraid that the reasons that are blocking the development of women's studies are the same reasons that are preventing us from thinking in new ways about education, from understanding the problems of the *banlieues* and from finding a type of multi-culturalism that can reconcile the recognition of differences with the preservation of the universalist principles without which no communication is possible. We encounter the same obstacles in all the great domains of social life. The main objection is that we must at all cost avoid talk of actors and actresses, their subjectivity and their projects, as the only sociological explanation is to look for the social determinants of personal and collective behaviours. The weaknesses of studies of social policies therefore seem to be a direct effect of the fear of innovation that characterized social thought in the second half of the twentieth century. Although some studies in philosophy enjoyed a dazzling success, we witnessed the continued existence of a school of thought that was intent upon destroying its own object, namely social behaviours that imply value-judgements, and in some ways it acquired even greater influence than before. In the same way, terrorist attacks have sought to replace the mobilization of mass movements and their hopes. But nothing could do more to reveal the mistakes that have been made and how to avoid going on making them than studies of women. The contrast between what is said about women and what women actually say is striking, and clearly shows the unreality of the pseudo-theories that shaped the dominant interpretive discourse whose errors and disastrous effects I continue to denounce.

Others. Difference

I introduced the key idea of the *end of the social* in order to identify a new principle of legitimacy that can be used to evaluate behaviours: the subject. All my subsequent efforts have been devoted to the same goal. The subject cannot be identified with any institution, value or social norm. The subject is, on the contrary, a counter-project and constantly fights the domination of external forces, be they economic, political or even biological. That is why the subject's position in society has yet to be determined, as it is defined solely by the attempt to escape the social system. It is, however, impossible to leave things at that, even though escaping the mechanisms of integration and socialization is still the primary task, as that alone allows us to perceive the subject.

The subject can only come into being by learning to recognize others and their differences. But not just any differences. The space that is allotted to difference is restricted by two boundaries. We must, on the one hand, refuse to identify modernity with the dominant societies, as that leads to an absolute rejection of all difference, which is immediately likened to inferiority. On the other hand, we must also reject the cultural 'differentialism' that eliminates all those elements that cultures and societies have in common. Differentialism makes it impossible for cultures and societies to communicate with one another, and that leaves only one way out: war.

I can only add that it is difficult to explain the full range of the differences we encounter. At one extreme, we accept that people dress differently and, more generally, have different ways of life, but only when we are talking about minorities. Our reaction is always one of tolerance. We can be very tolerant when there are a lot of minorities, as in Central Europe or the United States, to take only those familiar examples, but we find that our tolerance quickly runs out when the minority in question rebels, as minorities have done in Northern Ireland, the Basque Country and the Former Yugoslavia. It is difficult to talk about difference and equality when conflicts are exacerbated. It is also difficult when references to a dominant religion trap other religions into a situation of dependency. That Christianity played a central role in shaping European cultures is undeniable, but it is also true to say that the idea of the nation or republic, which was so important, derives from a different tradition. France experienced tensions between the supporters of Christianity and the supporters of the Enlightenment that came close to civil war. In many cases, talk of difference is so inadequate that no one uses the word. Relations between majorities and minorities are obviously unstable, and we have seen at close quarters minorities that begin by demanding safeguards sometimes go on to opt for secession. Because historical situations are so diverse, we have become suspicious of weak and over-general definitions of difference.

We therefore have to conclude that a society can always tolerate a certain diversity, especially if tolerance helps to ward off the threat of open conflict. We therefore arrive at a more positive notion, and one that is more helpful when it comes to analysing contemporary societies: the idea of *cultural rights* that must be defined and safeguarded as vigorously as the social rights over which so many battles have been fought since the nineteenth century. Cultural rights can be granted, but only if one elementary principle is accepted: the majority must recognize the rights of the minority, provided that the minority recognizes the rights of the majority. If that condition is not met, there is an open crisis and the only solution is rupture, independence and secession.

Preconditions for Inter-Cultural Communications

The communications field can be said to be open when the populations that meet within it refer in similar fashion to modernity, as I have defined it, or in other words with reference to principles that transcend all social and cultural loyalties, namely: scientific and technical reason and respect for individual rights that are regarded as universal. In the absence of that shared reference to the two basic components of modernity, the only outcome is war, separation or even self-segregation. The 'clash of civilizations' occurs when these shared references do not exist and when the encounter is one between cultures, civilizations or societies that regard themselves, and want to be regarded, as integrated, multi-dimensional wholes. It is these multi-dimensional wholes, which are often referred to as 'civilizations', that encourage war, whereas differences between economic, cultural and religious systems – assuming that they have been separated – are not obstacles to communication, even when communications are not perfect and when both partners agree not to interfere in domains that are considered to be either not worth discussing or not open to discussion, especially when a society's assertion of its specificity has a religious basis. This brings us to a preliminary conclusion: an individual's or group's identification with a social, cultural and political ensemble that is defined in holistic terms is an insurmountable obstacle to inter-cultural communications Given that the rejection of this 'holistic' analysis is a basic feature of modernity, any society that recognizes itself as modern must seek and find other ways of communicating with others. Societies that are trapped into a total identity cannot respect that point of view and reject it all the more vehemently in that other societies see it as a form of domination and colonization. That criticism is readily accepted by many the 'liberals' who admit that their country dominated, colonized and exploited large parts of the world. Brave as it may be, that response does not, on the other hand, prevent us from accepting that only one type of society, which we can describe as modern, permits communications with other societies. It is the recognition of universalism, reason and human rights that allows different societies to communicate with one another and to determine what they have in common and what makes them different.

There are therefore only two answers: a clash of civilizations that leads to mutual destruction, or a recognition, on the part of certain societies, of the universalist nature of modernity and, therefore, of the profound differences between those societies that accept universalism and those that do not. The universalism of modern societies is not a fact of nature; it is a historical reality, and therefore has its limitations. That, however, does not justify the claim that there is no difference between universalist societies, and societies that assert their radical difference and absolute superiority.

There can be no going back to the kind of cultural relativism that puts all 'civilizations' on the same level and defines each of them solely in terms of the differences between them and other societies. A visitor to a museum may well be content to contemplate the diversity between the gods and cosmogonies of different civilizations; social anthropology was a product of a rejection of the ethnocentrism of the dominant countries and of a desire to uncover the mistakes of an evolutionism that assumed that all civilizations were progressing in the same direction. But no approach is acceptable unless it recognizes the specific nature of modern societies which, unlike others, assert both their particular characteristics and their acceptance of the universalist principles that constitute modernity.

While there can be no going back on this conclusion, it does leave a number of important points unresolved and therefore requires further clarification.

The first mistake we have to avoid is identifying this idea with the belief in progress which, after having flourished in the eighteenth century and even the nineteenth, was gradually rejected in view of the twentieth century's numerous political disasters and wars. The emergence of Nazism in the heart of Europe destroyed for ever any possibility of believing in progress. That disenchantment does not, however, justify the objection that modern thought has disastrous consequences because it often reduces reason to its instrumental uses, turns into an instrument of power and a weapon, and thus becomes a major obstacle to inter-cultural communications and the recognition of the rights of individuals. Reason cannot be blamed for that: the guilty party is the communitarian 'holism' that defines nations, in particular, as specific cultural ensembles, and thus completely abandons universalism and undermines the spirit of modernity. Nationalism, in all its forms and in all societies, destroys the universalism of modernity, even when it claims to be extolling progress and freedom.

The lesson that is to be learned from this cultural and political pessimism is that rationalism is not *necessarily* associated with liberal individualism. It is not difficult to accept that similar criticisms can be made of individualism. The discourse of individual freedom can be no more than a crude capitalist ideology if it simply concludes that the most active and gifted individuals must be given a free rein, as that can lead to biological or historical explanations that are as far removed from the idea of modernity as nationalism.

Then what is that links the two components of modernity and thus creates the preconditions for communications between both individuals and civilizations? The answer, which I have already outlined, has to be repeated here: it is *the desire to extract universalist elements from every particular situation* that constitutes and sustains modernity. It is the desire to extract rationality from a diversity of customs and prejudices, and to recognize that all human beings are equal, irrespective of the colour of their skin, their level of income and the form of their laws. To put it in still more concrete terms, there must be a very close link between reason and humanism. That link allows us to identify a level of human existence and activity that clearly transcends both social loyalties and individual self-interest. Modernity is more than a juxtaposition of rationalism and individualism; it exists only when it creates a figure of the *subject* that unites the two. There can be no modernity without an awareness of modernity and the need for it, without universalist convictions or without faith in reason. The most important point is the assertion that modernity cannot exist without reference to the subject, who cannot exist in the absence of modernity, or in other words a combination of reason and individual rights. I am not trying to determine which is the cause and which is the effect; it is both necessary and sufficient to add the idea of the subject to the other two components of modernity: without this triad, inter-cultural communications are impossible.

Do we have to introduce another cause for concern? Do we have to take the view that this combination was a unique, or almost unique, historical event, and that our preoccupation with the problems of difference and multi-culturalism has a lot to do with the decline of our historical model and with the twentieth-century rise of totalitar-ian regimes, world wars and systematic massacres? Isn't this Western creation about to be buried, if not by a sandstorm, at least by the might of states that are identified with whole societies or of the weapons that are concentrated in nuclear arsenals or in the hands of terrorist groups? We can also put forward other hypotheses, such as that of a society that is increasingly invaded by consumerism, money or even a hedonism that knows no bounds. A rather different line of reasoning reminds us that, between 2001 and 2003, the United States ceased to be a scientific and democratic society, and became a reli-gious and bellicose society. Many people also take the view that Western modernity is bound up with slavery, class domination, the subordination of women and colonial conquests.

We have already encountered and endorsed this type of argument. European *modernization* was indeed based upon the dominance of a ruling class or elite. But the idea of *modernity* was a reaction against that modernization. And nor was modernity a product of the enlight-ened despotism that was adopted by a few European monarchs in a bid to catch up with Great Britain, Holland and France. The idea of modernity and the capacity for knowledge and communication that it generated were not products of war and conquest, or of the French and Spanish absolutisms to which so many free thinkers fell victim. And it was not, finally, religious powers that facilitated the triumph of reason and freedoms. Like many other peoples, the French have long had some clear ideas about this, and their concept of *laïcité* deserves to be better understood.

We were always going to reach conclusions that are far removed from both an apolitical rationalism and the peremptory assertions of multi-culturalisms that go so far as to celebrate the creation of communities. The goal of respect for *cultural rights* is as important, and as difficult to attain, as that of respect for social rights, and the only way to achieve that lofty goal is to establish closer and closer links between social and cultural rights and 'human', and especially political, rights, which are more general. There can be no more powerful call for tolerance and freedom, than the recourse to the idea of the *subject*, and it can ward off the threats of both communitarianism and truly religious movements. It gives the goal of living together with our differences a strong, positive meaning. The recognition of the rights of citizens made it possible to accept the construction of social and cultural rights. But those rights were, or will be, obtained only after long collective struggles. Only then will we really able to live together with our differences.

Today's Europe is far removed from the abstractly optimistic images that dominated its ideology until the catastrophes of the twentieth century occurred. There is a definite tendency to reject immigrants, and especially illegal immigrants. Undocumented immigrants are hunted down by the police. Those immigrants who are rejected retreat into their community of origin, which leads to a failure to integrate that alienates minorities still further from the majority. A few attempts are being made to understand Islam better, but Islamism and its extreme forms are more visible than Islam, in the sense of a religious culture.

At this point in our analysis, we can draw three conclusions: (a) radical multi-culturalism is full of dangers rather than attractive images, and communitarianism is leading to more and more serious conflicts; (b) the attempt to establish inter-cultural communications is highly positive in a world where cultural hybridity is on the rise, and where cultural worlds are no longer divorced from one another in any material sense; (c) we have to face up to the growing threat of confrontation by relying on the strongest possible interpretation of the theme of difference, but that theme is not enough to overcome indifference, segregation and hatred. We therefore have to appeal to the notion of recognizing the other as a subject.

The Social Bond

Theoretical and practical attempts to breathe new life into direct, face-to-face relations are always haunted by the fear that they will lapse into a celebration of homogeneous groups. There is also a growing trend, stemming sometimes from a very open interpretation of the theme of rational choice, and sometimes bound up with the process of interaction and, above all, the recognition of the other, to construct hierarchies, to establish distances and to place controls on the community. This has almost always been of interest to the writers and philosophers the French describe as *moralistes* because they are concerned with studying behaviours that reconcile the defence of private interests with an involvement in a certain order of social life.

Those who remind us that human life always involves us in interactions in the hope of winning a 'good reputation' or a lot of 'social capital', to borrow an expression from Putman, are right to think that they are taking us back to the basic problems of social psychology and sociology. That way of working is so far removed from what I am trying to do here that the two styles cannot but come into conflict. It is, on the other hand, impossible to defend such different orientations by asserting that they belong to the same corpus of knowledge and analyses. Sociology would not really exist if its various elements did not form a system and were not interdependent. The defining feature of a theory is its ability to demonstrate that interdependence.

It seems to me that sociology can only mean the study of societies that have a great capacity for acting upon themselves, and which therefore experience rapid change. Studies of interaction, recognition and reputation appear to me to come within the remit of the 'moral and political sciences', which reached their apotheosis during the relatively stable period ultra-hierarchical societies lived through before the upheavals caused by citizen revolutions and the birth of industrial society in Great Britain. Sociology is the study of the societies we describe, rather too vaguely, as 'modern', while work on interaction and the recognition of the other seems to me to pertain to the study of earlier societies in which creative and transformative action was less powerful. They were in fact orderly societies rather than societies in motion.

Fear of communitarian aggression is now so great that there is a growing desire to create 'social bonds'. The themes of loneliness and of the loss of social relations are everywhere. During the heat wave of 2003, large numbers of ill and old people were left abandoned, either in hospitals or in their homes; the result was a pathetic image of the breakdown of the social bond in France. The absence of social relations looks like the most serious pathology affecting our collective life. It was never a matter of choice for the inhabitants of São Paulo or London in the sense that it was for the anchorites of Mount Athos.

There are two main ways of reconstructing the social bond.

The *first* consists in establishing small local communities whose members derive self-esteem from the positive image others have of them. It is easier to reconstruct the social bond where, as in Italy, old networks of family or religious sociability still exist. The appeal to build such communities, which has nothing to do with any aggressive communitarian spirit, is being heard everywhere, but it is always defensive, and that restricts its import. A more disturbing variation on the same process is the establishment of groups, 'tribes' and communities defined by some common attribute, such as belonging to a shared space or a minority. Such groups can only come into being in opposition to other groups or communities, especially if they are defined in ethnic, linguistic or religious terms.

The *other* way of creating social bonds has a greater import. I refer to voluntary organizations. Many such organizations have humanitarian goals, but other, and more militant, groups then take up the defence of victims, denounce the guilty and resist the pressures that are brought to bear on them. In many countries, voluntary organizations have become more powerful than the trade unions and political parties. The actions of the social and political networks they create, and which, to recycle an old notion, we call *civil society,* have often featured in the present analysis. Voluntary organizations often do win important concessions from the authorities, but they do more to enhance the ability of individuals and groups to impose their interest on institutions, than to strengthen society. Weak and non-representative as they may be, they demonstrate an ability to change the rules and even the law. Indeed such changes now look like the ultimate victory for opinion-based campaigns that can mobilize strong feelings such as anger, hope or solidarity.

It is very superficial to attack the conception of the subject, and especially of the self-to-self relationship, that I am outlining by always appealing to the 'obvious' demands of social life and by recalling that human beings are social animals. The very nature of the subject, the way in which the subject so often comes into conflict with the rules of social life and protests against the unleashing of Eros and Thanatos, establish new and powerful non-traditional bonds. What is more important, they are voluntary and not transmitted.

The subject is not some contemplative figure or lone protestor that exists outside society. The self-to-self relationship must govern social loyalties. Involvement in collective actions is negative when their goals are not far removed from the logic of interest. I am not suggesting that we contrast loneliness with the crowd, be it the loneliness that is forced upon the excluded or the loneliness that is sought by the dandy. In all these cases, we have to ask whether the self-to-self relationship is present or absent in the way we judge a situation, from both inside and outside, and thus turn it into an issue.

Perhaps the accumulation of wealth and privileges does prevent us from effecting the reversal of perspective that creates a space for the emergence of the subject; affluence immobilizes those who both possess it and are possessed by it. But it is even easier to recognize that extreme deprivation destroys all capacity for action, forces its victims to identify with the images others have of them, takes away all initiative and denies them the ability to have any tight control over their own activities. Between these two extremes, to different degrees and in different ways, the actor is defined both by the situation within which he acts, its rules and its limitations, and by a relationship with himself that can range from a quasi-identification with some duty, to an almost complete rejection of an environment that is experienced as a denial of justice and a form of dependency.

All organizations strive to impose social bonds, representations and norms. All voluntary organizations, from churches and parties to groups of friends and neighbours, appeal to values that challenge norms and to desires that transgress the law. The subject comes into being only in those spaces where the opposing pressures are not contradictory, and where, on the contrary, it is possible to reconcile them without destroying either our sense of belonging or our self-to-self relationship. Which brings us back to the ever-present theme of the double and doubling.

If politics means the management of a community for which integration and flexibility are essential goals, the reference to the subject has nothing to do with politics. If politics serves the interest of rulers, either at home or abroad, it destroys subjectivation. But no living democracy reduces politics to management or domination. The defining feature of all democracies is that political power and institutions are explicitly made subordinate to principles that always prioritize what they call freedom, justice or solidarity. These are the attributes of what I call the subject in order to avoid the confusion inherent in the words 'man' and 'humanism'.

It is wrong to see such declarations as expressions of the old-fashioned idealism that often masks less noble intentions. In this domain, as in others, we have to reject the idea that modern societies are advancing further and further towards an instrumental rationalism, pragmatism, and trying to strike an unstable balance between conflicting pressure groups. The great political projects that are usually born of social movements degenerate into politicking, not to mention the transition from mysticism to politics that Peguy mentions in his well-known but over-ambitious comment on the Dreyfus Affair. But new projects can always be formulated and will always stimulate emotions that spread increasingly quickly in societies in which ever-denser communications networks transmit news so rapidly. Now that the political projects born of the labour movement, and which resulted in great social security and wealth-redistribution systems, have been exhausted, we can sense the forming of new sensibilities. They are ecological and humanitarian, defend minorities or nations, and they are already being voiced in political terms.

The Subject and the World Situation

This chapter has attempted to build some new bridges between the idea of the subject and several of sociology's main themes. I would now like to go further, and to extend these analyses which, in principle, only concern countries that have already entered into the new paradigm in which cultural categories take the central role that was once played by socio-economic categories in industrial society. I want to demonstrate that the same transformation can be observed all over the world, outside the most 'advanced' countries, and among all those populations that are already steeped in mass culture. That extension of the argument may, however, prove to be fragile and even shocking, as it might suggest that the whole world has no option but to follow in the footsteps of the so-called advanced countries. I have always rejected that evolutionism by contrasting the unity of *modernity* with the *plurality* of the roads to modernization. It becomes more absurd by the day to think that China or India will follow in the footsteps of the United States or Japan, or even post-Gorbachev Russia.

We have to recall that we are not dealing here with changes that have taken place in society or culture in general, as I did in *A New Paradigm*, but only with categories that analyse local actions, or in other words actions defined by social relations. That is the least demanding definition one could possibly give of the social sciences. My explorations are also limited by something else: can those who are steeped in mass culture and not sustained by some collective political or economic project, and who are therefore primarily consumers, in both rich and poor countries, behave as subjects? Can they accept my definition of modernity, and can they elaborate a representation of the other that escapes the friend/enemy dichotomy that most inhabitants of this planet accept so readily? Surely we have to accept that the greater part of humanity is hemmed in between powers, religions and forms of consumerism that effectively communicate only through the medium of war. To raise a related but more disturbing question, are we justified in thinking that the inhabitants of the most powerful developing countries, such as China, will act on the basis of the categories that I have identified? Can we support the seemingly paradoxical idea that women are the harbingers of a new culture, when they are subject to such violent domination and repression in so many regions of the world, and even within the territorial limits of countries where they are supposed to have been 'liberated'?

That the answer to these questions cannot be 'yes' borders on the self-evident. One would have to have a real taste for paradoxes to defend theses that so obviously go against what we can see with our own eyes. But it would be just as arbitrary to say that the answer is, *a priori*, 'no'. Perhaps other roads will open up if we introduce other elements that allow us to reconcile the unity and diversity of experience and representations in the contemporary world.

At the *global* level, we have got over the illusion of a generalized 'civility'. Competition between political powers supported by armies and the mass mobilization of populations has destroyed those elements of modernity that once characterized international life, just as wars between European states once destroyed them. And we do have to speak of war rather than of evolution. It is not Chinese civilization that is getting ready for a confrontation with Christian or Western civilization. It is an authoritarian regime backed by powerful armed forces and enjoying unprecedented economic expansion that is threatening a world system which is still dominated by the United States.

When the state is not strong enough, religion tries to play the principal role. It is, however, almost impossible for it to do so because religion has little capacity for political and military mobilization, even in the Islamic world, which is in fact very diverse and devoid of all unity. That is why Islamist intervention forces rely less and less upon tradition-bound populations, and more and more upon groups that belong to the world they are fighting by provoking serious attacks so as to reassert that arms are more powerful than the great powers' other resources.

Other countries, in contrast, are trying to imitate the Western model, and especially the rules of the market economy.

Other parts of the world are sinking into poverty, corruption, interethnic conflict and pandemics. But once again, we have to look upwards, and at leaders and their policies, and not downwards or at cultures and social organizations, to find an explanation for their successes and failures. That is why the United States has, thanks to

President Bush's decision to define it as a party of Good that is fighting a party of Evil, played down the economic and technological superiority that gave it its lead over Europe and even Japan.

Mass culture and Western – and especially American – technological culture have certainly penetrated almost everywhere, thanks largely to the Internet. But on the world scale, the main confrontations take the form of armed clashes, while ideologies are losing their strength, and while struggles between nations that follow the old European model trigger only local conflicts that do nothing to disturb the dominant powers.

Leaving behind the lofty spheres where cultures, societies and wars are shaped, it is more important – and more difficult – to go down to the level of the most day-to-day and personal lived experiences. We do not devote enough effort to thinking about the basis of our conception of Good and Evil, about the needs education has to fulfil, or even about the emergence and spread of new forms of sexuality. That is not because such themes are too far removed from us or have nothing to do with our behaviours, but because we do not yet know how to transform our desires into new issues and new commitments. It is so much easier to say 'that's life'. Love it or loathe it, that is the life we lead, and the life we make films, novels and songs about.

And yet we cannot accept this life as it is!

The Other and the Proletarian

We have to go all the way and accept that recognition of the other has eradicated the belief, which is so deeply rooted in the minds of so many people, that the strongest social relationship is that between the haves and the have-nots, or between proletarians and capitalists. There is no denying that these representations had an enormous influence and seemed, at times, to encompass all others: women were defined as men's proletarians, and the colonized as the victims of capitalist firms. We spoke, and still speak, of social capital or cultural capital, without, in most cases, making it clear if this was a metaphor, or an application of an economic term to non-economic domains. This 'classic' idea, which is so commonly identified with the Left or even, as the words of the *Internationale* explicitly state, revolutionary movements, is disappearing behind that of the other *qua* other in all kinds of situations. Which means that we have to accept that we need to reconcile different elements, and not elements that are defined by their different positions on the same ladder. We are not, for example, just talking about economics; in many cases we have to reconcile an economic component and a cultural/political component. This was the case in Mandela's South Africa, which eliminated apartheid but was careful not to follow the example of certain neighbouring cultures by driving out the creators of wealth. The case of New Caledonia is an extreme example. Tjibaou's campaign to have the rights of the Kanaks recognized led the French government to break with the policies that resulted in the brutal repression at Ouvéa, and, thanks to Michel Rocard, Christian Blanc and others, to recognize the existence of the Kanak nation and to grant it protection by placing restrictions on immigration, which was threatening to reduce the relative size of New Caledonia's Kanak population.

If we look at its central aspects, the wage-earners' struggle against their employers was in fact also predicated upon a recognition of the other. When it was at its apotheosis, working-class consciousness was not specifically economic; it was a demand for capital to recognize labour as a basic component in production. Representing the working class as a proletariat destroyed the meaning of working-class consciousness, and reduced it to agitation on the part of the have-nots or even, and why not?, the marginal. And that left the task of shaping a 'working-class consciousness' to the political and intellectual bourgeoisie.

I have stressed that the recognition that the adversaries involved are concerned with the same issues is an important element in social movements, but that certainly does not imply that there is no element of conflict. As the ecologists emphasize so strongly, domination is the enemy of diversity. The same comment might be applied to South Africa, where the abolition of apartheid has had almost no effect on social inequalities. The problem is that those who define the dominated as proletarians or even slaves cannot see any solution but revolution, which takes all power away from the dominated who are trying to liberate themselves by defining themselves in terms of their lack of knowledge, resources or education. That leaves the way clear for a new ruling elite. The opposite point of view may lead to the organization of political conflict, or in other words to a permanent combination of antagonisms and reforms.

The difference between contradiction and difference is so great that it is in the least modernized countries that the theme of difference emerges. Hence the exceptional influence of the work of Claude Lévi-Strauss, who has never stopped criticizing and dismissing the pretensions to universality of political models derived from Western capitalism by both liberals and Marxists.

The need to change our representations and attitudes is greater than ever, now that the dominated are so quickly being reduced to the status of victims, as though there could be no more national liberation movements, no more feminist campaigns and no more campaigns to defend all kinds of minorities. In that sense, there is a danger that many social and political conceptions will have only negative effects, and may even become obstacles that stop us seeing that social reality is being transformed more and more rapidly.

Ideas and Everyday Life

I cannot end this book without addressing the usual objection that there is an unbridgeable gulf between a theoretical analysis based upon concepts such as the subject, modernity and social movements, and the realities we see all around us. Political regimes seem quite alien to that intellectual world. In our daily lives, we experience constraints and set ourselves goals that are defined at the level of the individual rather than that of the subject. Individuals are demanding, that is, the right to be individuals. This complicated – but essential – formulation cannot easily account for the most widespread expectations and frustrations.

Depressing as it may be, we can easily accept this initially, as it does not represent a direct threat to my analysis. It is much more difficult to justify these analyses when we enter the domain of everyday life, self-interest, desire, happiness, competition and death. Popular culture and even great novels and plays are often built around very direct lived experiences that are very close to our day-to-day lives. No one would dare, on pain of being ridiculed, to claim that our only goal, at every moment in our lives, is to be recognized as subjects, to respect the principles of modernity or to fight anything that undermines subjectivity. And yet the answer to the question that has been asked does lie in that seemingly negative observation. Perhaps the question just seems to be insoluble.

Modernity, the subject and social movements are constructs based on a wide variety of direct lived experiences. If we divorce lived experience from constructs, and theory from practice, both everyday life and intellectual systems become quite meaningless. We then find ourselves in the equivalent to those societies that are furthest removed from democracy: societies based on order or caste societies based upon criteria other than non-social criteria. Our ideas, and therefore our cultural orientations, are, in contrast, effective only if the link between individual lived experience and general analytic principles is kept intact. It is in everyday life that we are beginning to see the recognition of the other as subject or, on the contrary, the desire to destroy the subject. It is in everyday life that the methods of production or forms of consumption that shape modes of subjectivation are implemented.

All that we can do at the most macro-social level is shore up our defences against war. At the most day-to-day level, which is directly experienced by everyone, the most important and most positive action we can undertake is to prevent the erection of barricades between what some call 'high' and 'low', or high culture and popular culture, or between the most elementary expressions of sexuality and the use of sexuality to construct more noble models of the personality. Simple as it may be, that conclusion must govern our practices, because there is always a temptation to divorce and separate levels of relations, thought and consumption, and therefore to contrast creative and rational elites with lazy and aggressive peoples. The most common and necessary expression of what we call democracy is the rejection of all these barriers and all these categories, which only serve to block the communications without which all modes of constructing the subject and modernity are impossible. Great cuisines can be developed by using only local produce such as bread, wine, rice and maize, and some people will taste them only in what are believed to be their most refined forms. For similar reasons, it is dangerous to try to ban what are indeed the crudest forms of sexuality in the name of its most refined forms. Nothing could be more foolish than trying to contrast carnal desire with the love of pure ideas.

This conclusion, which is very close to common sense, must help us to discover the most general meaning of this work of reflection and analysis. It is important to recognize the central role of notions such as the subject and modernity because they replace all the notions that erect insurmountable barriers between this world and the next, purgatory and paradise, capitalist exploitation and communist solidarity, between every form of aristocracy and elite and all plebeian forms of experience and ideas. As the meta-social guarantors of human experience disappear, human experience has to become self-reliant. Taking more responsibility for itself, it must be more ambitious about the great task of finding the meaning of its existence and its action within itself.

It is pointless to go on recalling expressions that are now so widespread. Our problem is finding the connection between what I call the subject and what we can now call 'life', or the great principles of *lived experience*, and above all finding the links between the desire for money, success, sex, protection and conquest, and the far-off and grandiose world into which I have settled almost naturally because my task is to discover and explore it.

To put it in even more commonplace terms, we live in a world that was created by mass culture, and in which creative mass action based upon the self-to-self relationship appears to have been swept away by the discourses of professors, preachers and politicians. But do we have to accept the usual answer and concede that those who are crushed by illness, unemployment, separation and death will always be with us, and that they coexist alongside those who draw up projects, write books and life stories, and those who trying to make money by running factories or by making people laugh or cry? All these lived experiences are so simple and so commonplace that there is, it would seem, nothing more to be said about them. They are primal, full of emotion, feeling and self-interest. They affect all of us, permeate our daily lives, and appear to be impervious to criticisms that apply only to those who have a little free time, enough to live on without having to worry about tomorrow, who are educated and who have a taste for intellectual work.

That is the answer I reject.

Where is the subject in the life of the individual? Where is the subject in your life, or mine? Here is a different answer: the evil that threatens us and that is devouring us consists in divorcing ideas from everyday life, free speech from obligations, pressures and drives from their sublimation into ideals, and the 'people' from the 'elites'. When these breaks are sharp, when the divorce is complete and when the barricades are high, everything, from great ideas to the simplest of lives, is debased. The world of the subject, modernity, social movements and recognition of the other is real and liberating only when it is constantly present in every aspect of the lives of all. That is the most profound meaning of democracy, which cannot be reduced to institutional mechanisms because those mechanisms cannot ensure that the heights and depths of society, in all their forms, are in constant communication with one another.

Sociologists have no difficulty in accepting this suggestion: they are accustomed to detecting in the most direct experiences the presence of the most complex constructs and the most highly charged issues. They chose their profession because they always wanted to relate field work to theoretical constructs.

The last thing we should do is to contrast the heaven of the subject with the hell of money, power or jealousy. Everything is mixed up with everything else, and we are involved in the work of reflection and interpretation that orient our lives and our institutions. Those who talk most are not the ones who are best able to reconcile their lives with their thoughts, lived experiences with constructs, or practice with theory. As I complete this book and emerge from the confinement to which it condemned me, I feel a need to open the window, turn on the television and go on to the Internet so that my thoughts can be carried away by the movement of the lives of each and every one of us, and be as present in everyday life as love is present in desire.

Point of Arrival

Where Have We Got To?

What route did we travel to get to this point? And why have I said on more than one occasion that our long and difficult journey has taken us from one country to another?

It is now possible to sum up in a few words the concrete meaning of what I am calling the 'end of the social', as there is a danger that such a weighty expression might obscure its decisive importance for every aspect of our lives, from the most material to the most political or ideological. Social life was torn apart by the triumph of capitalism, which has to be defined in terms of the breakdown or undermining of all forms of control over the economy. It destroyed those forms of thought and social organization that were based upon social relations, which were at once hierarchical and conflicted. When we speak of differences or inter-cultural relations, we are no longer living in the world in which we spoke of the division of labour or the class struggle. That does not mean that those categories or problems no longer exist, but it does mean that they no longer have the structuring role they had for so long, just as relations of kinship or neighbourliness no longer have the same meaning in some of those societies that are furthest removed from us.

It seems, however, appropriate to look at two more specific applications of this mutation, which goes far beyond what I have called a change of *paradigm*.

The *first* is that the categories of collective action no longer have any meaning. This is especially true of political parties and ideologies, as Jean-François Lyotard so clearly demonstrated with his celebrated remarks about the end of grand narratives. We no longer know, in any material sense, what we mean when we talk about socialism or, more simply, trade unionism. What we call the crisis in representation actually means both that political institutions are no longer representative, and that social interests have lost their capacity for being represented. Talk of the party of the working class or of the bourgeoisie means as much to us as talk of the conflict between the Armagnacs and the Burgundians meant in the France of Joan of Arc. But we cannot therefore conclude that there are no more conflicts, inequalities or domination in the changeable, multi-dimensional and 'liquid' society in which we live. Such a conclusion would not just be arbitrary; it is refuted day-by-day as we read the newspapers, watch television or surf the net.

The *second* application of this notion is the breakdown of the link between signs that proliferate, and referents that sink into obscurity and silence. Words, images and signs that 'mean nothing', and which refer to nothing but themselves, are much more attractive because using them means that we do not have to ask ourselves about what meaning might be lent them. The rapid spread of pornography will accelerate still further. Although our desire to do away with taboos is still very real, appeals to 'natural' morality and good morals, 'sexual liberation' no longer liberate anything. It liberates neither desire, love nor the attractions of the forbidden. We can apply the same reading to most of the messages we get from the media, and we have gradually come to understand what Jean Baudrillard predicted so long ago: a sign can be nothing more than a simulacrum that refers to no actor and no intention. Some messages appear to come from a virtual reality which may well deserve to be described as virtual but which is no longer a reality.

Trapped between these empty categories and these signs that refer only to themselves, we are disappearing and are lost in two senses. We can no longer define ourselves or situate ourselves with reference to the two worlds in which we move. We are absent from them, and we are strangers to ourselves.

That is why I wish to underline the extent of the change of perspective I am proposing. Like the idea of the state before it, the idea of society was central to social thought. It has to be cast down from its throne, even though we must not forget that it did advance our understanding of social life. Social situations and actions can no longer be judged in terms of their social functionality, and must be judged in terms of what they do to promote the freedom and creativity of the social subject. Institutions are no longer the architecture of the state; they must protect individuals and communities to the extent that they are subject, and when they threaten them, they must be checked and reformed.

A social life that is organized around individual or collective personal subjects may lose its way or even fall into deadly traps. It may confer illegitimate privileges on those who are most 'conscious' – who are often the most privileged – while the exiles, the dominated and the poor may become trapped into situations from which they cannot escape and which prevent them from developing any reflexivity. That threat can easily be warded off, as the experience of sociologists demonstrates that those who are dominated are often acutely aware of what they are suffering, while the rich and the powerful often identify with their social roles, their interests and their ideologies to such a degree that they are incapable of becoming aware of how others see them or even of how they see themselves.

The study of social movements all over the world demonstrates that it is easier to detect the subject among the poor than among the rich. The approach I have adopted, and therefore the methods I am using, must displace the analysis away from the higher social milieus in which it has so often been trapped, and towards the lived experience of those who live in hope and anger rather than by the wealth and power that may blind them.

We now inevitably come back to the prelude to this book, and to our critique of the long decay of a social thought that referred so often to the labour movement and Marxism, even though they were no longer alive and had drifted away. The influence of the thoughts and ideologies that hampered the development of the social sciences for several decades has increased because many of their adherents have a taste for power and for strategies of intimidation. Twenty years after the Berlin Wall came down, almost thirty years after Solidarity in Poland, and forty years after 1968 in Paris and New York and the Prague Spring, we are at last recovering from their deadly influence. It is about time . . .

The loss of meaning, not to mention our loss of awareness and the definite feeling that we live in a world that is controlled from outside and that no longer feels any need to look at its own internal process of decision-making, are everywhere, but they are not to be confused with nihilism, which is the antithesis of a voluntaristic assertiveness. Nihilism is a desire to destroy an order that has become unacceptable, as the Russian nihilists of the pre-revolutionary period wished to do.

I cannot leave things at that. The time for a purely negative critique of post-modernists ideas is gone, and we can see new actors and new issues emerging day-by-day. We are hearing new protests, and new and optimistic visions are being developed. We feel that a new type of social life is gradually being organized before our very eyes. How are we to define the new vision that is striving to replace the old, which is now either in ruins or reduced to tired formulae?

The most important point is that it is becoming apparent that there definitely are actors in this world of artifice, ideologies and objects, but they are no longer truly *social* actors. They can act because they have a greater capacity for resistance and freedom. These actors are no longer defined by their relationship with the norms and mechanisms of social life, but by the way they construct themselves. We are already committed to this work of liberation, and especially to the liberation of our bodies, our sexuality and everything we have been given in order to produce ourselves. We are mobilizing our past, and sometimes even our future, around our present.

The most visible and urgent task is the reconstruction and reinterpretation of the body. The women's movement, especially in its most recent phase, which began after the great legal and ideological victories of the previous generation, is now constructed around the central role that women accord to sexuality in their construction of themselves.

What is true at the individual level is also true at the collective level. We are no longer content with the global/local couple, which guarantees the absolute dominance of the impersonal forces of global systems. We want to find complex beings who combine the present with the past, and their heritage with new interventions. It is possible that these identities, which are usually national, will lead to the worst of catastrophes, including civil wars and genocide, but they may also result in the creation of actors who can create spaces for the initiatives and the freedom that will prevent a destructive clash between the global and the local. Not every element in the formation of this new collective consciousness – which may be national or even communitarian – is negative, provided that they do not become fascinated with their quest for identity. The quest for identity inevitably leads to racism, the rejection of differences and the quest for purity and homogeneity that now poses the most serious threat to the world.

Do I have to say yet again that the central role I am according to the personal subject, and therefore a certain conception of individualism, does not mean that we have to abandon collective actions and pursue an egotistic individual self-interest that is blind to both profound distress and great hopes? It is not worth refuting such accusations, which indicate such a crude lack of understanding that they can only be based upon bad faith or some malevolent intent.

What this book is in fact saying is that we have gone from living in a society that thought of itself in economic terms to living in one that thinks of itself in cultural terms, just as, before we lived in a society that thought of itself in economic terms, we lived in a different society where the most important categories were political. To put it in more colourful terms, we might say that we moved from the world of Rousseau and the French Revolution to the world of Marx and industrial society, and then entered the world of Freud and a society based upon communications, consumption and mass culture.

Why this series of images, and why place them in that order? We are usually suspicious of evolutionists, and never fail to ask them 'and then what?' What will happen after the final phase of evolution that you are describing? The answer is that the factor that drives evolution is the level of a society's ability to act upon itself. Jean Fourastié demonstrated in spectacular fashion that, after a long period of stagnation, there was a rapid increase in productivity per hour of labour in the twentieth century. I describe a society's capacity for creating, and therefore transforming, itself as its *historicity*. And a society's historicity increases as that capacity increases at every level of social life. I might add that society's capacity for self-transformation does not increase continuously. Roads and waterways had to be built, the weight of coins had to be standardized and banditry had to be repressed before the circulation of commodities could facilitate the specialization and extension of markets. That was a favourite topic for jurists and economists at the time when Europe witnessed the establishment of city-states and nation states that could protect trade. It was the political authorities that took responsibility for roads and currencies, prices, taxes and tolls.

A profound change occurred when not only trade but production were transformed both by the introduction of calculations into productive operations, and by the creation of increasingly powerful machines for both civilian and military purposes. In the mid-nineteenth century, a nation's modernity began to be measured in terms of its horse-power capacity. It was not until much more recently that the industrial mode of production was extended to all domains: consumption, communications and mass culture.

We do not necessarily find the same schema everywhere. An economy that is completely dominated by the state blocks the road that leads to the highest stage of modernity. But the phases I describe are found, in rather different forms, in most parts of the world.

To put it in different terms, this means that our analytic categories come closer and closer to our behavioural categories. In a political world, the origins of norms and institution lies in the power of a sovereign, which might be a prince, a city or a Pope. In industrial society, the individual is no longer simply a political figure, a citizen or the subject of a king, but a *worker* whose activity helps to construct a society based upon production, investment and innovation.

In a world that is defined in cultural terms, we are even more fully committed not only to our work, but also to our emotions, our values, and so on. The rights we demand and for which we fight were once *political* rights and then *social* rights that were extended to become *cultural* rights. Does this mean that we identify more and more completely with every aspect of our lives, with our interests, desires and opinions? I hope I have convinced the reader that those of us who live in a world that has, for better and for worse, a fantastic capacity for self-transformation, have moved away from the gods, who were not part of the human world, and from everything that deified history or reason. Increasingly, we come face-to-face both with ourselves and the double who transforms experiential beings into *de jure* beings. And as the reader must be aware by now, I call that being the *subject*. I do not believe in the power of the gods. I do not believe in the power of government apparatuses. And I do not believe that our minds and bodies are being manipulated by messages emanating from the machines that broadcast the news. We increasingly appeal to ourselves as the guiding principle in our lives.

I should add that our contemporary civilization is not the final stage of evolution. That is all the more obvious in that every year brings new innovations, and in that it is quite possible that even the biological identities of human beings may change. Some people dream that we will, in some virtual space, be able to create a being who will be our double, though they tend to speak of avatars, with which every creator, meaning every one of us, will be able to identify. Some find that vision exciting, but others find it disturbing. It would, I think, be wise to have active doubts about the possible effects of inventions that might eventually replace the real with simulacra, to use Jean Baudrillard's well-chosen expression. The positive side to the current wave of interest in avatars, or the *double mind* [English in the original], is that it helps us to understand how self-creation and self-control have become the main goal for all of us, whereas the triumphant images of industrial society are going into decline as they come under attack from the ecologists.

The will to be ourselves and to create and defend ourselves as individuals, with all our roots and branches, and in the full awareness that we are a tree, is now the only principle that can guide our behaviours and allow us to tell good from evil. While some are so foolish as to resist this individualism, which is, they claim, subordinating us

to the market and to every form of power, and others are so reactionary as to believe that defending the social rights we began to win over
one hundred years ago and the cultural rights we are now fighting
for, traps us into classes or communities – which would only be true
if we renounced our human rights – I feel so far removed from their
discourses that I have finally abandoned the attempt to convince
them. I want nothing more to do with artificial choices between two
equally unacceptable positions. The subject I am describing is both
universalist in the sense that the human rights of all must be defended
on all fronts, and *individualist* because it is a form of self-assertion,
the discovery that the self is a double, and the right to be a human
being with rights and the capacity to say 'I'. Such is the main demand
of all human beings today. The individual 'I' should not be the servant
of society; society and its institutions must be the servants of self-
creating individuals.

Many ask only to be integrated into the globalized economy and
to find a place within it; a second category is trying to protect social
groups which, not being defined by their economic function, are being
transformed into communities. Modernity defined us in terms of what
we 'did'; many people are now once more defining themselves in
terms of what they 'are', and not in terms of their jobs. They define
themselves with reference to a language, a nation, a religion or, at a
more restricted level, a neighbourhood, gang, kinship group or area.
They are all becoming dangerously trapped into their ideas, loyalties
or origins. There is, however, also a third category that no longer
wants to conquer the world, and which knows that reason and calculations often lead to violence and arbitrariness. Its members try to
find reasons for acting within themselves. They do not want to define
themselves in terms of their roots or jobs; they are asserting themselves and their universal rights.

The philosophy of the Enlightenment demonstrated to us that
individuals were the possessors of rights who could resist all powers,
including the power of tradition and the powers of conquest; individuals are no longer prepared to be defined in abstract terms. While
they do assert their political rights, the important point is that they
are also asserting their social and cultural rights. They are denouncing
violence and injustice, the accumulation of wealth and the exclusion
of the poor. They are defending all their rights, but they have not
abandoned the universalist definition of those rights and are, in other
words, refusing to give ground to communitarianism. I have until now
been talking mainly about this third group, as its response seems to
be the only creative response. This is because it is neither the growth
of production nor the rise in consumption that has really left its mark

on the twentieth century; it was above all the century of totalitarian-isms and bellicose or racist communitarianisms. That century will for ever be marked by death certificates and not by the achievements of life. How, in the face of such blinding evidence, can we not try to support the demands of individuals who are asking to be recognized as *de jure* subjects?

The demand 'to be myself' is being heard everywhere, and it is pregnant with hopes and demands, but we already know when an individual tries to look at himself, it is not himself that he discovers in the mirror; it is the subject, or his double as an individual. He sees not his conscience, but his demand to have a meaning for himself, and therefore his demand to have rights.

The subject confers upon the individual the right to be a social actor; the subject ensures that the individual's life is not broken down into a series of sequences that have no coherence in either existential or intellectual terms. Neither God nor master. No economic, political or religious God or master: we are no one's slaves. We are in control of our own lives, even if we can experience failure.

No material, political or social change is as important as the change that inverted our relationship with ourselves and turned it upside down. It has brought the individual face-to-face with the subject, the 'me' [*moi*] and the 'I' [*je*], and needs face-to-face with rights.

Throughout this book, and no matter whether I was speaking of education, religion or social movement, I have gradually been working towards this central conclusion. We find ourselves in a strange situa-tion: in a contemporary society in which the death of the subject has been announced so often, the subject is appearing in full daylight. The subject is aware that he can depend upon no one but himself and is asserting everywhere that he has rights that must apply to all and that define good and evil for all.

How did things stand in the past, when the situation was very dif-ferent? We had a strong sense of belonging to more than one com-munity. The world of objects was much more stable than it is today, and the maps were covered in *terrae incognitae*. We now have to complete this return to the past. At a time when so many voices are announcing the return of religion, we cannot retreat from our central assertion: the face-to-face encounter between the individual and the subject who confers rights upon the individual is taking place in con-temporary society. That society has acted upon itself more firmly and more completely than any other, and has therefore attained the highest level of historicity. When, in contrast, society has little ability to act upon itself, it becomes more difficult to find the subject, as he no longer appears in a social guise. In those conditions, subjectivation cannot be a purely internal process; it takes on forms that are further and further removed from human actors, and always imagines that human life has a non-human basis, and especially a religious basis. Until very recently, we put the subject at the centre of the idea of progress in the way that a cosmonaut sits in the cabin of his rocket. A few centuries earlier, we identified the subject with the order that fought all forms of disorder, violence and war. If we go back still further, we find the image of a divine creator and, even further away from us, gods whose existence was entwined with society's foundation myth.

As we travelled this road, which disappears into the night of time, we have the impression that we are entering the world of the subject that many people already evoke, even though it has been invaded by capitalist rationality and the explosion of desires and pleasures. Yet norms and values make a mockery of that impression. The states and tribes that defended, and still defend, social norms were certainly not defending the universalism of individual rights. The power of the sacred dominated the indirect and hidden figure of the subject, but was not actually a figure of the subject. The function of the sacred is to control the subject or the figure that conceals the subject.

Precisely because they are external to the individual, all figures of the subject have two aspects: the *universalist* subject establishes, but the world of the *sacred* conceals the presence of the subject. Religious systems and the systems that came after them, such as the 'religions' of the state or progress, held the subject prisoner and confined within a social space that they controlled.

In the industrial society we have just left behind, society occupied the position that once belonged to the gods, and then the state. The personal subject is now evicting it. Sociology identified with an idea that had long been accepted, taught in schools and defended before the courts: that which is socially functional and furthers the interests of the social system is good, and that which undermines the workings of society, its need for integration, and its ability to manage the requisite changes, is evil.

The statue of society has, however, been toppled by the triumph of capitalism, or in other words a globalization that has done away with every form of social and political control that might limit the freedom of our economic leaders. Companies are more powerful than the market; emigration causes populations to mingle and is erasing territorial boundaries; mass urbanization means that cities are no longer autonomous institutions.

We are uncertain about the role of education and we have stopped believing that there are such things as 'normal' families and families that are not normal. By dissociating a globalized economy from agencies that can no longer control it, the collapse of the social and its institutions clears the way for either the arbitrary power of the market and weapons or a fearful and troubled withdrawal into couples, tribes, identities and communities. The purpose of this book is both to drive back those enemies and to protect the space where the subject created by individuals and groups can emerge.

The history of ideas, of political life or of economic activity are simply not the threads that weave the fabric of a general history. We lost all faith in the various forms of the philosophy of history long ago. Yet these domains of reality and thought are not entirely independent of one another. For the post-war generation, political life was dominated by state interventionism; the end of that period saw the triumph of a capitalism that cannot be contained by any frontiers. We now have a growing feeling that we are looking for what once seemed to be an impossible combination of an open economy and the state interventions that are required to guarantee greater security and freedom for all. In France, as in other countries, the 'Left' is now exhausted because it identified itself with the direct management of society by the state. Now that Soviet power has collapsed and that the Communist parties have gone, it is both possible and necessary to pay more attention to the voices that were drowned out by the cries of the liberals and their adversaries.

To restrict the argument to France, the version of history that has almost become a vulgate must be completely rejected. A whole generation was shaped by Marxism but remained hostile to a Communist Party that had become sclerotic and dependent; most intellectuals are now said to be rallying to an increasingly conservative neo-liberalism, and some of them have reportedly joined the ranks of the American-style 'neo-cons'. This apologetic reading of the dominant interpretive discourse of the 1960s and 1970s confuses the work of great minds like Michel Foucault or Jacques Derrida with a 'spirit of the times' that refuses to see and understand the new problems facing the world: the recognition of differences, the treatment of minorities, ecological thought and feminism. The troupe of semi-intellectuals that has taken over most of the places where intellectual judgements are shaped is trying to convince us that, after the creative phase of recent decades, thought is losing both its intellectual qualities and its desire for social and cultural liberation. I am defending precisely the opposite position; for too long, we were held prisoner by a school of thought that might be described as posthumous because it referred to social forces and ideas that lost their driving force long ago. The world was already full of problems that intellectuals in many countries were trying to resolve, but the French intellectual milieu refused to introduce those problems into its programme of studies or to debate their themes. I certainly do not feel that we are living in the shadow of a great generation that has passed away; there is an urgent need to brush aside its over-possessive heirs, to look reality in the face, to examine the questions it raises, and to look at the new ways of thinking that are required if we are to answer them.

It is difficult to change a vision of reality, or to stop believing that the rationalization of production leads to progress. We need an interpretation of our acts that, while it does not reintroduce any semblance of a religious approach to the world, is certainly not satisfied with the image of social actors who are determined from outside by the impersonal logics of markets, technological change and wars, without any hope of escape or liberation. If the word 'humanism' had not been worn out by being used in so many different or even contradictory ways, it might provide the best description of my approach.

An Invitation

Everything I have said in this book and everything that I am summing up in these pages may seem to some to be bound up with what is already a distant past and to be too far removed from the modern world for them to feel concerned about both these polemics and these new ideas. If we had to turn the page and to stop using the words, ideas and debates to which I have referred so often, I would be the first to rejoice, so convinced am I that our representations are often archaic. But that is far from being the case. Political debates, the school curriculum and trade-union demonstrations are still full to overflowing with the ideas and words I have been fighting. Conversely, our society, and especially its representations, has until now taken almost no account of the transformations brought about by the women's movement or by the growing number of migrations. We are just beginning to think about the great question of how we can live together with our differences; ten years ago, that theme was already the title of one of my books. The invasive presence of ideas from the past is precisely what I am fighting; hence the need to go beyond a critique of the past, and to create new representations of both individual and collective life.

This book looks to the future, and beyond polemics directed at a past that is still with us. But the idea of the subject will not become an official ideology. The great difference between the idea of the subject and that of a state society or even God is that it is not central to a general vision of social life. The idea of the subject has no ambition to take the central role we accorded for so long and so foolishly to the state or the class struggle, nor to go back to the advent of Christianity. 'The subject' is not another name for the spirit of the times, post-industrial society or mass culture. It is never in the hands of a prince or party. Those who act and speak as such forceful subjects are neither saints nor wise men; they are often unknown or recognized as the 'righteous', in the sense that Israel awards that distinction to those who saved Jews from the persecution of the Nazis. The most eminent figure of the subject, at least in the countries of the democratic West, is the collective figure of women. That statement may seem excessive to the majority, but I constantly reaffirm it.

The best sociologists devote themselves to analysing the collapse of societies, the decay of institutions and the increase in violence, racism and job insecurity. When we were working on a book together, Farhad Khosrokhavar criticized me for not doing enough to recognize the presence of evil, and that is a serious criticism, coming from a man who was brought up in the culture of Shi'ism. I admit that I am attracted to images of good and have an aversion for images of evil. I do not approve of those who speak of workers, women and minorities only as victims. I always look for the actor behind the victim, and I know that the actor can be found everywhere, and has even been discovered in the Ringelbaum papers that were found in the Warsaw Ghetto. But it is now necessary, just it was necessary in the past, to look day-by-day for, and find new forms of evil, crisis and decay.

The general meaning of these conclusions may emerge more clearly if I briefly recall the differences between them and various highly influential currents within contemporary thought.

The appeal to the subject, human rights and freedom of consciousness, and especially the idea that human beings can create their collective and personal destiny, are far removed from Marxism, whose main strength lies in its ability to explain social facts in terms of the state of an economic situation. The ideas expressed here are still further removed from the neo-liberalism that is suspicious of all voluntaristic interventionism because it puts its faith in the market's adaptive mechanisms. It should also be clear that I have nothing in common with any 'sociologism' that evaluates behaviours in terms of their effects on the social system. Turning, finally, to the other conceptions I reject, without condemning them, mention must be made of inter-actionism, which, in my view, does not accord enough importance to the processes whereby categories are constituted or the problems that govern the lives of communities.

Having rejected all those theories, the most limpid response is, perhaps to go back to the notions I have evoked most often: the subject, modernity and social movements. They broadly outline the space in which I see social action taking place. But why should according these notions a central importance prevent us from looking for new definitions of good and evil that can explain many of the behaviours and struggles that are transforming institutions? I believe that the task to which I am devoting myself is all the more useful in that many people still refuse to recognize the intellectual, social and cultural mutations that have transformed the last half-century and insist on looking at the present through the spectacles they were given when they were young, at school, in political parties, in the press or in novels. Thirty years ago, talk of the subject was scandalous; the word has now recovered its place in the vocabulary of the social science. In future, and as soon as possible, it will be used in every domain of knowledge about the human science of organized social action, and to introduce institutional reforms.

It would not be difficult to indicate what effect my way of thinking might have on political action, and on social policies in particular. At the time of writing, the political crisis is too acute for me to do that, but I would like to make up for that reticence by expressing the strong conviction that this approach is both necessary and relatively easy because the representations that still influence political life have become unreadable, given that they still belong, directly or indirectly, to industrial society. 'Civil society', which has been so profoundly transformed and revitalized by today's voluntary organizations, is more willing to accept new representations of society and social action. The task of revitalizing political life on the basis of a new representation of society should therefore appeal to the many women and men who are resolved to reform public life, collective action and democracy.

We have come a long way since the days when social thought set itself the task of detecting false choices and false consciousnesses and revealing the effects of the determinisms to which social action was subject! That programme was developed by a sociology that was more concerned with promoting an ideology than with shedding light on real behaviours, which are never reducible to such operations. The goal of this book is therefore not to move from one conception to another, or from one ideology to another as though everything to do with the social sciences was a matter of opinion. At no point has my attempt to define certain notions distracted me from looking for tools that will help us to understand observable behaviours. As for my final attempt to define a field of analysis that has rarely been identified, and still more rarely seriously cultivated, it has very quickly revealed the problems we have to face up to more and more often in our individual and collective lives. This conclusion should therefore be seen as an introduction to sociology that has at last been reconstructed.

Is it still possible to reconstruct sociology? Can we still try to understand a society, an era or a milieu? We have been living in a divided world since the end of the post-war period and, perhaps, especially since 1968: on the one hand, quantitative data, much of it economic and, increasingly, international; on the other, ideas, interpretations and the polemics intellectuals, and not just French intellectuals, use to construct images of the present that are usually so tragic that they seem to come from the beyond, as though all their discourses began: 'It is already too late.' Reality is no longer real; policies have no effect. Does history itself exist outside the images that are shown by CNN and the other televisions channels? They keep telling us that anything that does not look completely objective can only be completely subjective. Political philosophers occupy all the zones that have not been colonized by the economists.

This is the self-image of an era that no longer believes it can understand itself, or in other words understand actors and investigate the meaning of collective or individual choices. The self-image this era has bequeathed us is one of an empty theatre that is illuminated by lighting effects and shaken by subterranean rumblings.

Social thought has ebbed so rapidly, and the messages we receive from the places it once occupied have become so indecipherable, that I have to ask myself, now that this book has been written, if it isn't the book that is unreal, if it isn't an unidentified flying object in the intellectual space the telescopes are scanning.

The situation of social thought, as I have just described it, is not as depressing, and therefore unacceptable, as many people think. I wanted to reject both established conceptions of social life and the excommunications pronounced by those who aspire to living outside society, history and above all sociology – a word which they may already find incomprehensible. I wanted to outline a way of thinking about social life ... but a *different* way of thinking about it. I wanted to bring social actors back on stage and make them talk, laugh and cry, even though they had been driven away. I wanted to build the set around the figure of the *subject*, which has miraculously escaped all the firing squads. It would be dangerous for us not to think for ourselves, both individually and collectively, and to abandon that essential task because we are afraid, or afraid of upsetting someone. Yes, we can and must think, but we must think differently.

At the Gates of Hell

Before I leave the reader, I must remind him or her that when I decided to write this book, I took a big risk by deciding to study the decay of one type of society, and especially its replacement by another. I have argued against a discourse that spoke in the name of the great intellectual revolutions of the nineteenth century, but which was no more than a caricature of those great schools of thought. Having made a critique of a social thought that had become dissociated from any historical practice, it was therefore devoted to the positive task of reconstructing a social thought that was associated with the upheavals and creations of the twentieth century. That was and is my choice: to construct a new way of thinking about social facts and, therefore, of analysing human behaviours.

What seems to be missing here is the din of wars, totalitarian societies, widespread violence, and institutions that are breaking up like icebergs in a warm spring, The content and tone of this book are so removed from the conflicts, the acts of terrorism and the genocides, but also the liberation of the life drives and death drives that were until recently contained by laws, churches, families and schools, that it may give the impression that it was written in an enclave of peace that has, for the time being, been spared the conflicts and destruction that affect the rest of the world. I do not reject that image completely, but it does have to be given a different form. This is not a nice book written for middle-class retirees in one of the richest countries in the Western world. Let us use the terms that have to be used: we are standing before the gates of hell, and we have to identify and arm the only force that can resist the depersonalization of the world, and the reign of power, speculation, arbitrariness and hatred. That force cannot be an army, and still less can it be the intervention of some higher power that can stop the fighting. Violence secretes its own weapons, and the archangels have become corrupt. The story of how divine grace can save humanity from original sin has become incomprehensible to most of us, me included.

The only power that can resist the violence that has been unleashed, and the only metal that can stand such high temperatures is the will of every individual and every group to promote universal rights, both for themselves and for everyone else. Some reject the universal nature of the appeal to human rights, which define, they claim, only those highly industrialized societies that have a great capacity for reflexivity and self-transformation. I believe that, on the contrary, any individual can possess universal rights that apply both to him and others and can be aware that we are all free and possess universal human rights. Such an individual is the only thing that can stand up to the hurricanes that are destroying everything in their path. That is what the Frankfurt School began to understand when it denounced the reduction of reason to its instrumental role during the years that announced the triumph of Nazism in Germany. To extend that critical thinking, I am saying that the defence of human rights cannot be divorced from the defence of what Weber called 'material' reason.

Neither political conflicts nor social struggles are the central issues today; as the apocalypse reaches its climax, the central issue is the advent of a human subject who is aware of his universal rights. The birth is not taking place in Bethlehem or on some campus in California, but wherever human beings are capable of asserting themselves in terms that are neither social nor territorial, but which refer to them as free subjects.

Such a declaration immediately meets with a chorus of objections. How can we talk about universalism *and* modernity? If universalism is a defining feature of the modern enlightenment, surely it is a historical phenomenon that cannot always be found everywhere. Why accord such general importance to the idea of a subject who belongs only to a Western civilization that is, at least in part, dominated by the spirit of the Enlightenment?

I will not surrender an inch of ground to these objections, powerful as they may be, because, as I have already said, the reason why the unveiled subject has been so late in appearing is that veiled figures of the subject – be they religious or the products of philosophies of history – are everywhere, or at least wherever society has embraced and is enhancing its ability to transform itself. It is not the pure, unveiled form of the subject that is universal; it is the individual's construction of a double that confers rights upon him or her and at the same time rescues the individual from the power of the guardians of the sacred.

The construction to which I have devoted so much work has nothing to do with the construction of a country house or a sports stadium. I am concerned with a consciousness that fights non-consciousness, with a universal that fights omnipotence, and with rights that outweigh duties. The apparent weakness of the subject conceals a strength that is greater than that of the death rays let fly by invaders from another planet. The reader's struggle is not over. What I am offering here is not a bed of rest, but a suit of armour that will help him or her to slay dragons.

Post-Scriptum: In a Few Words

(1) This, then, is our point of arrival: the social, which was central to our vision and which claimed with such arrogance to be independent and explicable only in its own terms, has been cast down from its throne. I am actually saying that social action is always subordinate to the least social thing about it: the human *subject* who creates rights that are superior to social laws.

We used to speak of the social functions of the individual; we now have to talk about how the function of the social organization promotes or threatens the freedom of the subject, Above all, we must fight, at the level of the state, economic power and the power of the media, and their attempts to grow stronger. We must subordinate them to the higher goals of defending human beings against the degradation of their environment, and the breakdown of humanity into 'races', nations, genders and age-cohorts, with some being defined as being superior to others. Schools must no longer be seen as agencies for socialization, but as milieus for subjectivation and the construction of the subject.

We all find it difficult to extract ourselves from a mode of thought that is dominated by social categories. And yet, casting off that worn, torn garment is a matter of urgency, just as it was necessary, when we began to industrialize, to get away from a political discourse about social facts, and to adopt the social discourse we now have to abandon because it is holding us prisoner in its decayed forms, and blocking creative action and authentic behaviours.

I am neither proposing nor announcing the advent of a new social thought. That thought is already present in our representations and our behaviours. What some people still invoke as though it were still alive and even 'progressive' belongs in a museum. We have to pay enough attention to what we do and what we think to be able to explain the categories and arguments that already organize our lives. We began to change the way we think fifty years ago, and it is high time we realized it.

(2) We already define and evaluate our situations and behaviours in terms of our desire to be recognized as *de jure* subjects who are present in all human beings and who therefore transcend powers and the norms they impose. The theme of 'human rights', which was so important at the time of the French Revolution and the American War of Independence, was marginalized during an industrial period that accorded a dominant importance to 'functionalist' analysis and

evaluation, or in other words to the positive or negative effects behaviours had on society, its integration or its crises. That theme has now returned. It is stronger than ever, and goes far beyond humanitarian action. We speak, in particular, of cultural rights, meaning that everyone has the right to partake of the main aspects of their own culture: language, religion, food, forms of sexual relations and of family organization. Those rights are no longer restricted by the preconditions for participation in larger or different ensembles. For centuries, we spoke of the general interest, the common good and of our duties toward society, and it was inculcated into us that we become individuals who are capable of being free by becoming citizens who do their duty, respect the authorities established by the law, and contribute to the common good. We are now committed only to ourselves, but as beings with universal rights that apply to all human beings. Talk of dignity has become more important than references to duties or functions.

This is not a desocialization that leads to 'every man for himself' and therefore to the survival of the fittest, but an increasingly demanding universalism which is openly opposed to the inequality and domination political and administrative forces imposed in the name of the market. It is in that very demanding sense that we can speak of a transition from a social era to an ethical era.

(3) I have defined and adopted this approach throughout my work. I have demonstrated that the struggles of the working class could not, as was almost always claimed, be explained in terms of the crises of capitalism, and had to be explained in terms of a working-class autonomy that was coming under threat from management methods that corresponded to an attempt to maximize profits. The emergent labour movement was quickly absorbed into the overtly political programmes of Socialist, Communist, Social-Democratic and other parties, but what I called *working-class consciousness* was never completely dissolved into political action. Throughout my life, I have studied *social movements* that are not reducible to the political and ideological formulae that claim to speak in their name. In addition to studies of the 'new social movements' that emerged after 1968, I have demonstrated the meaning of great historical events such as Solidarity in Poland, Popular Unity in Chile and the Zapatista movement in Mexico after 1990.

(4) Over this long period, the demands and expectations of social actors almost everywhere in the world became further and further removed from the ideologies and from parties inscribed in types of

society. The fall of the Berlin Wall and of the Soviet Empire were the key moments in that shift. But the social-democratic regimes were also undermined by transformations that they were increasingly unable to understand or manage.

France is an extreme case. François Mitterrand could only evict the Communist Party from its dominant position by adopting the radical spirit and language of its programme. Once it had got rid of Michel Rocard, who was a great reformer, the new Socialist Party then become trapped into a blind managerialism that did little but mediate in struggles between different factions inside the party. It then suffered a major defeat in 2002, and then another with the rejection of the proposed European Constitution, which was in fact a rejection of a social-democratic model that had been implemented in most of Europe. This nonsense led to another defeat in 2007, and its scale was revealed by the number of voters who abandoned the Socialist Party in the first round and supported François Bayrou's convincing attempt to build a party of the centre. The whole vocabulary of politics is now meaningless. As the great movements that promoted freedom and political, social and rights, look more and more like a thing of the past, social thought becomes subdivided into two currents of equally polluted water. One endorsed the intellectuals' submission to political powers that were usually totalitarian. The other, which was less powerful but had a wider influence and which is still there, wanted to create the image of a world in which there were no actors, no beliefs and no hopes. It was a dead world, and only the words of philosophers gave it any semblance of life.

I much prefer those who still refer to industrial society, its social movements and its ideals, which still mean a lot to me because they give us an example of a coherent historical ensemble. In a world of accelerated change, where globalization is being forced upon us by new information technologies and networks of financial and economic exchange, I am astonished at how many people believe that nothing can change. If we fail to understand new forms of production, we reduce social life to the reproduction of order and domination. The heirs to the old revolutionary movements are more clear-sighted when they try to understand the reasons why the alterglobalists clashed with the police in Seattle or Genoa. They can at least see that the world is in motion, even if they do not really know how to analyse the reasons and the direction in which it is moving.

The self-destruction of the militant Left leaves us with very limited theories that that look into how the social bonds that have been destroyed by accelerated changes in every domain can be reconstructed. It is much more important to define the demands and protests that are shaping new actors, new social issues and, in a word, a new figure of the subject.

(5) I cannot define our point of arrival simply by listing the territories we have crossed, the ideas we have abandoned and the social movements that have fallen into decay. Quick, we have to throw overboard everything that has lost its meaning and that can only be used by commentators who have nothing new to say. If we do that, we will be able to see how the great themes that will characterize our new century are already embodied in new representations, new sensibilities and new forms of action.

They are easily identified. For centuries, the world was conquered by reason, by technologies and by arms; we are now entering a space in which all roads lead to us, to a self-construction that will begin by trying to put together what a certain rationalism took apart. Hence the increasingly central importance of political ecology. This is also why a society of men is being replaced by a world of women, because they are the main victims of a polarization that put them in an inferior position. Women have begun to reconstruct a whole that has been cut in two, by re-establishing the links between body and mind, reason and feeling, public life and private life, and male and female. Male chauvinism already looks archaic, even residual.

And how, finally, can we not end by saying something that should have been said from the outset: the whole world is the space for the creation and development of the new cultural and social life we have already begun to lead. This will not lead to the demise of states, nations or local communities, but we have to understand that, if we do not make room for what we might call a 'global' level of analysis, there is a danger that our analysis will lose much of its utility. We have to be both for and against globalization, for and against new technologies, just as we must be for and against our self-transformation, be it physical, psychological or relational. The meaning of our behaviour is no longer supplied by a philosophy of history based upon great principles, or by a 'natural' morality that is dictated by the will of God or the traditions of particular groups. Human life is meaningful only because it is human beings themselves who define what is human and what is meant by respect for the right of every individual to enjoy freedom in every domain of personal and collective life. Our last word must be that everyone has the right to be the subject who creates his or her rights.

This working programme is deliberately moving further and further away from sociologies that are defined by the search for the social basis for social behaviours. It should have demonstrated its radical nature by abandoning the term sociology, but let us not waste our time playing with words. Above all, we have to understand how today's actors are formulating their rights and directing their action; we also have to understand the battles they are fighting, and the ways in which they are trying to embody a subject who is already more discernible than he was when we were blinded by ideological discourses. Sociology was the study of social systems; it must now be defined in different terms as the study of the struggles of social actors who are fighting for their freedom and their rights insofar as they are subjects.

Bibliography

Agacinski, Sylvaine (2007), *Engagements*, Paris: Seuil.

Alba Vega, Carlos and Bizberg, Ilan, eds (2004), *Democracia y globalización en México y Brasil*, México: Colego de México.

Anderson, Perry (2004a), 'The Fall of France', *London Review of Books*, vol. 26, no. 17, 2 September.

—— (2004b), 'The Normalizing of France', *London Review of Books*, vol. 26, no. 18, 23 September.

—— (2005), *La Pensée tiède. Un Regard critique sur la culture française, suivie de La Pensée rechauffée (Réponse de Pierre Nora)*, Paris: Seuil.

Archer, Margaret (1996), *Culture and Agency: The Place of Culture in Social Theory*, Cambridge: Cambridge University Press.

Aron, Raymond (1957), *The Opium of the Intellectuals*, trans. Terence Kilmartin, London: Secker and Warburg [original French publication 1955].

—— (1968), *Democracy and Totalitarianism*, trans. Valence Ionescu, London: Weidenfeld and Nicolson [original French publication 1965].

—— (1972), *Progress and Disillusion: The Dialectics of Modern Society*, Harmondsworth: Penguin [original French publication 1969].

—— (1969), *D'une Sainte Famille à une autre*, Paris: Gallimard.

—— (2002), *Le Marxisme de Marx*, preface by J. C. Casanova, Paris: Desclée de Brouwer.

Baca, Laura (1986), *Bobbio: Los intelectuales y el poder*, México: Oceano.

Badinter, Elisabeth (1986), *L'Un est un autre*, Paris: Odile Jacob.

Barber, Benjamin, R. (1995), *Jihad vs McWorld*, New York: Times Books.

Baudrillard, Jean (2005), *The Intelligence of Evil or, The Lucidity Pact*, trans. Chris Turner, Oxford: Berg [original French publication 2004].

Bauman, Zygmunt (2000), *Liquid Modernity*, Cambridge: Polity.

Bayard, Jean François (1996), *L'Illusion identitaire*, Paris: Fayard.

Beck, Ulrich (1992), *Risk Society: Towards a New Modernity*, trans. M. Ritter, London: Sage [original German publication 1986].

—— (1996), *The Reinvention of Politics*, trans. Mark Ritter Cambridge: Polity, 1996 [original German publication 2002].

—— (2005), *Power in the Global Age: A New Global Political* Economy, trans. Kathleen Cross, Cambridge: Polity [original German publication 2002].

—— and Giddens Anthony and Lash, Scott (1994), *Reflexive Modernization Politics*, Stanford: Stanford University Press.

Ben Rafael, Eliezer and Sternberg, Yitzak, eds (2005), *Comparing Modernities*, Leiden and Boston: Brill.

Benhabib, Seyla (2002), *The Claims of Culture: Equality and Diversity in the Global Era*, Princeton: Princeton University Press.

Berlin, Isaiah, Sen, Amartya, Mathieu, Vittorio, Vattimo, Gianni and Veca, Salvatore (1990), *La Dimensione etica nelle società contemporane*, Turin: Fondation Agnelli.

BID (1998), *Desarrollo económico y sociedad en los umbrales del siglo XXI*, Washington: BID (InterAmerican Development Bank).

Bindé, Jérôme, ed. (2004), *Où sont les valeurs? Entretiens du XXIe siècle II*, Paris: Albin Michel.

Birnbaum, Norman (1969), *The Crisis of Industrial Society*, New York: Oxford University Press.

—— (2001), *After Progress: American Social Reform and European Socialism in the Twentieth Century*, Oxford: Oxford University Press.

Bobbio, Norberto (1996), *The Age of Rights*, Cambridge: Polity [original Italian publication 1990].

—— and Viroli, Maurizio, *Dialogo intorno alla republica*, Rome and Bari: *Laterza*, 2001.

Bottomore, Tom (1979), *Political sociology*, London: Hutchinson.

Bourdieu, Pierre (2001), *Science de la science et réflexivité*, Paris: Raison d'agir.

Bouretz, Pierre (1996), *Les Promesses du monde: philosophie de Max Weber*, Paris: Gallimard.

—— (2002), *La République et l'universel*, Paris: Gallimard.

Bréchon, Pierre (2000), *Les Grands Courants de la sociologie*, Paris: PUF.

Brubaker, William (1992), *Citizenship and Nationhood in France and Germany*, Cambridge, MA: Harvard University Press.

Bulmer, Martin and Rees, Anthony, eds (1996), *Citizenship Today: The Contemporary Relevance of T.H. Marshall*, London: UCL Press.

Cahiers Internationaux de Sociologie (1999), *La Différence culturelle en question*, Paris: PUF.

Calabro, Ana Rita (1997), *L'Ambivalenza come risorsa*, Rome and Bari: Laterza.

Camus, Albert (2002), *The Plague*, trans. Robin Buss, Harmondsworth: Penguin [original French publication 1947].

Cassirer, Ernst (1951), *The Philosophy of the Enlightenment*, trans. Fritz C. A. Koelln and James P. Pettegrove, Princeton: Princeton University Press [original German publication 1932].

Castel, Robert (2002), *From Manual Workers to Wage Laborers: Transformations of the Social Question*, trans. Richard Boyd, New York: Transaction Publishers [original French publication 1995].

Castells, Manuel (1983), *The City and the Grassroots: A Cross-Cultural Theory of Urban Social Movements*, Berkeley: University of California Press, 1983.

—— (1989), *The Informational City: Information Technology, Economic Restructuring and Urban Regional Process*, Oxford and Cambridge, MA: Blackwell.

—— (1996; 2000), *The Information* Age. Oxford: Blackwell, 3 vols.

—— ed. (2004), *The Network Society: Cross-Cultural Perspectives*, Northampton: Edward Elgar.

Castoriadis, Cornelius (1987), *The Imaginary Institution of Society*, trans. Kathleen Blamey, Cambridge [original French publication 1975].

—— (2005), *Une Société à la dérive (entretiens et débats, 1974–1997)*, Paris: Seuil.

Ceri, Paolo (2002), *Movimenti globali*, Rome and Bari: Laterza.

Cohen, Daniel (2006), *Trois leçons sur la société postindustrielle*, Paris: Seuil.

Cohen, Jean and Arato, Andrew (1992), *Civil Society and Political Theory*, Cambridge, MA: MIT Press.

Cousin, Olivier (1998), *L'Efficacité des collèges. Sociologie de l'effet établissement*, Paris: PUF.

Crespi, Franco (1985), *Le Vie della sociologia*, Bologna: Il Mulino.

—— *Teoria dell'agire* (1999), Bologna: Il Mulino.

Crespi, Franco and Moscovici, Serge (2001), *Solidarietà inquestione*, Rome: Meltemi.

Dagnaud, Monique (2000), *L'État et les média*, Paris: Odile Jacob.

Daniel, Jean (2006), *Avec Camus. Comment resister à l'air du temps*, Paris: Gallimard.

Debray, Régis, *Revolution in the Revolution* (1968), trans. Bobbye Ortiz, Harmondsworth: Penguin [original French publication 1967].

—— (1981), *Teachers, Writers, Celebrities: The Intellectuals of Modern France*, trans. David Macey, London: Verso [original French publication 1979].

—— (1983), *Critique of Political Reason*, trans. David Macey, London: Verso [original French publication 1981].

Delmas Marty, Mireille (2007), *La Refondation des pouvoirs*, Paris: Seuil.

Dreyfus, Hubert and Rabinow, Paul (1982), *Michel Foucault: Beyond Structuralism and Hermeneutics*, Hemel Hempstead: Harvester Press.

Dubet, François (1982), *Le Déclin de l'institution*, Paris: Seuil.

—— (1987), *La Galère, jeunes en survie*, Paris: Fayard.

—— (1994), *Sociologie de l'expérience*, Paris: Seuil.

—— (2008), *L'Expérience sociologique*, Paris: La Découverte.

Dubet, François and Duru-Bellat, Marie (2000), *L'Hypocrisie scolaire*, Paris: Seuil.

218 Bibliography

Dubet, François and Lapeyronnie, Didier (1992), *Les Quartiers d'exil*, Paris: Seuil.

Dubet, François *et al.* (2006), *Injustices. L'Expérience des inégalités au travail*, Paris: Seuil.

Dupas, Gilberto (2006), *O Mito do Progresso, Sao Paolo*, Unesp.

Duval, Julien *et al.* (1998), *Le 'Décembre' des intellectuels français*, Paris: Raison d'agir.

Ehrenberg, Alain (1995), *L'Individu incertain*, Paris: Calmann-Lévy.

Eisenstadt, Shmueel (1963), *Modernization, Growth and Diversity*, Bloomington: Indiana University.

Etzioni, Amitai (1968), *The Active Society*, New York: Free Press, 1968.

Fabietti, Ugo (1995), *Identità etnica*, Rome: La Nuova Italia Scientifica.

Fernandez, Alfred and Gowland, Geoffroy (2006), *Towards Human Rights*, Geneva, Diversité.

Ferrer, Aldo (1996), *Historia de la Globalización*, Mexico: FCE.

Foucault, Michel (1970), *The Order of Things: An Archaeology of the Human Sciences*, London: Tavistock [original French publication 1966].

—— (1977), *Discipline and Punish: The Birth of the Prison*, trans. Alan Sheridan, London: Allen Lane [original French publication 1969]

—— (1987), *The Use of Pleasure: The History of Sexuality, Volume 2*, trans. Robert Hurley, Harmondsworth: Penguin [original French publication 1984].

—— (1998), *The Care of the Self: The History of Sexuality, Volume 3*, trans. Robert Hurley, Harmondsworth: Penguin [original French publication 1984].

—— (2001), *Dits et ecrits II: 1970–1975*, ed. Daniel Defert and François Ewald, Paris: Gallimard.

—— (2005), *The Hermeneutics of the Subject: Lectures at the Collège de France 1981–1982*, trans. Graham Burchell, London: Palgrave MacMillan [original French publication 2001].

Fouque, Antoinette (2004), *Il y a deux sexes*, Paris: Gallimard.

—— *Gravidanza, féminologie II* (2007), Paris: Des femmes.

Franq, Bernard (2003), *La Ville incertaine*, Louvain-la-Neuve, Bruylant Academia.

Furet, François (1981), *Interpreting the French Revolution*, trans. Elborg Foster, Cambridge: Cambridge University Press [original French publication 1978.

—— (1985), *In the Workshop of History*, trans. J. Mandelbaum, Chicago: University of Chicago [original French publication 1982].

Galli, Carlo, ed. (2006), *Multiculturalismo*, Bologna: Il Mulino.

Gans, Herbert, ed. (1988), *Middle American Individualism*, New York: Free Press.

Garreton, Manuel Antonio (2003), *Incomplete Democracy*, Chapel Hill, NC: University of North Carolina Press.

Gauchet, Marcel (2002), *La Démocratie contre elle-même*, Paris, Gallimard.

Gellner, Ernest (1993), *Postmodernism, Reason and Religion*, London: Routledge.

Giddens, Anthony (1979), *Central Problems in Social Theory: Action, Structure and Contradiction in Social Analysis*, London: MacMillan.

Gitlin, Todd (1980), *The Whole World is Watching: Mass Media in the Making and Unmaking of the New Left*, Berkeley, CA: University of California Press.

Glissant, Edouard (1987), *Traité du Tout-Monde*, Paris: Gallimard.

Global Civil Society (2001), Oxford: Oxford University Press.

Göle, Nilüfer (1993), *Musulmanes et modernes. Voile et civilisation en Turquie*, Paris: La Découverte.

Green, André (2001), *Life Narcissism Death Narcissism*, trans. Andrew Weller, London: Free Association Books [original French publication 1983].

Guénif-Souilamas, Nacira, ed. (2006), *La République mise à nu par son immigration*, Paris: La Fabrique.

Habermas, Jürgen (1987), *The Philosophical Discourse of Modernity*, trans. Frederick G. Lawrence, Cambridge: Polity [original German publication, 1985].

Halevi, Ran (2007), *L'Expérience du passé*, Paris: Gallimard.

Harvey, David (1990), *The Condition of Post-Modernity*, Oxford: Blackwell.

Héritier, Françoise (2002), *Masculin/Féminin II*, Paris: Odile Jacob.

Hervieu-Leger, Danièle (1993), *La Religion pour mémoire*, Paris: Cerf.

Hirschman, Albert (1991), *The Rhetoric of Reaction: Perversity, Futility and Jeopardy*, Cambridge, MA: The Belknap Press of Harvard University Press.

Honneth, Axel (1995), *The Fragmented World of the Social*, New York: SUNY Press.

—— (2001), *Disrespect: The Normative Foundations of Critical Theory*, Cambridge: Polity.

Hopenhayn, Martin (1999), *Después del nihilismo*, Santiago: Andres Bello.

Huntington, Samuel P. (1997), *The Clash of Civilizations and the Remaking of World Order*, London: Simon and Schuster.

Irigaray, Luce (1994), *Thinking the Difference: For A Peaceful Revolution*, trans. Karin Montin, New York: Routledge [original French publication 1989].

Jameson, Frederic (1991), *Postmodernism*, Durham and London: Duke University Press.

Jasper, James (2000), *Restless Nation: Starting Over in America*, Chicago: University of Chicago Press.

Jeanson, Françis (1955), *Sartre par lui-même*, Paris: Seuil.

Joas, Hans (1996), *The Creativity of Action*, trans. Jeremy Gaines and Paul Keast, Cambridge: Polity [original German publication 1992].

Judt, Tony, *Marxism and the French Left: Studies on Labour and Politics in France 1830–1981,* Oxford: Clarendon Press, 1986.

Kepel, Gilles and Richard, Yann (1990), *Intellectuels et militants dans l'Islam contemporain*, Paris: Seuil.

Khosrokhavar, Farhad (2001), *l'Instance du sacré*, Paris: Cerf.
—— (2005), *Suicide Bombers: Allah's New Martyrs*, trans. David Macey, London: Pluto Press [original French publication 2002].
Konrad, George and Szelenyi, Ivan (1979), *The Road of the Intellectuals to Class Power*, trans. Andrew Arato and Richard E. Allen, New York: Harcourt Brace Jovanovich.
Kristeva, Julia (1991), *Strangers to Ourselves*, trans. Léon S. Roudiez, New York: Columbia University Press [original French publication 1988].
Kymlicka, William (1985), *Multicultural Citizenship*, New York: Oxford University Press.
Kymlicka, William and Mesure, Sylvie, eds. (2000), *Comprendre les identités culturelles*, Paris: PUF.
Laclau, Ernesto (1977), *Politics and Ideology in Marxist Theory*, London: NLB.
Lacorne, Denis (1997), *La Crise de l'identité américaine. Du melting pot au multiculturalisme*, Paris: Fayard.
Lamy, Pascal (1997), *La Démocratie-monde*, Paris: Fayard.
Larana, Enrique and Gusfield, Joseph, ed. (1994), *Los Nuevos Movimentos sociales*, Madrid: CIS.
Lash, Scott (1990), *Sociology of Postmodernism:* London: Routledge.
Lash, Scott and Friedman, Jonathan (1992), *Modernity and Identity*. Oxford: Blackwell.
Lash, Scott and Robertson, Robert, eds (1992), *Global Modernities in Featherstone*, London: Sage.
Lash, Scott and Urry, John (1987), *The End of Organized Capitalism*, Cambridge: Polity.
Latour, Bruno (1991), *Nous n'avons jamais été modernes*, Paris: La Découverte.
Lefort, Claude (1976), *Un homme en trop. Réflexion sur l'Archipel du gulag de Soljénitsin*, Paris: Seuil.
—— (1988), *Democracy and Political Theory*, trans. David Macey, Cambridge: Polity, 1988 [original French publication 1986].
—— (1999), *La Complication*, Paris: Fayard, 1999.
—— (2007), *Le Temps présent. Ecrits 1945–2005*, Paris: Belin.
Lepenies, Wolf (1988), *Between Literature and Science: The Rise of Sociology*, trans. R. J. Hollingdale, Paris and Cambridge: Maison des sciences de l'homme and Cambridge University Press [original German publication 1985].
Levinas, Emmanuel (1995), *Altérité et transcendence*, Saint-Clément: Fata Morgana.
Lévy, Bernard-Henri (2000), *Le Siècle de Sartre*, Paris: Grasset.
—— (2004), *War, Evil and the End of History*, trans. Charlotte Mandell, London: Duckworth [original French publication 2001].
Lyotard, Jean François (1984), *The Postmodern Condition: A Report on Knowledge*, trans. Geoff Bennington and Brian Massumi, Manchester: Manchester University Press [original French publication 1979].
Maalouf, Amine (1998), *Les Identités meurtières*, Paris: Grasset.

MacKinnon, Catherine A. (1974), *Only Words*, London: HarperCollins.
—— (1983), *Feminism Unmodified. Discourses on Life and Law*, Cambridge, MA: Harvard University Press.
Maffesoli, Michel (1995), *The Time of the Tribes: The Decline of Individualism in Mass Society*, trans. Don Smith, London: Sage [original French publication 1988].
Makhaiski, Jan Waclav (1979), *Le Socialisme des intellectuels*, Paris: Seuil.
Mannheim, Karl (1952), *Ideology and Utopia*, London: Routledge and Kegan Paul [original German publication 1929].
Maturana, Humberto (1991), *El sentido de la humano*, Paris: Hachette.
Mauss (Collectif), *Une Théorie sociologique générale est-elle possible?* Paris: La Découverte, 2004.
Mead, George H. (1934), *Mind, Self and Society: From the Viewpoint of a Social Behaviourist*, Chicago: University of Chicago Press.
Meda, Dominique (1995), *Le Travail: une valeur en voie de disparition*, Paris: Aubier.
Melucci, Alberto (1996), *Challenging Codes: Collective Action in the Information Age*, Cambridge: Cambridge University Press.
—— and Diani, Mario (1982), *Nazioni senza stato y movimenti etnico nacionalie in occidente*, Milan: Feltrinelli.
Mendras, Henri (1971), *Vanishing Peasants: Innovation and Change in French Agriculture*, trans. J. Lerner, Cambridge MA: MIT Press [original French publication 1967].
—— (1988), *La Seconde Révolution française (1965–1984)*, Paris: Gallimard.
Minc, Alain (2004), *Ce Monde qui vient*, Paris: Grasset.
Mongardini, Carlo (1993), *La Cultura del presente*, Turin: Franco Angelli.
—— (1989), and Maniscalco, Marie-Louisa, *Moderni et postmoderni*, Rome: Bulzoni.
Mongin, Olivier (2005), *La Condition urbaine*, Paris: Seuil.
Morin, Edgar (2001), *L'Identité humaine (La Méthode V)*, Paris: Seuil.
—— (2008), *California Journal*, trans. Deborah Cowell, Portland, OR: Susses Academic Press.
Moscovici, Serge (1988), *La Machine à faire des dieux*, Paris: Fayard.
—— (2001), *Mélanges en l'honneur de Serge Moscovici. Penser la vie, le social, la nature*, Paris: Éditions de la MSH.
—— (2002), *De La Nature*, Paris, Métailié.
Mouffe, Chantal (1993), *The Return of the Political*, London and New York: Verso.
Negri, Antonio (2008), *Goodbye Mister Socialism*, trans. Peter Thomas, London: Serpent's Tale.
Nisbet, Robert (1967), *The Sociological Tradition*, New York: Basic Books.
Nussbaum, Martha (2000), *Women and Human Development*, Cambridge: Cambridge University Press.
Ossowski, Stanislas (1963), *Class Structure in the Social Consciousness*, London: Routledge and Kegan Paul.

Perivolaropoulou, Nina and Despoix, Philippe, eds (2001), *Culture de masse et modernité: Siegfried Kracauer, sociologue, critique, écrivain*, Paris: Éditions de la MSH, 2001.

Peyrelevade, Jean (2005), *Le Capitalisme total*, Paris: Seuil.

Pirsig, Robert (1974), *Zen and the Art of Motorcycle Maintenance*, New York: William Morrow and Co.

Protzel, Javier (2006), *Procesos interculturales. Texturas y complejidad de los simbélicos*, Lima: Universidad de Lima.

Raynaud, Philippe (2005), *L'Extrême gauche plurielle*, Paris: Autrement.

Renaut, Alain (1999a), *The Era of the Individual: A Contribution to the History of Subjectivity*, trans. M. B. DeBevoise and Franklin Philip, Princeton: Princeton University Press [original French publication 1989].

—— (2004), *Qu'est ce qu'une politique juste?* Paris: Grasset.

—— ed. (1999b), *Le Critique de la modernité politique*, Paris: Calmann-Levy.

Rocard, Michel (1996), *Les Moyens d'en sortir*, Paris: Seuil.

—— (2005), *Si la gauche savait*, Paris: Robert Lafont.

Roman, Joël (1998), *La Démocratie des individus*, Paris: Calmann-Levy.

Rosanvallon, Pierre (1979), *Le Capitalisme utopique*, Paris: Seuil.

—— (1999), *L'État en France*, Paris: Seuil.

—— (2004), *Le Modèle politique français*, Paris: Seuil.

—— (2008), *Counter-Democracy: Politics in an Age of Distrust*, trans. Arthur Goldhammer, Cambridge: Cambridge University Press [original French publication 2006].

Sandel, Michael, ed. (1984), *Liberalism and its Critics*, New York: New York University Press, 1984.

Sartre, Jean-Paul (1949), *Situations III (Lendemains de guerre)*, Paris: Gallimard, 1949.

—— (1961), *Crime Passionnel*, trans. Kitty Black, London: Methuen Drama [original French publication 1948].

—— (1964), *Situations VI (Problèmes du marxisme)*, Paris: Gallimard.

—— (1965), *Situations VII (Problèmes du marxisme II)*, Paris: Gallimard.

—— (1967), *Words*, trans. Irene Clephane, Harmondsworth: Penguin [original French publication 1964].

—— (1968a), 'Materialism and Revolution,' in *Literary and Philosophical Essays*, trans. Annette Michelson, London: Hutchinson [original French publication 1946].

—— (1968b), *The Communists and Peace, with A Reply to Lefort*, trans. Hazel Barnes, New York: Brazillier.

—— (1972), *Situations VIII (Autour de 68)*, Paris: Gallimard.

—— (1982a), *In Camera*, in *Three Plays*, trans. Stuart Gilbert, Harmondsworth: Penguin [original French publication 1944].

—— (1982), *Lucifer and the Lord*, in *Three Plays*, trans. Stuart Gilbert, Harmondsworth: Penguin [original French publication 1951].

—— (2000), *Nausea*, trans. Robert Baldick, Harmondsworth: Penguin [original French publication 1938].

—— (2001), *The Age of Reason*, trans. E. Sutton, Harmondsworth: Penguin [original French publication 1945].

—— (2007), *Existentialism is a Humanism*, trans. Carol Macomber, New Haven: Yale University Press [original French publication 1946].

Schnapper, Dominique (1998a), *Community of Citizens: On the Modern Idea of Nationality*, trans. Severine Rosée [original French publication 1994].

—— (1998b), *La Relation à l'autre*, Paris: Gallimard.

Sedgwick, Eve Kosofsky (1990), *Epistemology of the Closet*, Berkeley: University of California Press.

Sen, Amartya (1992), *Inequality Reexamined*, Oxford: Oxford University Press.

Sennet, Richard (2006), *The Culture of the New Capitalism*, New Haven: Yale University Press.

Serres, Michel (2001), *Hominescence*, Paris: Le Pommier.

Simmel, Georg (1984), *On Women, Sexuality and Love*, New Haven and London: Yale University Press.

Singly, François de (2003), *Les Uns avec les autres*, Paris: Armand Colin.

Stasi, Bernard, ed. (2003), *Laïcité et République* (Rapport au Président de la République), Paris: La Documentation française.

Tabboni, Simonetta (2006a), *Norbert Elias. Un Ritratto intellectuale*, Bologna: Il Mulino.

—— (2006b), *Lo Straniero et l'altro*, Naples: Liuguori.

Tarrius, Alain (2002), *La Mondialisation par le bas*, Paris: Balland, 2002.

Taylor, Charles (1992a), *The Ethics of Authenticity*, New Haven: Yale University Press.

—— (1992b), *Multiculturalism and the Politics of Recognition: An Essay*, Princeton: Princeton University Press.

—— (2004), *Modern Social Imaginaries*, Durham and London: Duke University Press.

Tezanos, José-Felix (2005), *La Sociedad dividida*, Madrid: Biblioteca Nueva, 2005.

Touraine, Alain (1995), *Critique of Modernity*, trans. David Macey, Oxford: Blackwell, 1995 [original French publication 1992].

—— (2006), *Le Monde des femmes*, Paris: Fayard.

—— (2007), *A New Paradigm for Understanding Today's World*, Cambridge: Polity [original French publication 2005].

Touraine, Alain and Khosrokhavar, Farhad (2000), *La Recherche de soi. Dialogue sur le sujet*, Paris, Fayard.

UNESCO (2001), *Keys to the 21st Century*, ed. Jérôme Bindé, Paris: UNESCO.

—— (2005), *Vers les societés du savoir*, ed. Jérôme Bindé, Paris: UNESCO.

Vattimo, Giani (1991), *The End of Modernity: Nihilism and Hermeneutics in Post-Modern Culture*, trans. Jon R. Snyder, Cambridge: Polity [original Italian publication 1985].

—— (2004), *Nihilism and Emancipation: Ethics, Politics, Law*, trans. William McCuaig, New York: Columbia University Press [original Italian publication 2003] *Nihilismo ed emancipazione*, Milan: Garzanti.

Veca, Salvatore (1990), *Cittadinanza*, Milan: Feltrinelli.

Vidal, Daniel (1977), *L'Ablatif absolu*, Paris: Anthropos.

Wallerstein, Emmanuel (1995), *Impenser la science sociale*, Paris: PUF.

Walzer, Michael (1997), *On Toleration*, New Haven: Yale University Press.

—— (2004), *Politics and Passion: Toward a More Egalitarian Liberalism*, New Haven: Yale University Press.

Weil, Dominique, eds (1992), *Hommes et sujets*, Paris: l'Harmattan.

Wieviorka, Michel (2008), *Violence*, trans. David Macey, London: Sage [original French publication 2004].

—— ed. (1996), *Une Société fragmentée*, Paris: La Découverte.

Wieviorka, Michel *et al.*, eds (2001), *La Différence culturelle. Une reformulation des débats. Colloque de Cerisy*, Paris: Balland.

Wolton, Dominique (1997), *Penser la communication*, Paris: Flammarion.

—— (2003), *L'Autre Mondialisation*, Paris: Flammarion.

Young, Iris Marion (1990), *Justice and the Politics of Difference*, Princeton: Princeton University Press.

Zapata, Francisco (2001), *Cuestiones de teoría sociológica*, México, Colegió de México.

Index